Newnes

C++

Pocket Book

Second Edition

Newnes
C++
Pocket Book
Second Edition

Conor Sexton

Newnes
An imprint of Butterworth-Heinemann
Linacre House, Jordan Hill, Oxford OX2 8DP
A division of Reed Educational and Professional Publishing Ltd

A member of the Reed Elsevier plc group

OXFORD   BOSTON   JOHANNESBURG
MELBOURNE   NEW DELHI   SINGAPORE

First edition published 1993, reprinted 1995
Second edition, first published 1996
© Conor Sexton 1993, 1996

NOTICE
The author and the publisher have used their best efforts to prepare this
book, including the computer examples contained in it. The computer
examples have been tested. The author and the publisher make no warranty,
implicit or explicit, about the documentation. The author and the publisher
will not be liable under any circumstances for any direct or indirect
damages arising from any use, direct or indirect, of the documentation or
computer examples contained in this book.

TRADEMARKS/REGISTERED TRADEMARKS
Computer hardware and software brand names mentioned in this book are
protected by their respective trademarks and are acknowledged.

British Library Cataloguing in Publication Data
A catalogue record for this book is available from the British Library.

ISBN 0 7506 2539 2

Typeset by P K McBride, Southampton
Printed and bound in Great Britain by The Bath Press, Bath

Contents

Dedication

To Sam McQuade,
long-suffering bank manager

Preface to the First Edition

C++ is a compatible superset of the C programming language, providing extensions to support the object-oriented programming (OOP) methodology.

C++ was developed in the early 1980s at AT&T Bell Laboratories by Dr. Bjarne Stroustrup. It was originally called *C With Classes*, reflecting the fact that its major extension to the syntax of C was the implementation of the class construct.

When development of C++ began, C had already been in wide use for a number of years. Certain weaknesses in C's syntax had become apparent and new techniques, especially those of object-oriented programming, could not be expressed adequately in C. In 1983, the ANSI X3J11 committee convened and began the process of defining an American National Standard for C, which, in 1989, resulted in Standard X3.159 – ANSI C. A number of early C++ innovations, especially the syntax of function prototypes, were incorporated in the ANSI C standard.

Because a great amount of C code already existed throughout the world, the C++ designers had to ensure that the new language was compatible; any C program should compile and execute properly within the C++ environment. At the same time, desirable extensions to C were added. A very high degree of compatibility was achieved; there are a few changes, as opposed to additions, to the syntax of C++ from ANSI C, but almost all ANSI C programs run in the C++ environment.

In November 1985, the first major release of C++, Release 1.0, was made available by AT&T. The 'compiler' was in the form of a front-end translator, referred to as *cfront*, which converted C++ code into C. The C code was then processed to executable code by the C compiler and local loader.

After the release of Release 1.0, Stroustrup published the first definitive text on C++, *The C++ Programming Language*, in 1986. In July 1986, Release 1.1 became available. It provided several extensions to the original definition of the language, including **protected** class members and pointers to class members.

Release 1.2 was shipped in September 1987. It improved code generation and naming of generated variables, allowing the C++ front-end translator to be used with more C compilers.

In 1988, the first full C++ compilers appeared; many of these are now available, especially for the PC and workstation environments. Release 2.0 appeared in 1989 and was a major improvement to C++, including most importantly multiple inheritance of classes. The current C++ Release is 3.0, which introduces templates. Exception-handling features are scheduled to be included in Release 4.0, the version of the C++ language on which the future ANSI standard will be based.

An important objective of the C++ system was that executable code for a given program should not give worse performance than the equivalent program written in C. In the event, this objective was achieved.

C++ extends traditional C in three ways:

- It encourages and supports development of Abstract Data Types (ADTs).

- It supports program design and construction using object-oriented programming (OOP) principles.

- It implements many smaller extensions and improvements to the syntax of the C language.

Abstract Data Types are types defined by the programmer in addition to those supplied as part of the language. The nearest approach in traditional C to ADT is the typedef mechanism, with which the user creates a new type often based on a structure declaration. An ADT in the OOP context, however, also includes definition of the operations which may be carried out on its data components. The internal implementation of an ADT is hidden from all other operations which are not part of the ADT.

C++ implements ADTs using the object-oriented design and programming approach. Because of the way ADTs package their data and operations, software designed with them tends to be more modular and less complex than code designed with traditional methods. The interfaces between modules are well-defined and interdependencies across modules are few. This promotes easy division of tasks among software developers. Because the internal implementation of an ADT is hidden, there is some assurance that a module will not be tampered with by outside code.

More specifically, C++ implements ADTs and OOP in these ways:

- It implements *objects*, defined as *classes*, which incorporate not just the data definitions found in C structures but also declarations and definitions of functions which operate on that data. This *encapsulation* of data and functions in a single object is the central innovation of C++.

- *Instances* of classes may automatically be initialised and discarded using *constructors* and *destructors*. This eliminates program initialisation errors.

- The way in which C++ classes are defined enforces *data hiding*; data defined in a class is by default only available to the member functions of that class. External, or client, code which uses a class cannot tamper with the internal implementation of the class but is restricted to accessing the class by calling its member functions.

- C++ allows *overloading* of operators and functions. More than one definition of a function may be made having the same name, with the compiler identifying the appropriate definition for a given function call. Ordinary operators such as ++ and -> can also be overloaded with additional meanings.

- C++ allows the characteristics of the class type – data and functions – to be inherited by sub-classes, called *derived classes*, which may in turn add further data and function definitions. This encourages re-use of existing code written in the form of shareable class libraries and consequent savings in the cost of the software development process.

- With effect from C++ Release 2.0, *multiple inheritance* is possible: sub-classes can inherit characteristics from more than one base class.

- C++ additionally allows classes to define *virtual functions*: more than one definition of a function, with the decision as to which one is selected being resolved at program run-time. This is *polymorphism*, with the run-time selection among function definitions being referred to as *late binding* or *dynamic binding*.

- With Release 3.0 of C++, *template* classes can be defined which allow different instances of the same class to be used with data of different types but with unchanged code. This further promotes code re-use.

C++ facilities for object-oriented programming are characterised by classes, inheritance and virtual functions. These facilities make C++ particularly suitable for writing software to handle a multitude of related objects. Perhaps the most appropriate use of C++ is in implementing graphical user interfaces (GUIs), where many different but related objects are represented on a screen and are allowed to interact. Using the object-oriented approach, C++ stores these objects in class hierarchies and, by means of virtual functions, provides a generic interface to those objects (e.g. 'draw object'), which saves the programmer from having to know the detail of how the objects are manipulated. This makes it easier for the programmer to develop and maintain code, as well as rendering less likely introduction of bugs into existing code.

While C++ is intended to be used for OOP, it is a hybrid language and can be used in a purely procedural way. This is shown by the fact that almost all C programs, which are by definition procedural, run in the C++ environment. The hybrid nature of C++ is probably its most controversial characteristic.

Data type-checking and conversion in C++ are stronger than in traditional C. The syntax of function prototypes makes transfer of parameters at the function call interface less error-prone than in C. Strong type-checking with function prototypes is a C++ innovation which was included in the 1989 ANSI C definition.

C++ provides a large number of smaller syntactic improvements over C. It provides a new *reference* mechanism, complementing the pointer-dereferencing approach of C. It simplifies the process of dynamically allocating and de-allocating memory. It also implements a new Stream I/O library, which defines in a class hierarchy streams for input and output.

C++ is an extension of C which, by facilitating improved design practices, promises software that better reflects the 'real world', reduces complexity and code amounts, and increases reliability.

This book covers the whole definition of the C++ language as it currently stands (Release 3.0), with the exception of some of the 'darker corners' of the language syntax. It is intended to be readable for a C programmer; to be short, yet quite comprehensive. In terms of comprehensiveness, it is somewhere between the introductory primers — of which many have appeared — and the definitive *Annotated Reference Manual* (*ARM*) by Ellis and Stroustrup. The purpose of this book is different from that of the *ARM*; its aim is to allow experienced C programmers quickly to get up and running with C++. The style and layout of the ARM, while exhaustively comprehensive, does not suit that purpose.

When the C language is referred to in this book, what is meant is the ANSI C definition of the language. It is assumed that the reader is already familiar with at least the original K&R C language definition. Knowledge on the part of the reader of ANSI C is, however, better, as no attempt is made to explain the differences between K&R C and ANSI C. Syntax differences between C++ and C are presented using ANSI C as the baseline. Readers who are unsure about whether they meet these pre-requisites are referred to the earlier book in the same series, *The C Pocket Book*.

Readers of *The C Pocket Book*, will notice a strong similarity in style and symmetry in layout between it and this book. Many of the examples in the C book are adapted here to reflect the object-oriented design and implementation approach. Care is taken to make the examples as short as possible, although the need to define class hierarchies makes this difficult. One of the reasons programmers buy and read books is for quick answers to awkward language questions: 'How do I use constructors to initialise an array of classes?' This book attempts to address that need in a way which is short, terse and yet readable.

In much the same way as *The C Pocket Book*, the first chapter of this book leads the reader on a 'tour' of C++.

In ten short sections, all the fundamental C++ extensions to the C language are introduced. At the end of this chapter, the reader should understand the differences between C++ and C, not alone in syntax but also in the object-oriented design approach.

Chapter 2 is a summary, with examples, of the syntax differences between C++ and C which are outside the context of classes, inheritance, virtual functions and the other C++ language constructs that facilitate the object-oriented design approach. This chapter is a useful reference to the improvements made in C++ to C language syntax.

Chapter 3 explains the C++ class and its special cases, structures, unions and bit fields. A straightforward presentation on classes is given using as a basis the program 'dates.cpp', which will be familiar to readers of *The C Pocket Book*.

Chapter 4 goes into constructors and destructors, demonstrating many of the ways in which they can be used with classes. More complex — and typical — class implementations are shown using string and list classes.

Chapter 5 treats function and operator overloading, as well as friend functions put to their best use, which is in declaring overloaded-operator functions. The string class implementation introduced in Chapter 4 is extended to demonstrate these C++ features by example.

Chapter 6 covers class inheritance, including multiple inheritance. It treats the crucial area of virtual functions, the C++ implementation of polymorphism, which characterises the object-oriented programming approach. A number of examples are presented, culminating in the list example first shown in Chapter 4 being adapted to illustrate implementation, using polymorphism, of a list of generic objects.

Chapter 7 explains the contents of the C++ Stream I/O library and shows, with examples, how it is used as an alternative to the C I/O library and stdio.h.

Finally, Chapter 8 deals with the newest features of the C++ language: templates; and gives an introduction to the exception-handling constructs, which will be part of Release 4.0.

Even experienced C programmers, if they do not already know C++ and the principles of object-oriented programming, will need to read all the chapters in this book to get a good understanding of both. C++ is a difficult set of extensions to a language, C, which is itself not simple.

This book does not address itself to any of the commercial C++ implementations currently available. Neither does it deal with any particular class libraries, of which there are many commercially available for applications including graphics and communications. This means, for example, that the reader is not shown how to draw a Microsoft Windows dialogue box, because that would introduce code dependent on the environment of one supplier. It should not be difficult for the reader to substitute for a system-independent print class member function the function required by a particular GUI.

The treatment of C++ presented by this book is generic and applies to all C++ implementations conforming to the Annotated Reference Manual, which is the basis for the current ANSI C++ standardisation effort.

Preface to the Second Edition

The first edition of this book was published in 1993 and reprinted in 1995. It was my second book; in light of experience with the first (*The C Pocket Book*), it was exhaustively researched and received uniformly good reviews. Unlike C, which has reached stable maturity, C++ is still changing and its American National Standard is not yet finalised. To my knowledge, no book is yet available that addresses as a whole the C++ language as defined by the ANSI Draft Standard. This Second Edition is an attempt to fit in a slim volume the essential facilities of C++ as specified by that ever-expanding Standard.

In their seminal 1978 publication *The C Programming Language*, Brian Kernighan and Dennis Ritchie asserted that C is not a big language and is not well served by a big book. It seems that some of the minimalism espoused by early versions of UNIX, and the C and C++ languages, has been abandoned in the C++ standardisation effort. Fully one-half of the approximately-800-page C++ Draft Standard Working Paper is taken up with definitions of library functions and facilities. Yet C and C++ have traditionally made a virtue of the fact that their language specifications have excluded built-in functions, relegating them to libraries in the name of smallness and portability between disparate computing environments.

This book presents the essential subset of the ANSI Draft Standard C++ language and environment. Every facility of the language is addressed, but the new libraries and header files — for strings, exceptions and others — are only mentioned. In a book of this size, intended as a description of the C++ language, considerations of space preclude any comprehensive treatment of those libraries. They are, in any event, strictly not part of the language at all. New language facilities, for example runtime type identification (RTTI) and namespaces, are dealt with. The coverage of templates and exception handling is updated, as is that of many other aspects of the language. I have (I hope) improved the exposition of such topics as memberwise initialisation and assignment; multiple inheritance and virtual base classes; and the internal implementation of virtual functions. The example programs in this book are more real-world and comprehensive than those presented in the First Edition and, additionally, are available on disk.

Limitations imposed by the Pocket Book format make it impossible to typeset these programs to *appear* the same as those on the disk. I guarantee that the disk programs are the same semantically as those in this book.

The order of presentation of topics in this book is essentially the same as that of the First Edition. In response to suggestions that the book should integrate treatment of the C and C++ languages, Chapter 1 reviews the essentials of C while Chapter 2 conducts the reader on a tour of the main facilities provided by C++. It should therefore be possible for a reader with no prior experience of either C or C++ to adopt this book as a single reference.

Chapter 2 is expanded to 11 sections in which the fundamental constructs of the C++ language are introduced. A section summarising the characteristics of templates is added.

Chapter 3 explains the C++ class and its special cases, structures, unions and bit fields. The model used to illustrate fundamental class characteristics is now that of a bank account; this seems more real-world and less abstract than the Date class model used in the First Edition. In the last section, the coverage of pointers to class members is improved.

Chapter 4 goes into constructors and destructors, demonstrating many of the ways in which they can be used with classes. More complex — and typical — class implementations are shown using String and List classes. The String class is more comprehensive than that presented in the First Edition, while the explanation of issues surrounding memberwise initialisation and assignment is, I believe, significantly improved.

Chapter 5 treats function and operator overloading, giving the more formal set of rules used by ANSI C++ for overload resolution. The String class implementation introduced in Chapter 4 is extended to demonstrate these C++ features by example.

Chapter 6 covers class inheritance, including multiple inheritance. The Clock model used in the First Edition is replaced by the Employee model. This seems, again, more real-world and more plausibly illustrates multiple inheritance and virtual base classes. The treatment of virtual functions is also improved, with additional explanation of their internals as implemented with virtual tables. The List example first shown in Chapter 4 is adapted to illustrate implementation, using polymorphism, of a list of generic objects.

Chapter 7 is largely new. It describes the major extensions to the original definition of C++ that have been accepted for inclusion in the ANSI Standard. These are templates, exception handling, namespaces and runtime type identification. At the time of the First Edition, only templates had been widely implemented; the final three sections of Chapter 7 are therefore completely new. While not all the minor changes mandated by the Standard are mentioned in this book, a number of the more significant ones are integrated at appropriate points in the text.

Chapter 8 acknowledges the enormous expansion of the C++ Library since the First Edition and then proceeds to explain the contents of the Stream I/O component of that library. The First Edition's Chapter 2, with some changes, has become Appendix A. It summarises the non-class syntax differences between C++ and C. In de-emphasising C as a language in its own right, it seemed reasonable that considerations of migration from C to C++ should be relegated to an appendix. The material it contains, however, is still important as a description of C++ syntax and its basis in C.

This book is intended to be a useful general reference and guide to the ANSI Draft Standard C++ language. Its audience extends from novice programmers with no knowledge of C or C++ to experienced developers. Given the expansion of the C++ language and environment, and the sheer scale of the Standard, this book cannot be an exhaustive reference but it should certainly be sufficient for programmers requiring an up-to-date text covering the essentials of the standard language.

Conor Sexton.

February, 1996.

1 Review of the C Language

1.1 The C Subset of C++

All but a few ISO C programs are also valid C++ programs. This chapter introduces the C subset of C++, treating it as an integral part of the C++ language. In the years after C++ first appeared, it was conventional to assume that those learning it would in the main be programmers converting from C. This is no longer a valid assumption, with many programmers embarking directly on C++, bypassing the C-first route.

Like its C++ counterpart, a C program is a set of one or more functions and data, known as *source code*, written by the programmer with an editor program. The source code is stored in a file with an arbitrary name, by convention followed by the suffix '.c'.

A C program is preprocessed, compiled and linked according to the steps described at the start of Chapter 2. A source code file comprising code restricted to the C subset of C++ can nonetheless be named with the '.cpp' suffix that tells the compiler to treat it as a C++ program. This book henceforth treats all such code as C++ code.

1.2 Simple C Programs

The following is the minimal C (and C++) program:

```
main()
{
}
```

which does nothing. Every C++ program must contain one and only one main function, no matter how many program source code files make up the program. The main function header has no return type or argument list. If an integer return type is specified:

```
int main()
{
  return(0);
}
```

a return statement should also be included to return an integer value to the operating system environment. If the return statement is omitted, the compiler issues a warning or error message. A void argument list can additionally be used:

```
int main(void)
```

As is noted in Appendix A, this is never necessary in C++, but is still correct syntax. The parentheses, (), enclose the names of *parameters* that may be received by the function. There are no parameter names here, but rules for inclusion of these are given later in this chapter.

The curly braces {} are a *compound statement*: in fact a null compound statement because they do not contain any statements. The program, as might be expected, produces no output.

This program is more meaningful:

```
/*  greet.c - program to display a greeting */
#include <stdio.h>
int main(void)
{
    printf("Hello C World\n");
    return(0);
}
```

This is a C (and a C++) program that works normally when compiled in the C++ environment.

printf is a call to a library function. It is not part of the C++ language itself. The printf line is nonetheless a statement, which is (and must be) terminated by a semicolon. The text within the parentheses is an *argument* to the called library function printf.

Executing this program causes the text:

```
Hello C World
```

to appear on the computer's *standard output* device, which is probably a terminal. The \n, one of the ways in C++ of specifying advance to a new line, causes the output to advance one line after the text is displayed.

The stdio.h header file must be included in C++ programs if C Standard I/O library functions are used. With both traditional and ISO C, if a function returns a value of type int, as printf does, it need not have a function prototype declared earlier, although the ISO standard specifies that this should be done. C++ requires that printf be declared and this is done by including the header file.

1.3 Functions

A function is a body of C++ code executed from another part of the program by means of a function call. Functions usually contain code to perform a specific action. Instead of duplicating that code at every point in the program where the action is required, the programmer writes calls to the function, where the single definition of the code resides. Every C++ program is a collection of functions and declarations.

main, as shown in the previous section, is a special function: it must be present in every C++ program. When the program is run, the operating system uses main as the *entry-point* to the program. main in turn usually contains calls to an arbitrary number of programmer-defined functions.

The following is a simple general form for all functions:

```
<returntype> <functionname>(<arglist>)
{
    <statements>
}
```

Here is a C++ program containing two functions:

```
// Two-function program

void myfunc(void);      // 'myfunc' declaration

int main(void)
{
    printf("Hello C World\n");
    myfunc();
    return(0);
}

void myfunc(void)
{
    printf("Hello C World again\n");
}
// End of program text
```

In this program, main contains three statements: first the printf we have already seen; second a call to the function myfunc, which contains a further, slightly different, printf statement; and lastly a return statement that passes control back to the operating system by terminating execution of main.

When it is run, this program displays the lines of text:

```
Hello C World
Hello C World again
```

on the standard output device.

The statement

```
myfunc();
```

is the call from main to the function myfunc.

On execution, control is passed to myfunc from main. When the single statement in myfunc has been executed, control is returned to the first statement in main after the function call. In this case, that statement is return and the whole program immediately stops execution.

The function myfunc is expressed in three parts, the *declaration* (also called a function *prototype*):

```
void myfunc(void);
```

which announces to the compiler the existence of myfunc; the call:

```
myfunc();
```

and the *definition* of the function itself:

```
void myfunc(void)
{
   printf("Hello C World again\n");
}
```

Note that the function call is a statement and must be terminated with a semicolon. The prototype is not a statement but is distinguished from the header of the called function by a terminating semicolon. The header must not be appended with a semicolon.

Every C++ function must be fully described in three parts using a declaration, call and definition.

The text of comments, announced by a leading double-slash on a line has no effect on the execution of the program. The compiler ignores following text on the same line and does not generate object code for it.

Especially for short comments, the // notation is preferred to the /*....*/ sequence. If the trailing */ is left out, the compiler will keep on searching for it until the end of the program and the compilation process will fail. Additionally, if the characters in /* or */ are separated by one or more spaces, for example / *, the compiler will not recognise the text between them as comments. The comment delimiters are pairs of characters.

Double-slash comments must not be nested:

/* Comment text /* nested */ in error */

In this case, the first */ ends the comment. When the compiler tries to interpret in error */, a compilation error results. Double-slash comments can, however, be nested within /*....*/ blocks and vice-versa.

The double-slash form of comment should be used for long, block, comments:

```
/************************************************
*
* Function:    myfunc
*
* Purpose:     Simple output
*
* Arguments:   None
*
************************************************/
```

1.4   Simple Data Representation

Variables in C++ are data objects that may change in value. A variable is given a name by means of a definition, which allocates storage space for the data and associates the storage location with the variable name.

The C++ language defines five fundamental representations of data:

    boolean
    integer
    character
    floating-point
    double floating-point

Each of these is associated with a special type specifier:

bool	specifies a true/false value
int	specifies an integer variable
char	specifies a character variable
float	specifies a fractional-number variable
double	specifies a fractional-number variable with more decimal places

Any of the type specifiers may be qualified with the type qualifier const, which specifies that the variable must not be changed after it is initialised.

A data definition is of the following general form:

    <type-specifier> <name>;

A variable name is also called an identifier. The following are some examples of simple data definitions in C++:

```
int      goals;     // integer variable
char     c;         // character value eg: 'b'
float    balance;   // bank balance
const    double x = 5.0;
                    // high-precision variable
                    // value fixed when set
bool     cplusplus = TRUE;
```

1.5   Operators

C++ has a full set of arithmetic, relational and logical operators. It also has some interesting operators for direct bit-level manipulation of data objects. This is another of the likenesses of some C++ constructs to their assembler equivalents.

The binary arithmetic operators in C++ are:

+	addition
-	subtraction
*	multiplication
/	division
%	modulus

There is no operator for exponentiation; in line with general C++ practice, this is implemented as a special function in an external library.

Both + and - may be used as unary operators, as in the cases of -5 and +8. There is no difference between +8 and 8; for completeness, the unary plus operator was first required in the ISO C standard.

The modulus operator, %, provides a useful remainder facility:

    17%4   // gives 1, the remainder after division

The assignment operator, =, assigns a value to a memory location associated with a variable name. For example:

    a = 7;

    pi = 3.1415927;

Relational operators in C++ are:

    <   less than

    >   greater than

    >=   greater than or equal to

    <=   less than or equal to

    !=   not equal

    ==   test for equality

Care is needed in use of the equality test ==. A beginning programmer will at least once make the mistake of using a single = as an equality test; experienced programmers do it all the time! Writing

    x = 5;

assigns the value 5 to the memory location associated with the name x. The statement

    x == 5;

on the other hand, tests the value at the memory location associated with the name x for equality with 5.

Confusion here can result in serious program logic errors. It is a good idea, with the editor, to check all usages in the source code of = and == manually. The compiler will not catch these mistakes for you.

Logical operators provided by C++ are:

&&   AND

|| OR

!   NOT (unary negation operator)

If two variables are defined and initialised like this:

    int   x = 4;

    int   y = 5;

    then

    (x == 4) && (y == 5)   is TRUE

    (x == 4) > (y == 3)   is TRUE

    !x   is FALSE

In C++, any non-zero variable is inherently TRUE; its negation is therefore FALSE. The quantities true and false are defined by ANSI C++ for use with boolena variables (type bool).not themselves part of the C++ language; they must be defined with the preprocessor:

By convention in C++, truth is defined as non-zero and falsehood as zero. This, unfortunately, is the opposite of the interpretation adopted by operating systems including UNIX. Thus, while a C++ program will use zero internally to represent a failure of some kind, it will probably, when it terminates, return zero to the operating system to indicate success.

1.6   Expressions and Statements

An expression is any valid combination of function names, variables, constants, operators and subexpressions. A simple statement is an expression terminated by a semicolon.

The following are all expressions:

    a = 5

    cout << "Hello World\n"

    a = b + c

    a = b + (c * d)

Every expression has a type, depending on the types of its constituents, and a boolean value. An expression may be assigned to a variable:

```
a = printf("Hello World\n");
```

In this statement, a is assigned the value returned by the library function printf – the number of characters output by printf. More usefully:

```
a = b + c;
```

assigns to a the sum of the values of variables b and c.

Expressions in C++ may be extremely complex. Here is a slightly less simple one:

```
a = b + c * d
```

In this case, the order of arithmetic evaluation is important:

```
a = b + (c * d)
```

is not the same as

```
a = (b + c) * d
```

because the precedence of the operators is different. We can summarise the order of precedence of common C++ operators as follows:

()	Sub-expressions surrounded with parentheses (high precedence)
! -	The unary negation operator and unary minus
* / %	The arithmetic operators
+ -	The plus and minus binary arithmetic operators
< <= > >=	The relational operators
!= ==	The equality operators
&& >	The logical operators (low precedence)

Statements may optionally be grouped inside pairs of curly braces {}. One or more statements so grouped form a compound statement:

```
{
    printf("Two statements...\n");
    printf("that are logically one\n");
}
```

That a compound statement is a single logical entity is illustrated by the conditional statement:

```
if (s == 2)
{
    printf("Two statements...\n");
    printf("that are logically one\n");
}
```

If the variable s has the value 2, both printfs are executed. Where the two statements are simple and not compound:

```
if (s == 2)
    printf("Two statements...\n");
    printf("that are logically distinct\n");
```

the second printf is executed even if s is not equal to 2.

1.7   Standard Device I/O

The concept of *standard device* is important in C++. If you are using a terminal, you may think of the *standard input* as being the keyboard and the *standard output* as the screen.

A C program may read text from the standard input by means of the getchar library function and send text to the standard output using printf, which we have already seen, or the putchar library function.

The equivalent C++ program reads text from the standard input using the get member functions of the istream object and sends text to the standard output using the cout object of type ostream. For details of these techniques, see chapters 2 and 8.

printf is the name of a library function. Its declaration is stored in the header file stdio.h. The '.h' suffix is a convention used to denote a header file.

Header files are included in C++ programs by means of the #include directive, as follows:

```
#include <stdio.h>
```

stdio.h contains many declarations of library functions, such as printf, as well as other useful definitions, including those for NULL (binary zero) and EOF (end-of-file, usually represented as -1).

The printf function call includes at least one argument. The first argument is always a string and is called the *format string*. The format string contains two kinds of objects: ordinary characters, which are copied to the standard output device, and format codes, which are prefixed by a %. The format string causes printf to output any following arguments in the manner specified by the format codes.

If they are specified, the second and subsequent arguments to printf are variables or expressions. Here is an example:

```
#include <stdio.h>

int main(void)
{
   int      num = 6;
   float    e = 2.718282;

   printf
   ("Number is %d, fraction is %f\n", num,e);

   return(0);
}
```

The printf call causes the following display on the standard output device:

```
Number is 6, fraction is 2.718282
```

Fundamental printf format codes are:

%d   decimal integer

%f   floating-point number

%g   double floating-point number

%s   string

%c   character

With these codes, and variations on them, quite sophisticated text output can be generated using printf.

The getchar function reads the next input character from the standard input device and returns that character as its value. Consider the following code segment:

```
int c;

c = getchar();
```

After its execution, c contains the next character read from the standard input. The statement

```
putchar(c);
```

writes the character represented by the value stored at c to the standard output device.

1.8   Conditional Statements

The if statement is used to allow decisions and consequent changes in the flow of control to be made by the program logic. The following is the general form of if:

```
if (<expression>)
  <statement1>
else
  <statement2>
```

The else part is optional: an if statement with one or more subject statements and no alternative provided by else is legal. For example:

```
if (nobufs < MAXBUF)
  nobufs = nobufs + 1;
```

Here, if the number of buffers used is less than the allowed maximum, the counter of used buffers is incremented by one.

Two or more statements may be made subject to an if by use of a compound statement:

```
if (day == 1)
{
  printf("Monday\n");
  week = week + 1;
}
if (day == 2)
{
  printf("Tuesday\n");
  run_sales_report();
}
```

else should be used where the program logic suggests it:

```
if (day == 1)
```

```
{
  printf("Monday\n");
  week = week + 1;
}
else
if (day == 2)
{
  printf("Tuesday\n");
  run_sales_report();
}
```

Use of else here stops execution of the Tuesday code if the value of day is 1.

It is possible to nest if statements:

```
if (month == 2)
  if (day == 29)
    printf("Leap Year!!\n");
  else
    printf("February\n");
```

Nesting of ifs can be performed to arbitrary depth and complexity while the whole construct remains syntactically a single statement.

1.9   Iteration

Where the if statement allows a branch in the program flow of control, the for, while and do statements allow repeated execution of code in loops.

```
#include <stdio.h>

int main(void)
{
  int x;

  x = 1;
  while (x < 100)
  {
    printf("Number %d\n",x);
    x = x + 1;
  }

  return(0);
}
```

This program displays all the numbers from 1 to 99 inclusive.

```c
#include <stdio.h>
int main(void)
{
   int x;
   for (x = 1; x < 100; x = x + 1)
      printf("Number %d\n",x);

   return(0);
}
```

This program does exactly the same. The for statement is often used when the condition limits – in this case 1 and 100 – are known in advance. The general form of the for statement is this:

```c
for (<expr1>;<expr2>;<expr3>)
   <statement>
```

Any of the expressions may be omitted, but the two semicolons must be included. For example, the statement:

```c
for (;;);
```

results in an infinite loop.

The do statement is a special case of while. It is generally used where is it is required to execute the loop statements at least once:

```c
do
{
   c = getchar();
   if (c == EOF)
      printf("End of text\n");
   else
      /* do something with c */
} while (c != EOF);
```

The *symbolic constant* EOF is defined in stdio.h as the numeric value -1. The keystroke sequence required to generate this value is system-dependent. On UNIX systems, EOF is generated by *Ctrl-D*; on PCs by *Ctrl-Z*. Use of do instead of while is relatively rare: perhaps 5% of all cases.

Review of the C Language   15

The following example illustrates use of putchar, getchar, if and one of the iterative statements.

```
/*
 * Program to copy standard input to
 * standard output but stripping out
 * newlines
 */
#include <stdio.h>

int main(void)
{
    int c;

    while ((c = getchar()) != EOF)
    {
        if (c != '\n')
                putchar(c);
    }

    return(0);
}
```

Notice the getchar function call embedded in the while condition expression. This is legal and also considered good practice in concise programming.

1.10 Arrays and Structures

An array is an aggregate data object consisting of one or more data elements all of the same type. Arrays contrast with structures – aggregate data objects consisting of members of possibly different types. Any of the data objects we have seen may be stored in an array. An array of ten integer variables may be defined like this:

```
int   num[10];
```

The value within the square brackets, [], is known as a *subscript*. In the case above, ten contiguous memory locations for integer values are allocated by the compiler. In this case, the subscript range is from zero to 9. When using a variable as a subscript, care must be taken to count from zero and stop one short of the subscript value. Failure to do this will result in unpleasant program errors.

A structure groups data objects of usually different types:

```
struct stock_type
{
   char      item_name[30];
   char      part_number[10];
   double    cost_price;
   double    sell_price;
   int       stock_on_hand;
   int       reorder_level;
};
```

An instance of a structure is created in the computer's memory like this:

```
struct stock_type item;
```

and an individual structure member is accessed using the dot operator:

```
item.part_number;
```

The following is a simple example of use of arrays:

```
/*
 * Fill integer array with zeros, fill
 * character array with blanks
 */

#include <stdio.h>

int main(void)
{
   int n[20];
   char      c[20];
   int i;

   for (i = 0; i < 20; i = i + 1)
   {
      n[i] = 0;
      c[i] = ' ';
   }

   return(0);
}
```

Notice that i starts the iteration with value zero and finishes at 19. If it were incremented to 20, a memory location outside the bounds of the array would be accessed. No array-bound checking is done by the C++ compiler or run-time system. To implement such checking, it is necessary to implement the [] enclosing the array bounds as an *overloaded operator* (see chapters 2 and 5).

A string is a character array terminated by the null character '\0', also known as *binary zero*. The standard library contains many functions that perform operations on strings. Here are three, which are needed for the program examples:

```
gets(<string>); // Read a string into an array
atoi(<string>); // Convert ASCII to integer
atof(<string>); // Convert ASCII to float
```

Using the following definitions:

```
char        instring[20];
int         binval;
double      floatval;
```

the statement

```
gets(instring);
```

reads from the standard input device a string of maximum length 20 characters, including the null terminator '\0'. There is nothing to stop the entry of data greater than 20 characters long; if there are more than 20 characters, truncation will ensue.

The terminated character array instring may then be converted into its integer numeric equivalent value using the library function atoi:

```
binval = atoi(instring);
```

instring may be converted into its double floating-point numeric equivalent value using the library function atof:

```
floatval = atof(instring);
```

1.11 Pointers

A pointer is the address of a data object in memory. More than any other construct, pointers set C and C++ apart from all other languages. PL/1 and Pascal have pointers in their syntax, but these are not as flexible in use as C++ pointers. Use of pointers in C++ code is ubiquitous.

A variable definition allocates space for the data and associates a name with that data. The data name refers directly to the data stored at the memory location. Pointers, on the other hand, are data objects which point to other data objects.

A character variable is defined as follows:

```
char c;
```

A character pointer is defined like this:

```
char *cptr;
```

cptr is a *pointer to* a data object of type char.

The statement:

```
cptr = &c;
```

assigns the address of c to the character pointer cptr.

Before this assignment, cptr pointed nowhere in particular; after it, cptr points to the memory location associated with the data name c. After the assignment of the address of c to cptr:

cptr points to (contains the memory address of) c.

*cptr is the *contents* of or the *object at* the pointer cptr.

*cptr equals c.

To use a pointer such as cptr before it is assigned a memory address is always an error. In fact, it is one of the most common serious runtime errors encountered in C++ programming. It is easy even for experienced programmers to neglect pointer initialisation. This has led to inclusion in the C++ language of the *constructor* mechanism to guarantee it.

Let us make a character pointer point to an array:

```
char instring[20];
```

First, we define a character pointer:

```
char *cptr;
```

Now, we want to assign the address of the array to the character pointer. The address of a simple data item, such as c above, is found using the address operator &. In the case of an array, *the address of the array is the name of the array itself.* No & operator is needed. This is a syntactic inconsistency in the C++ language that can cause confusion for inexperienced programmers. The statement

```
cptr = instring;
```

assigns the address of the array instring to the pointer cptr. cptr now points to the first element of the array.

*cptr is the contents of the first element of the array and is the same in meaning as instring[0]. Similarly, *(cptr+1) represents the contents of the array's second element, as does instring[1].

The relationship between the pointer, the array's name (address) and the contents of the array – assumed here to be the character sequence 'J', 'K', 'L' – can be described graphically:

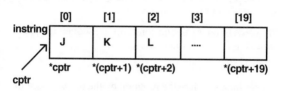

Data objects of all types – including pointers themselves – may have pointers. In this introduction, we have only seen character pointers.

1.12 C++ Preprocessor

Before a C++ program is compiled, the source code is processed by the C++ preprocessor. The preprocessor deals only with lines of code which have a # character (*hash* in Europe, *pound* in North America) as the first non-whitespace character in a line of source code.

The # must be followed by a preprocessor directive. The full set of preprocessor directives includes the following:

define	if
include	ifndef
ifdef	endif

For the moment, we will consider only the first two.

We may define symbolic constants with #define thus:

```
#define    PI    3.1415927

#define    MAX   20
```

Wherever MAX is subsequently used in the body of the program source code, the preprocessor, before compilation, converts it into the associated value – in this case, 20. Preprocessor definitions must not be terminated with semicolons.

Defining symbolic constants using the preprocessor gives a number of benefits. First, it helps eliminate *magic numbers* from the program source. PI makes more sense, especially to a non-mathematician, than 3.1415927.

Secondly, if it is decided to change the value of MAX, it is changed once, where it is defined, rather than at every occurrence throughout the program.

By convention, symbolic constants are written in upper-case, C++ variables in lower-case.

```
#include <stdio.h>
```

causes inclusion into the program by the preprocessor of the full text of the standard input/output header file stdio.h.

There are other standard header files, such as math.h and string.h, which may be similarly included. The standard header files collectively provide declarations for the functions and macros made available by the C++ Library.

In addition to using the standard header files, the programmer may write and include original files. Writing one's own header files is good practice for grouping in one place a definitive copy of data declarations. Rather than incorporating the declarations explicitly in the program source code, they are #included using the preprocessor. This means that all program files that include the header file are using the same declarations, giving a reduction in compile-time errors and inconsistencies.

2 A Tour of C++

2.1 Compilation and Execution

A C++ program is a set of one or more functions and data, known as source code, 'written' by the programmer with an editor program. The source code is then stored in a file which, by convention, has an arbitrary name followed by one of several possible suffixes.

The filename suffix for C programs is universally '.c'. C++ filename suffixes are not so standardised. On computers running the UNIX operating system, the C++ source code filename may end with either '.c' or '.C'. For many C++ systems running on PCs and workstations, the suffix is '.cpp'. Some PC-based C++ compilers require the suffix '.cxx'. This text uses exclusively the suffix '.cpp'.

First, the C++ program source code is scanned by the C preprocessor. The preprocessor performs the same function as for C programs: text substitutions and header-file inclusion. Because C++ supports constant values (as does ISO C) and *inline functions* (shown later in this chapter), C++ programs use the preprocessor mainly for including header files and conditional compilation, with the #define directive being largely supplanted. After the preprocessing step, the changed source code is passed to the C++ compiler.

The first C++ systems were based on the AT&T *cfront* translator. A number of C++ cfront implementations are available today. The C++ source code is translated — one can argue that this is a compilation process — into equivalent C code, which is then processed into object code by the local C compiler.

Other C++ systems comprise both a C compiler and a full C++ compiler, which are independent. Depending on the source filename suffix, '.c' or '.cpp', one or the other is used.

Whichever method is employed, the name of the object code file output is the same as that of the source code file, except that it is suffixed with either '.o' or '.obj'.

Next, the *linkage editor*, or *loader*, combines the object code with the object code of library files and the runtime system. Variable references are resolved and an executable program file for the target computer and operating system is produced. The executable program file may then be run on the computer.

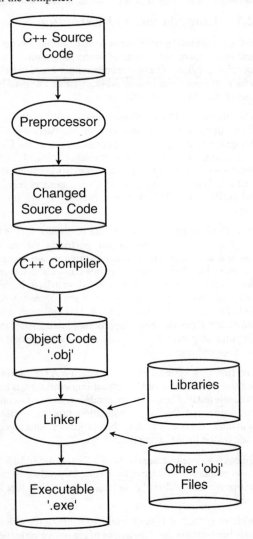

Conventional C++ Program Build Sequence

Large software systems written in either C or C++ usually consist of many source code files, known as *translation units*, which are compiled separately and then loaded together at the end of the process. In C++, this is particularly appropriate.

Declarations of classes, including data, function prototypes and inline functions, are typically stored in header files that are included by the preprocessor in the program file containing the main function. main acts as a driver, calling the functions declared as part of the classes. The definitions of the functions declared in the classes are often stored in another program file.

This organisation of files allows class declarations and the definitions of their member functions to be stored in files that can be compiled and then reused by other programmers, who do not have to be aware of how the classes and functions are implemented.

This text does not deal further with characteristics of particular compilation environments. Options are always available in these environments to control the sequence referred to above.

2.2   Simple C++ Programs

Here is the C++ program of the conventional *Hello World* type:

```
//  greet.cpp - program to display a greeting

#include  <iostream.h>

int main()
{
   cout << "Hello C++ World\n";
   return(0);
}
```

The double-slash comment notation unofficially introduced in many C implementations is accepted in C++: all characters following the double slash // on the same line are ignored. The /*..........*/ notation of C is retained in C++ but, for short comments, // is preferred.

stdio.h is replaced by the header file, iostream.h. This contains class and function declarations that are included by the preprocessor in the source code file and are necessary for the facilities of the C++ *Stream I/O Library* to be used.

One such facility is cout, which is an object representing the standard output stream. The characters to the right of the << operator are sent to cout, which causes them to be displayed on the user's terminal screen, assuming that is the standard output device. The << operator is in fact the bitwise left-shift operator *overloaded* by the C++ system to mean 'insert on a stream'. The C++ Stream I/O system is fully explained in Chapter 8.

Here is a program that uses an elementary class construct and does the same thing as 'greet.cpp':

```
//   clgreet.cpp - program using a simple C++
//   class to display a greeting

#include <iostream.h>

class message
{
private:
public:
   void greeting()
   {
      cout << "Hello C++ World\n";
   }
};

int main()
{
   class message user;

   user.greeting();
   return(0);
}
```

The program's comments and inclusion of iostream.h are as before. The declaration of the class type message is new. Classes are treated further in Section 2.4 and in detail in Chapter 3. For now, message is briefly explained.

Everything within the enclosing curly braces following message is a member of the class message. All the members of message are declared public; they are generally accessible. message only has one public member, a function called greeting which has no return type or argument list.

In the function main, an instance of the message class, called user, is defined. The greeting function is called and the Hello C++ World message displayed by the function call:

```
user.greeting();
```

Use of a class in this case is overkill, but it demonstrates the general form and one of the simplest possible uses of the class construct.

2.3   C++ Extensions to C

This section deals briefly with the most important changes to the syntax of C++ from ISO C, apart from the addition of object-oriented programming facilities and the Stream I/O, template and other libraries. A more exhaustive list of extensions is given in Appendix A.

STATEMENTS

In ISO C, a simple, rather than compound, statement is an expression followed by a semicolon. In C++, declarations followed by semicolons are also statements. Because a declaration and semicolon is a statement, declarations do not have to come first in a statement block but can follow other statements:

```
#include <iostream.h>

int main()
{
  for (int x = 5; x < 10; x++)
    ;
  cout << "First declaration: " << x << "\n";
  int y = 6;
  cout << "Both declarations: " << x << " "
          << y << "\n";
  return(0);
}
```

This order of declarations and statements is valid C++ syntax. Also, a variable can be declared and initialised as part of the controlling expression of a for loop. The result produced by this program is:

```
First declaration:  10
Both declarations:  10 6
```

CLASS AND STRUCTURE TAGS

The tag of a class, structure or enumerated type is itself a type. In C, a structure is declared like this:

```
struct list
{
  int      x;
  double   y;
};
```

An instance of the structure, inst, is defined like this:

```
struct list inst;
```

In C++, it can be done in the same way or with the shortened form:

```
list inst;
```

KEYWORDS

C++ introduces a number of new keywords, including:

class	delete	friend
inline	new	operator
private	protected	public
template	virtual	

These are all explained later in this chapter and a full list is given in Appendix A. Any C program containing any of these keywords as variable names is not a valid C++ program.

DYNAMIC MEMORY ALLOCATION

As an alternative to the malloc and free function family of C, C++ introduces the new and delete operators, which perform dynamic memory allocation and deallocation:

```
#include <iostream.h>

int main()
{
  int *x;
  x = new int;
  *x = 5;
```

```
    cout << "Allocated-integer value: "
                    << *x << "\n";
    delete x;
    return(0);
}
```

new allocates memory heap space for an integer and returns a pointer to that space to **x**. Pointer-dereferencing is used thereafter to access the contents of **x**.

FUNCTION PROTOTYPES

Although ISO C got its function prototyping mechanism from C++, there is one important difference in this respect between the two languages. In ISO C, the prototype:

```
int myfunc();
```

means that the function **myfunc** takes zero or more parameters. In C++, it means that **myfunc** takes no parameters. This closes a loophole in ISO C type checking.

Every function in a C++ program that is called before its definition must be declared, before the function call, with a prototype. For functions with return values of type int, this is unnecessary (though recommended) in ISO C.

FUNCTION CALL-BY-REFERENCE

In C, when a variable is passed as an argument between functions, it is by default passed by value, or copied, to the called function. The variable's value in the calling function is not changed by whatever happens in the called function. To make a change to the variable have effect in the calling function, a pointer to the variable must be used as the argument in the function call. C++ additionally provides a true call-by-reference mechanism, using the *reference type*:

```
#include <iostream.h>

void myfunc(int&);  // prototype

int main()
{
    int x = 5;
    myfunc(x);
    cout << "Changed value: " << x << "\n";
    return(0);
}
```

```
void myfunc(int& x_ref)
{
    x_ref = 10;
}
```

Although the initial value of x is 5, the value is changed
to 10 in main after the call to myfunc. x is passed to
myfunc as a reference. x_ref is not a copy of or a pointer
to x but an alias, or alternative name, for it. The reference
is likely to be implemented internally by the C++ system
with pointers and dereferencing (although the C++
language specification does not require this), thus freeing
the programmer from having to supply pointers as
arguments and dereference them in the called function.

INLINE FUNCTIONS

When an ordinary function is called, a jump to the
function's *entry point* (address) is executed. If a function
is called often, and especially if it is small, this overhead
may be prohibitive. C++ provides the inline keyword,
which is prefixed either to the function's declaration or
its definition. The function myfunc in the last example
can be declared and defined as inline thus:

```
#include <iostream.h>

inline void myfunc(int& x_ref) { x_ref = 10; }

int main()
{
    int x = 5;

    myfunc(x);

    cout << "Changed value: " << x << "\n";
    return(0);
}
```

inline acts as a prompt to the compiler to treat myfunc as
a macro: the same as if the code were embedded in the
body of main. This avoids the function call overhead.
Use of inline does not guarantee that the function will be
treated as such and is, in that sense, similar to a register
declaration. Because the inline function myfunc is defined
at the place of its declaration, the function prototype may
be omitted.

Large functions should not be declared inline. As is explained in the next section, implicitly inline functions may be defined within C++ classes.

OPERATOR AND FUNCTION OVERLOADING

C++ allows operators from its basic operator set, such as + and ==, to be given additional meanings defined by the programmer. For example, == can be used to compare structures for equality, an operation which is illegal in C. Examples of operator overloading are given in Section 2.7 and Chapter 5.

Functions may be declared and defined more than once with different argument lists. Calls to the different instances of the functions may be made, and the compiler resolves the calls based on the differences between the argument lists they specify. Here are two function prototype declarations:

```
double sqr_func(int);
double sqr_func(float, float); // overloaded
```

The function call:

```
result = sqr_func(1.732, 1.732);
```

causes the compiler to select the second function definition for execution.

Function overloading is the generalisation of operator overloading and is covered in full in Chapter 5.

2.4   Classes

DEFINITION

C++ introduces classes to provide language support for the object-oriented programming approach. The class is a generalisation of the structure (struct) construct found in C. The class, along with inheritance and virtual functions, is the central innovation made by C++.

Like a structure, a class consists of a number of *members*. Unlike the structure, the members can be functions. A class is used to describe a real-world object.

For example, consider the case of a clock. A clock records information including (at least) hours and minutes.

At least two operations are possible on this information: the minutes may be advanced by 1 and the hours may be advanced by 1. In C++ the clock's information and possible operations might be recorded like this:

```
class clock
{
private:
  int  minutes;
  int  hours;
public:
  void adv_minute();
  void adv_hour();
};
```

This is a class declaration; to define an instance of the class – often also referred to as a *class object* or *class variable* – is similar to definition of a struct instance in C:

```
class clock wall_clock;
```

or

```
clock wall_clock;
```

The second definition takes account of the fact that, in C++, the tag name, clock, is itself a type.

CHARACTERISTICS

There are two parts to the class clock, private and public. The private keyword means that the class members declared following it are only accessible to member functions of the class clock– adv_minute and adv_hour. The public keyword means that any other class or function may make a call to either of the functions adv_minute or adv_hour.

Before making such a call, an instance of the class must be defined as above. Then the call looks like this:

```
wall_clock.adv_minute();
```

The *data hiding* that is enforced by the private part of the class means that the private members cannot be directly used by code other than that defined in the member functions of the same class. All that is available to outside code is the class's *function call interface*; the internal implementation of the class remains a *black box*.

This mechanism results in the production of highly modular code that may be reused by many programmers, without their having to know anything about the code other than how to call it.

The general class clock as declared above can be refined. Further classes can be designed that take on the characteristics of clock and add new ones. For example, the class digital might add seconds and a stopwatch function; and the class analog might add a large bell. This is an intuitive example of class inheritance.

LIST CLASS EXAMPLE

Here is an example program that uses a class to define a rudimentary (one-element!) linked list. This example is built on for the remainder of this chapter and used to illustrate, in as simple a manner as possible, some of the principal facilities provided by the C++ language.

```
// list.h -- include file for elementary
// list-handling program

class list
{
private:
  struct element
  {
    int    x;
    double y;
    element *next;
  };
  element* instance;
public:
  void get_element_data(int&, double&);
  void assign(int a, double b)
  {
    instance = new element;
    instance->x = a;
    instance->y = b;
    instance->next = NULL;
  }
  void display();
};
```

The class list has as its private members a declaration of the structure element and the definition of a pointer, instance, to a structure of type element. The public

members get_element_data and display are prototypes
of functions that carry out operations on the structure.
The definitions of these functions are in the program file
'listfunc.cpp'. The function assign has an implicitly
inline definition. This prompts the compiler to treat
assign as a macro, without incurring the overhead of a
function call. It should only be used for short, often-used
functions.

Here are the definitions of the member functions:

```cpp
// listfunc.cpp – defines element-handling
// functions.

#include <iostream.h>
#include "list.h"

void list::get_element_data(int& a, double& b)
{
  cout << "Enter an integer: ";
  cin >> a;
  cout << "Enter a double: ";
  cin >> b;
}

void list::display()
{
  if (instance)      //      list not empty
  cout << "Integer: " << instance->x <<
      " Double: " << instance->y << " \n";
}
```

The Stream I/O header file is included, as is list.h. The
function header notation for functions declared as part of
the class list needs explanation. In both cases, :: is the
C++ *scope resolution* operator. In the case of display, it
specifies that display is in the scope of class list and has
no return value (void). In this way, another display
function in another class can be distinguished.

get_element_data is similarly in the scope of list and
has no return value. Its argument list matches the prototype
given in the declaration of list and specifies that the
function is supplied with arguments that are references to
one integer and one double floating-point variable.

get_element_data also contains the first use we have
seen of cin, the standard input stream object. This is the

reverse of cout. It causes input from the standard input (typically the keyboard) to be assigned to the variable following the >> operator. Input is terminated by EOF, defined in iostream.h.

Lastly, here is the main function, stored in the program file 'list.cpp', which acts as a driver for the functions declared in the class list:

```cpp
// Program 'list.cpp' – creates a
// single-element linked list

#include <iostream.h>
#include "list.h"

int main()
{
    int x;
    double y;

    list list1, list2;

    // call by reference
    list1.get_element_data(x, y);
    // call by value
    list1.assign(x, y);
    list2.get_element_data(x, y);
    list2.assign(x, y);
    list1.display();
    list2.display();
    return(0);
}
```

First, the header files are included. The integer variable x and the double y are defined within main to act as storage areas for user-input data. Two instances of the class list, list1 and list2, are defined.

The function calls follow. Note that each function call must be made in a way that explicitly specifies the function as being a member of a particular instance of the class list. Using, for example, the call:

```cpp
get_element_data(x,y);
```

instead of:

```cpp
list1.get_element_data(x,y);
```

causes the compiler to generate a message claiming that the function prototype is absent. In fact, the function prototype is in the list1 instance of list and the function call must be prefixed with 'list1.' for the call and the prototype to be matched.

All the function calls qualified with 'list1.' operate on the list1 instance of list. Those qualified with 'list2.' operate on the list2 instance of list.

Both calls to get_element_data are calls by reference; x and y are passed to reference declarations in the function header argument list. This causes the changed values of the two variables on return from get_element_data, after user input, to be seen in main.

The function assign is called with arguments x and y by value; assign does not change their values but merely assigns x and y to a newly-allocated list element.

The statement:

```
instance = new element;
```

allocates memory space for a new instance of the nested structure element and assigns the address of that memory to the pointer instance, which is also of type element. Assignments are made to the member variables in the ordinary way:

```
instance->x = a;
instance->y = b;
instance->next = NULL;
```

The two calls to the function display:

```
list1.display();
list2.display();
```

cause the contents of both instances of the class list to be displayed on standard output.

It is illegal for the private members of the class list to be accessed directly other than by the member functions of the class. Therefore, to enter a line such as this in main:

```
list1.instance->x = a;
```

is an error. A direct operation such as this is only legal within the member functions of list. Within one of the member functions of list1, use of the 'list1.' prefix is unnecessary.

The organisation of program files shown here is typical.

Class declarations are stored in one or more header files defined by the programmer. The definitions of the member functions of the class or classes are in a program file separate from the one containing the main function – in this case 'listfunc.cpp'. main, acting as a driver, is in 'list.cpp'.

Compilation procedures vary between C++ implementations but it is usually possible to use a command-line operation such as this, used by Borland C++ 4.5:

```
bcc list.cpp listfunc.cpp
```

or this, used in UNIX environments:

```
CC -o list list.C listfunc.C
```

After the program files have been compiled and loaded, the executable program may be run.

2.5   Constructors and Destructors

In the example shown in the last section, the programmer has to remember to allocate space for element and to initialise it. This is done in the assign function. A common source of errors in all programs is when the initialisation is omitted. In this case, if the programmer forgets the allocation and initialisation, every subsequent use of the pointer instance is an error.

In cases where memory is dynamically allocated, especially in list and text processing, the programmer should take care to return storage to the system's free list when it is no longer required. When an element is deleted from a linked list in a C program, it should be explicitly discarded and returned to the system using the free library function call. Again, the programmer may forget to do this. Failure to free storage is less serious than leaving out the initialisation but it can in extreme cases exhaust system memory.

In C++, automatic initialisation and discarding are done using constructors and destructors. This makes C++ programs more reliable than their C counterparts.

A constructor is a member function of a class which initialises a variable of that class. The constructor function name is always the same as the class name.

A destructor is a member function of a class which performs housekeeping operations, and perhaps deallocates memory used by a class object, before the class object is itself destroyed. The destructor function name is the same as the class name and is prefixed with a tilde, '~'.

The constructor function is called as part of the variable definition; the destructor is called not explicitly but automatically when the variable goes out of scope.

Here is the list class reworked to use constructors and destructors. First, list.h:

```
// list.h – include file for elementary
// list-handling program

class list
{
private:
  struct element
  {
     int    x;
     double  y;
     element *next;
  };
  element* instance;
public:
  list() { instance = new element; }
  void get_element_data(int&, double&);
  void assign(int a, double b)
  {
     instance->x = a;
     instance->y = b;
     instance->next = NULL;
  }
  void display();
  ~list() { delete instance; }
};
```

The constructor list() is called every time an instance of the class list, such as list1 or list2, is defined and each time causes a new instance of element to be allocated. The memory is discarded when the variables go out of scope.

As is explained in Chapter 4, constructor function calls may be specified with arguments, while destructors must not. The program files 'list.cpp' and 'listfunc.cpp' are unchanged.

LIST25: IMPROVED USE OF CONSTRUCTORS AND DESTRUCTORS

Although the class declaration above uses constructors and destructors, it does not take full advantage of them. When they are used well, constructors and destructors often dramatically reduce the size of C++ programs. In the list example, the code of the assign function can – and should – be subsumed by the list constructor. Here is the entire program, consisting of the header file, list.h and the program files 'listfunc.cpp' and 'list.cpp':

```
// list.h – include file for elementary
// list-handling program

class list
{
private:
  struct element
  {
     int    x;
     double y;
     element *next;
  };
  element* instance;
public:
  list();

  void display();

  ~list() { delete instance; }
};


// 'listfunc.cpp' – program file for 'list'
//  member functions

#include <iostream.h>

list::list()
{
  instance = new element;

  cout << "Enter an integer: ";
  cin >> instance->x;
  cout << "Enter a double: ";
  cin >> instance->y;
  instance->next = NULL;
}
```

```
void list::display()
{
  if (instance)                    //         list not empty
  cout << "Integer: " << instance->x <<
       " Double: " << instance->y << " \n";
}

// Program file 'list.cpp'
#include <iostream.h>
#include "list.h"

int main()
{
  list list1, list2;

  list1.display();
  list2.display();
  return(0);
}
```

Here, the list constructor function is made to do all the
work of initialising list class objects. This leads to
elimination of the functions get_element_data and
assign as well as the the intermediate storage variables
x and y. The result is a program no more than half as long
as that in which constructors are used naïvely.

2.6   Friends

In a strict OOP world, only public member functions of
a class are allowed direct access to the private member
variables. Things are not that simple, however, and C++
provides the friend mechanism, which allows the rules to
be bent.

A function may be specified within a class declaration
and prefixed with the keyword friend. In such a case, the
function is not a member of the class, but the function is
allowed access to the private members of the class. This
is illustrated again using the list example. First, list.h:

```
// list.h – include file for elementary
// list-handling program

class list
```

```
{
private:
  struct element
  {
    int    x;
    double y;
    element *next;
  };
  element* instance;
public:
  list() { instance = new element; }
  void get_element_data(int&, double&);
  void assign(int a, double b)
  {
    instance->x = a;
    instance->y = b;
    instance->next = NULL;
  }
  friend void access_element(const list&);
  void display();
  ~list() { delete instance; }
};
```

There is only one change: a prototype for the friend function access_element is added. This function is defined in 'listfunc.cpp' as follows:

```
void access_element(const list& l)
{
  // get and do something with the list's
  // private data members

  cout << l.instance->x
       << " "
       << l.instance->y;
}
```

The function is called from main in 'list.cpp':

```
int main()
{
  //  'main' unchanged to here
  //  call by value
  list1.assign(x, y);

  //  call 'friend' function
  access_element(list1);
```

```
    list2.get_element_data(x, y);
    list2.assign(x, y);

    //   call 'friend' function
    access_element(list2);

    list1.display();
    list2.display();

    //   destructor called when list1 and
    //   list2 go out of scope
    return(0);
}
```

access_element is a friend of class list. It is not a member of list or of either of the instances of list, list1 or list2. It is not, therefore, called as a class member with the 'list1.' or 'list2.' prefix. In 'listfunc.cpp', it is defined as an ordinary function; the scope resolution operator is not necessary since access_element is not a member of any class.

Because this is so, access_element must be called with each class instance as an argument for the members of list1 and list2 respectively to be added. This is done using a reference declaration, qualified with const, in the prototype and function header.

To underline the effect of the friend function declaration, consider main. main is not a member or friend of any class. To use a member variable of list like this:

```
    list1.instance->x
```

in main directly is an error; main does not have direct access to the private members of the class. Because the function access_element is a friend, the same usage within access_element is valid.

As well as having friend functions, a class can have friend classes. In the following case:

```
    class list
    {
    private:
      .
      //   private members unchanged
      .
```

```
public:
    .
    // public members unchanged to here
    .
    friend class spreadsheet;
    void display();
    ~list() { delete instance; }
};
```

the class **spreadsheet** is declared to be a **friend** of **list**. We do not need to know the contents of **spreadsheet** to understand this: all member functions of **list** have access to the private members of **list** and so do all member functions of **spreadsheet**.

The **friend** mechanism is a dilution of the principles of object-oriented programming and, as such, has caused controversy. Use of **friend** declarations is discouraged unless:

- A function must have access to the private members of two or more classes.

- They are put to their best use, which is in defining overloaded-operator functions.

Overloaded operators are dealt with in detail in Chapter 5.

2.7   Overloading

C++ provides two kinds of overloading: *function overloading* and *operator overloading*. This section gives an example of both, using the **list** class.

Function overloading allows more than one version of a function with the same name to be used, with the appropriate version being called according to the parameter types used by the function.

Operator overloading allows a standard C++ operator to take on a new meaning.

Here is the **list.h** file, with the **list** class declaration changed to include an overloaded function and an overloaded operator. The **friend** function **access_element** is omitted.

```
// list.h – include file for elementary
// list-handling program

class list
{
private:
  struct element
  {
    int    x;
    double y;
    element *next;
  };
  element* instance;
public:
  list() { instance = new element; }
  void get_element_data(int&, double&);
  void assign(int a, double b)
  {
    instance->x = a;
    instance->y = b;
    instance->next = NULL;
  }
  void display();
  void display(int, double);
  friend int operator==(list&, list&);
  ~list() { delete instance; }
};
```

The function display is overloaded. Prototypes of two versions of it are declared. The appropriate version is selected depending on the absence or presence of arguments in the function call.

The operator == is overloaded. In C and C++, it is illegal to use the basic equality operator== to compare structures. Here, the == is made to do so. The keyword operator announces that the == operator is to be applied to the list1 and list2 instances of class list, allowing comparison of their members.

operator== is a function declaration, specifying a return type of int. For reasons explained in Chapter 5, it is declared as a friend of class list; it has access to the private members of list without being a member function.

The new display and operator== functions are incorporated in 'listfunc.cpp':

```
void list::display()
{
  if (instance)    //      list not empty
  cout << "Integer: " << instance->x <<
       " Double: " << instance->y << " \n";
}

void list::display(int a, double b)
{
  //    Display the input data
  cout << "Data Input: \n";
  cout << "Integer " << a <<
              " Double " << b << "\n";
}

int operator==(list& list1, list& list2)
{
  if ((list1.instance->x == list2.instance->x)
     && (list1.instance->y == list2.instance->y))
     return (1);
  return (0);
}
```

The display function with argument list consisting of a and b displays these variables, which contain the data input by the user. The display function that already existed takes no parameters and displays the contents of an instance of list. One or other of the functions is selected depending on the arguments specified in the function call.

The operator== function specifies that when two instances of class list are used with the overloaded == operator like this:

list1 == list2

for both, the members x and y of the single list element are compared. Note that the use of == within the function is not overloaded; they are comparing operands of types other than list. Depending on the result of the comparison, either a 1 (TRUE) or a 0 (FALSE) is returned by the function.

Now we can look at the main function:

```cpp
// Program 'list.cpp' - creates a single-
// element linked list

// Many C++ features are exercised,
// including constructors and destructors,
// function and operator overloading and
// 'friend's

int main()
{
   int x;
   double y;

   list list1, list2;

   // call by reference
   list1.get_element_data(x, y);

   // overloaded 'display' function
   list1.display(x, y);

   // call by value
   list1.assign(x, y);

   list2.get_element_data(x, y);
   list2.display(x, y);
   list2.assign(x, y);

   // overloaded '==' operator!
   if (list1 == list2)
      cout << "List elements are equal: \n";
   else
      cout << "List elements are different: \n";

   // calls to original 'display' function
   list1.display();
   list2.display();
   return(0);
}
```

Depending on the argument list in the display function calls, the compiler selects the right version. The == operator is overloaded, allowing simple comparison of list1 and list2.

Functions for overloading operators do not have to be members or friends of a class. Full rules for their use are given in Chapter 5.

2.8   Inheritance

Class inheritance is one of the main characteristics of the OOP approach. If a base class is declared, a derived class may also be declared that takes on all the attributes of the base and adds more. The derived class is said to inherit the base class. Hierarchies of derived classes of arbitrary depth may be built.

Single inheritance occurs when a derived class has only one base class; multiple inheritance is when a derived class has more than one base class. Multiple inheritance is covered fully in Chapter 6.

Here is a simple example of single inheritance based on a class, declared in the header file accounts.h, that might be used to implement a simple bank-account model:

```
class cust_acc
{
protected:
  float   bal;
  int     acc_num;
public:
  // 'cust_acc' member functions
};
```

The keyword private, which might be expected in the base class cust_acc, is instead protected so that its characteristics can be inherited by the derived class deposit.

Member functions of derived classes are allowed access if protected is used. A derived bank-account class, deposit is declared:

```
class deposit : public cust_acc
{
private:
  float int_rate;
public:
  // 'deposit' member functions
};
```

deposit inherits all non-private data and function members of the base class cust_acc. deposit adds the data member int_rate. A member function of deposit can now directly access any of the data members bal, acc_num or int_rate.

None of these data members can be accessed directly by code other than member functions of the class hierarchy. Member functions of the base class cannot access members of the derived class.

deposit inherits all member functions of the base class. If in deposit inherited functions are redeclared, those redeclarations are said to *override* the inherited functions. Inherited functions, however, need not be overridden; they may be declared for the first time in a derived class and join inherited data and functions as members of the derived class.

The main function defines a1 and a2 as objects of type cust_acc and deposit respectively:

```
#include <iostream.h>
#include "accounts.h"

int main()
{
    cust_acc a1;
    deposit a2;

    // Calls here to 'cust_acc' and 'deposit'
    // member functions
    return(0);
}
```

With large class hierarchies base and derived classes should be stored in separate header files. If the declaration of a derived class changes, code declaring and using the base class need not be recompiled and relinked.

2.9   Virtual Functions

Overloaded functions are matched to their corresponding function calls and selected for execution at compile time. This process is referred to as *early binding*.

If a member function declaration in a base class is preceded by the keyword virtual and followed by identical redeclarations of the same function name in one or more derived classes, then *late binding* or *dynamic binding* takes place.

CLOCK29: VIRTUAL FUNCTIONS

Here is an example, using a clock class hierarchy, that is of value for its brevity:

```cpp
#include <iostream.h>
class clock
{
protected:
  int hours, minutes;
public:
  virtual void display()
  {
     cout << "Generic clock\n";
  }
};

class digital : public clock
{
private:
  int hours, minutes, secs, tens;
public:
  virtual void display()
  {
     cout << "Digital stopwatch\n";
  }
};

class analog : public clock
{
private:
  int hours, minutes;
public:
  virtual void display()
  {
     cout << "Analogue clock\n";
  }
  void chime_on_hour()
  {
     if (minutes == 0)
             cout << "\a\a\a\a"; //   chime
  }
};

int main()
{
   clock *cptr[3];

   cptr[0] = new clock;
```

```
    cptr[1] = new digital;
    cptr[2] = new analog;

    for (int i = 0; i < 3; i++)
        cptr[i]->display();
    return(0);
}
```

Three classes are declared: the base class **clock** and the derived classes **digital** and **analog**. Each class declares the function **display** identically.

In **main**, an array of pointers to classes of type **clock** is defined. These pointers are in turn assigned addresses of new class objects.

A pointer to a base class, in this case **clock**, can also point to a class derived from that base. The selection of which virtual function to call is made at runtime depending on which class object is pointed to by the pointer. The selection is transparent to the programmer.

Use of the **virtual** keyword in the base class is necessary for the correct version of **display** to be selected at run time. It is not necessary to qualify the redefinitions of **display** in the derived classes as **virtual**, but it is useful for making it obvious in all classes in the hierarchy that the **display** function is virtual.

The output from the program is this:

```
Generic clock
Digital stopwatch
Big Ben
```

Along with classes and inheritance, virtual functions are a major characteristic of the OOP approach.

2.10 The C++ I/O System

The C++ environment provides a complete alternative to the ISO C Standard I/O library. This is called *Stream I/O* and is based on the declarations contained in the header file iostream.h. This section introduces some of the simple facilities offered by Stream I/O, which is fully described in Chapter 8.

iostream.h overloads the shift operators >> and << to be input and output operators. These operators are used with the four standard input and output streams:

cin	Standard input stream
cout	Standard output stream
cerr	Standard error stream
clog	Buffered equivalent of cerr, suitable for large amounts of output

The standard input stream typically represents the keyboard; the standard output stream the screen. cin is of type istream, a class declared in iostream.h. The other three streams are of type ostream, also declared in iostream.h.

If four variables are defined:

```
char    c;
int     i;
float   f;
double  d;
```

their values may be displayed with the following insertion on the output stream:

```
cout << c << i << f << d << endl;
```

The class ostream defines several *inserter types*, one of which is selected automatically to match the type of the variable being displayed. Therefore, the contents of the four variables are output as would the C statement:

```
printf("%c %d %f %g\n", c, i, f, d);
```

The predefined ostream operation endl has the effect of inserting on the output stream a newline ('\n') and also flushing the output buffer.

Reading from the input stream is done in much the same way:

```
cin >> c >> i >> f >> d;
```

This is similar in effect to the C statement:

```
scanf("%c %d %f %g", &c, &i, &f, &d);
```

Here are two program examples showing some other C++ I/O facilities:

```
#include <iostream.h>
int main()
{
    char c;
    while (cin.get(c))
        cout.put(c);
    return(0);
}
```

The get member function of class istream extracts one character from the input stream and stores it in c. The put member function of class ostream inserts one character on the output stream.

```
#include <iostream.h>
const int MAX = 80;
int main()
{
    char buf[MAX];
    while (cin.getline(buf, MAX))
    {
        int chars_in;
        chars_in = cin.gcount();
        cout.write(buf, chars_in);
    }
    return(0);
}
```

getline extracts at most MAX - 1 characters from the input stream and stores them in buf. getline by default finishes extracting characters after a newline is entered. The while loop above stops when EOF – defined in iostream.h, on PCs usually represented by *Ctrl-Z* and on UNIX by *Ctrl-d* – is encountered.

gcount returns the number of characters extracted by the last call to getline. write inserts at most chars_in characters on the output stream.

The effect of these two programs is to copy characters and strings from standard input to standard output.

The more-sophisticated C++ formatted-input and output facilities are dealt with in Chapter 8, which also describes a full set of alternatives for the C Standard Library file I/O functions.

2.11 Templates

The ANSI C++ Standard includes a number of new facilities, for example *runtime type identification* (RTTI) and *namespaces*. The base document for ANSI C++ was the *C++ Annotated Reference Manual* (Ellis and Stroustrup, 1990). A number of language facilities that, in the ARM, are listed as experimental have since been finalised in form and accepted as part of the C++ language specification. The most significant of these are templates and exception handling.

This section briefly introduces templates; the other innovations are described in later chapters.

Templates allow the types of function arguments and class members to be parameterised. In this way, a function can be defined as a family of functions capable of operating on arguments of any type. Similarly, a class can be defined as a family of classes containing data and function members of any type. If a class generalises an object, it can be said that a class template generalises a class.

Templates are suitable for implementing the so-called *container classes* – those that describe collections of objects of similar type. Templates further promote code re-use and are an elegant means of generating, from one declaration, many functions and classes to manipulate data objects or arbitrary data type.

There are two categories of template in C++: the class template and the function template. An instance of a class template is called, confusingly, a template class. In the sense that member functions of class templates are themselves function templates, this section deals primarily with class templates.

CLASS TEMPLATES

Class templates are declared by prefixing a class declaration with a template specification. This is the **template** keyword followed by a pair of angle-brackets containing one or more identifiers representing parameterised types or constant initialising values.

Using class templates, a class can be declared and defined in terms of any type. Such a class is said to be parameterised. Consider this simple example of a generic number class:

```
//  class template declaration
template <class numtype>
class number;

     .
     .

//  definition of a class instance
number<int> ni;

     .
     .

//  class template definition
template <class numtype>
class number
{
private:
  numtype n;
public:
  number()
  {
     n = 0;
  }
  void get_number() { cin >> n; }
  void print_number() { cout << n << endl; }
};
```

Using conventional C++ (or C), to define a class or structure capable of representing numbers of arbitrary types is difficult, if not impossible. Class declarations cannot be overloaded – it is illegal to declare more than one class of a given name. Usually, it is necessary to take the brute force approach and declare a class type for every type of number that is required.

With the class template shown, it is possible to *instantiate* that class for a number of any type. Instantiation occurs when the template name is used with its list of parameters. An instance of the class for integer numbers is defined thus:

```
number<int> ni;
```

Now the identifier ni is a class object of type number<int> that specifies the characteristics of an integer number, including some operations which are possible on it. The above definition causes the built-in type specifier int to be substituted for the class template parameter numtype and to be used thereafter in the class declaration in place of numtype. This is exactly as if the class declaration:

```
class number
{
private:
  int n;
public:
  number()
  {
    n = 0;
  }
  void get_number() { cin >> n; }
  void print_number() { cout << n << endl; }
};
```

were explicitly made and the instance ni defined in the ordinary way:

```
number ni;
```

The class template above is declared, instantiated and defined in that order. In practice, the forward template declaration is often dispensed with and the template is defined at a point in the program source code before the instantiation.

NUM211: A NUMBER CLASS WITH TEMPLATES

Here is the full number class program:

```
#include <iostream.h>

template <class numtype>
class number
{
private:
  numtype n;
public:
  number()
  {
    n = 0;
  }
  void get_number() { cin >> n; }
  void print_number() { cout << n << endl; }
};
```

```cpp
int main()
{
  number<char> nc;
  cout << "Enter a character: ";
  nc.get_number();
  cout << "Character is: ";
  nc.print_number();

  number<int> ni;
  cout << "Enter an integer: ";
  ni.get_number();
  cout << "Integer is: ";
  ni.print_number();

  number<double> nd;
  cout << "Enter a double: ";
  nd.get_number();
  cout << "Double is: ";
  nd.print_number();

  return(0);
}
```

Three template class instantiations are made, one each for char, int and double data types. For each instance, the private member n is defined in turn as char, int and double.

The member function get_number extracts a value from the standard input stream and stores it in n. The first time it is called, cin uses the extractor operator overloaded for type char and expects a character to be input. On the second call to get_number, cin expects input of an int and on the third call a double. If the numbers are not input in this order, the input operation fails. When the program is executed, its input-output sequence is this:

```
Enter a character: r
Character is: r
Enter an integer: 7
Integer is: 7
Enter a double: 2.64575
Double is: 2.64575
```

FUNCTION TEMPLATES

If the function get_number were defined outside rather than as part of the template, the following function declaration and definition would be used:

```
//   function declaration in template
void get_number();

//   function definition externally
template <class numtype>
void number<numtype>::get_number()
{
  cin >> n;
}
```

The header syntax is complex but may make sense when we see that the equivalent non-template header is:

```
void number::get_number()
```

The definition of the template function get_number must be prefixed with the template specification template<class numtype> and specified as being in the scope of the type number<numtype>.

A member function of a template class, such as get_number, is implicitly a template function, which uses the class template parameters as its own parameters.

Class templates obey the normal scope and access rules that apply to all other C++ class and data objects. They must be defined in global scope (never within a function) and must be unique in a program. Class template definitions must not be nested.

3 Classes

3.1 The Class Construct

The C++ class construct is a generalisation of the structure. The **class** and **struct** are the same except that the members of the class are by default of private (restricted) access while those of the structure are public. Structures and classes as implemented by C++ can have functions as members as well as data objects, while C structures can only have member data objects.

Here is the general form of a class:

```
class [<class name>]
{
  [ private: | public: | protected: ]

  <type specifier1> <member1>;
  <type specifier2> <member2>;
      .
      .
  <type specifierN> <memberN>;
}[<variable list>];
```

The class name is optional. If it is omitted, the usefulness of the class is reduced: it cannot be initialised or used as a function argument or return value.

The access-control keywords **private**, **public** and **protected** may appear anywhere between the curly braces. The variable list is optional and usually omitted in favour of a later definition.

If none of the access-control keywords is used in a class declaration, then all its members are by default **private**. In a **struct** declaration, omission of all these keywords means that all members of the structure are by default **public**. This is the only difference between the **class** and **struct** constructs in C++.

Private members of a class may only (**friends** excepted) be accessed by code within functions that are members of the same class. To be useful, a class must have some accessible (usually public) functions that may be called from *client code* (outside code, not part of a member function of the class) to access indirectly the private data and function members of the class.

Consider an example of a class date:

```
class date
{
   int dd;
   int mm;
   int yy;

   void get_data();
   int  validate();
   int  find_day();
   void disp_day(int);
};
```

None of the members is accessible by any outside code. Because the function members cannot, therefore, be called, the data members are useless. A class becomes useful with the inclusion of public:

```
class date
{
   int dd;
   int mm;
   int yy;
public:
   void get_data();
   int  validate();
   int  find_day();
   void disp_day(int);
};
```

Now only the data members are private; the member functions are callable by any client code for which they are in scope.

It is legal but unnecessary to insert the keyword private before the data members. Although, in a class, all members are private by default, the preferred form is to use private explicitly. private and public may appear anywhere, in any order, between class members within the curly braces:

```
class date
{
public:
  void    get_data();
  int     validate();
  int     find_day();
  void    disp_day(int);
  int     dd;
private:
  int     mm;
public:
  int     yy;
};
```

This declaration is unlikely but legal. It means that only the data member mm is inaccessible to client code. Class member data and member functions may be interspersed in any order. It is customary, but not necessary, for the data members to be defined first and to be followed by the member functions.

An instance of the date class is defined by either of the following:

```
class date    day;

date          day;
```

An array of class instances is defined like this:

```
date          day_arr[20];
```

The terms *class object* and *class variable* are often used to mean the same thing as *class instance*.

We may define and initialise a pointer to the class instance day:

```
date   *clptr = &day;
```

Use of pointers with classes and class members is covered in Section 3.6.

It is usually illegal to initialise a class or structure with an initialiser list in the way structures are initialised in C:

```
date   day = {14,7,84};
```

This causes a compilation error where date is either a class or a structure. The only classes that may be initialised in this way are those known as *aggregates*: classes

without **private** or **protected** members, member
functions and base classes. Structures that are aggregates
are the same as C structures.

Classes and structures should be initialised with
constructor functions, which are dealt with in Chapter 4.

The **typedef** storage class specifier may be used with
classes and structures in much the same way as it is used
with the structure in C:

```
typedef class date
{
private:
  int    dd;
  int    mm;
  int    yy;
public:
  void   get_data();
  int    validate();
  int    find_day();
  void   disp_day(int);
}DATE_TYPE;

DATE_TYPE day;
```

The newly-defined type is then used to define an instance
of the class, **day**. All the following definitions mean the
same thing:

```
class date        day;
date              day;
DATE_TYPE         day;
```

Use of **typedef** here is unnecessary and **typedef** is, in
general, used much less in C++ than in C code.

Members of a class are in scope for the whole outer block
of the class declaration – between the curly braces. This
means that member functions can directly access the
other function members. In the case of the class variable
day above, client code must access the **public** members
of the class, which are all functions, by qualifying them
with the class object **day** and the member-of (dot) operator:

```
day.get_data();
```

The code within the definition of **get_data** is allowed
access the other members directly:

```
void date::get_data()
{
  char c;

  cout << "Enter the day number: ";
  cin >> dd;
  cout << "Enter the month number: ";
  cin >> mm;
  cout << "Enter the year number: ";
  cin >> yy;

  // Flush the last RETURN from input stream

  c = cin.get();
}
```

After defining the class type DATE_TYPE with typedef, the types date and DATE_TYPE are interchangeable. In C++, a typedef name that names a class is itself a class name. Therefore, in the header of the get_data function, scope of the function may be resolved (using the scope-resolution operator, ::) to either of the types date or DATE_TYPE.

BANK31: THE BANK ACCOUNT CLASS

Here is program implemented with classes in C++ that provides a simple model of the operation of a bank account. It is organised in three files: the header file accounts.h; the function program file 'accfunc.cpp'; and the main program file 'accounts.cpp', which acts as a driver for the functions declared as part of the class cust_acc. First, the accounts.h header file:

```
class cust_acc
{
private:
  float bal;
  int acc_num;
public:
  void setup();
  void lodge(float);
  void withdraw(float);
  void balance();
};
```

accounts.h declares the cust_acc class, which has two private data members and four public member functions.

The definitions of those member functions are given in
'accfunc.cpp':

```cpp
/*
 *
 * Program file 'accfunc.cpp'
 * defines 'cust_acc' member functions.
 *
 */
#include <iostream.h>
#include "accounts.h"

//
// customer_account member functions
//
void cust_acc::setup()
{
   cout << "Enter number of account to be opened:";
   cin >> acc_num;
   cout << "Enter initial balance: ";
   cin >> bal;
   cout << "Customer account " << acc_num
                   << " created with balance "
                   << bal << endl;
}

void cust_acc::lodge(float lodgement)
{
   bal += lodgement;
   cout << "Lodgement of " << lodgement
       << " accepted" << endl;
}

void cust_acc::withdraw(float with)
{
   if (bal > with)
   {
      bal -= with;
      cout << "Withdrawal of " << with
              << " granted" << endl;
      return;
   }
   cout << "Insufficient balance for withdrawal of "
      << with << endl;
   cout << "Withdrawal of " << bal
      << " granted" << endl;
   bal       = (float)0;
}
```

```
void cust_acc::balance()
{
   cout << "Balance of account is" << bal << endl;
}
```

Finally, here is the 'accounts.cpp' program file. It contains a main function that acts as a driver of the functions declared in the class cust_acc. In the simulation, an account object called a1 is created. The function setup is called immediately after the creation to initialise the object in memory. This is done by prompting the program's user for initial balance and account-number values. Then, an amount of 250 is lodged to the account and 500 withdrawn. The account balance is reported after each of these operations.

```
/*
 * Program file 'accounts.cpp'
 * drives the 'cust_acc' class
 */

#include <iostream.h>
#include "accounts.h"

int main()
{
   cust_acc a1;

   a1.setup();
   a1.lodge(250.00);
   a1.balance();
   a1.withdraw(500.00);
   a1.balance();
   return(0);
}
```

The header file iostream.h is included in both 'accfunc.cpp' and 'accounts.cpp'. It contains, among other things, all declarations necessary to allow use of the input and output streams cin and cout. accounts.h is also included in both files, making the class declaration of cust_acc visible throughout the program.

The four member functions of the class cust_acc are called from main, in each case being qualified by the class object a1. To call the functions from main without qualification would result in compilation errors. The data

members of cust_acc can only be used within those
functions.

The bank-account program is a very straightforward use
of classes and the object-oriented programming approach.
It is modified in this chapter and the next to illustrate
other C++ constructs.

3.2   Class Members

DATA MEMBERS

Data members of a class are declared within the class in
the same way as ordinary (non-class-member) data
objects. The class cust_acc:

```
class cust_acc

  {
  private:
    float bal;
    int acc_num;
  public:
    // member functions
  };
```

can equally well be written:

```
  class cust_acc
  {
  private:
    float bal; int acc_num;
  public:
    // member functions
  };
```

Data members of a class cannot be declared with any of
the storage class specifiers auto, register or extern. If a
data member is declared static, only one copy of that data
object is allocated by the compiler in memory, regardless
of how many instances of the class are defined. A static
member therefore acts as a global variable within the
scope of a class and might reasonably be used as a global
flag or counter variable.

Here is a simple example:

```
#include <iostream.h>

class run_total
{
private:
  static int accum;
public:
  void increment() { accum++; }
  void pr_total()
  {
    cout << "Accum: " << accum << "\n";
  }
};

int main()
{
  run_total total1, total2;

  total1.increment();
  total1.pr_total();
  total2.increment();
  total2.pr_total();
  return(0);
}
```

Two instances of the class run_total, total1 and total2, are defined. After the first call to increment, the value of accum is 1. After the second call to increment –albeit with a different class instance – the value of accum has become 2. This program relies on the fact that static member variables are initialised by the compiler to zero.

Static data members of a class exist independently of the existence of any instances of that class: space for them is allocated at compile-time. Nevertheless, a static data member declared in this way is not a runtime definition.

Static data members should be defined outside the class declaration. The definition must be explicit, because defining an instance of the class of which it is a member does not have the effect of defining the static member.

The following example defines the static data member accum.

```
class run_total
{
private:
  static int accum;
```

```
public:
   void increment() { accum++; }
   void pr_total()
   {
      cout << "Accum: " << accum << "\n";
   }
};
```

The static member, accum, is defined in file scope using the class name and scope-resolution operator (not an instance of the class) and initialised with the value 5:

```
//   definition of static member
int run_total::accum = 5;

int main()
{
   run_total total1, total2;

   total1.increment();
   total1.pr_total();
   total2.increment();
   total2.pr_total();
   return(0);
}
```

With accum initialised in this way, the successive calls to pr_total yield the values 6 and 7. Static data members must not be initialised in this way more than once in the program. The static member variable accum can alternatively be set to a value by defining an instance of its class type, and then assigning a value to it:

```
int main()
{
   run_total total1, total2;

   total1.accum = 5;

   total1.increment();
   total1.pr_total();
   total2.increment();
   total2.pr_total();
   return(0);
}
```

The fact that the static member variable accum is qualified by 'total1.' has no effect on the operation; the single static instance of accum is assigned the value 5.

It is illegal for either static or non-static data members of a class to be directly initialised as part of their declaration.

Compilation errors result:

```
class cust_acc
{
private:
  static int acc_num  = 1234;
  float bal = 1000000.00;
public:
  //   Member functions here
};
```

If a local class is declared – within the body of a function – it is not visible outside that function. A local class must not have static data members. The subscript bounds of array members must be explicitly defined. The following code causes a compilation error:

```
class cust_acc
{
private:
  float bal;
  char accountName[];   // illegal, no bounds
public:
  //   Member functions here
};
```

Classes (including structures) may be data members of a class. The declaration of the member class must already have been encountered by the compiler:

```
class cust_details
{
private:
  char accountName[30];
  int age;
public:
  // 'cust_details' member functions
};

class cust_acc
{
private:
  float bal;
  int acc_num;
public:
  cust_details resume;
  // 'cust_acc' member functions
};
```

Here, the class cust_details is declared before an object of its type is defined in the cust_acc class. The following declaration sequence is equivalent:

```
class cust_details;    // Forward declaration

class cust_acc
{
private:
  int acc_num;
public:
  cust_details resume;
  // 'cust_acc' member functions
};
// Declaration of 'cust_details' class follows
```

FUNCTION MEMBERS

Class member functions may be declared or defined in a class declaration. Either of two function specifiers may optionally be used: inline and virtual.

If a function is specified inline as part of its declaration, the compiler is requested to expand the body of the function into the program code at the point of its call. In this way, it is treated much as a preprocessor macro: the function is expanded inline and the overhead of the function call is eliminated. If a class member function is defined as part of its declaration, it is implicitly inline:

```
class cust_acc
{
private:
  float bal;
  int acc_num;
public:
  void zero_bal() { bal = 0.0; }
  //   Other member functions here
};
```

Prefixing the inline specifier to the function definition within cust_acc is unnecessary and makes no difference to the definition of zero_bal: The function zero_bal as shown can be regarded as implicitly inline.

It is not necessary to include a function's entire definition in a class declaration for the function to be inline. A member function can be declared inline and defined later:

```
class cust_acc
{
private:
  float bal;
  int cust_acc;
public:
  .
  .
  inline void balance();
  .
};
  .
  .
// function definition
void cust_acc::balance()
{
  .
  .
```

A particular type of implicitly inline function, called the *access function*, is very often used to promote hiding of private member data objects. For example:

```
class cust_acc
{
private:
  float bal;
  int acc_num;
public:
  int isOverdrawn() { return(bal < 0.0); }
  // Other member functions here
};
```

Here, the boolean value of the equality test bal < 0.0 is returned by isOverdrawn. With this mechanism, it is no longer necessary to access the variable bal to check the customer's creditworthiness; it can subsequently be done with the function call:

```
cust_acc a1;
  .
  .
if (a1.isOverdrawn())
    // don't give her the money
```

A short function like this is particularly suitable for inline specification. Access functions are very common. They make it unnecessary for client code directly to access data members. The data hiding that results allows the class designer, in principle, to change the class definition while having no effect on the operation of the client code.

Virtual functions, declared with the function specifier
virtual, are dealt with in detail in Chapter 6.

Ordinary member functions are those not specified inline
or virtual and which are defined outside the class
declaration. Their function headers must contain the
scope resolution operator, as in the case of lodge from
the cust_acc class:

```
void cust_acc::lodge(float)
```

Private member data objects of the class cust_acc are
accessed directly and without qualification from within
member functions such as lodge.

A class data member must not be declared twice in the
same class.

A member function may be declared twice in the same
class but only if the two declarations have different
argument lists. Rules for declaration of overloaded
functions are given in Chapter 5.

A member data object and a member function must not be
declared with the same names.

A member function can be static but not auto, register
or extern.

A static member function must not have the same name
and argument list as a non-static member function.

A static member function is allowed access only the static
members of its class, unless it uses a class object with one
of the operators '.' or '->' to gain access.

To illustrate, here is a modified version of the run_total
example from earlier in this section:

```
#include <iostream.h>

class run_total
{
private:
  static int accum;
public:
  static void increment() { accum++; }
  void pr_total()
  {
    cout << "Accum: " << accum << "\n";
  }
```

```
};
int run_total::accum = 5;

int main()
{
   run_total total1, total2;

   total1.increment();
   total1.pr_total();
   total2.increment();
   total2.pr_total();
   return(0);
}
```

Now, as well as accum, the function increment has been declared static and can still access accum. If, however, the static keyword is removed from the declaration of accum, a compilation error results. The function increment can access a non-static data member of the same class by using, in this case, a class object to qualify accum:

```
#include <iostream.h>

class run_total
{
private:
   int accum;        // non-static
public:
   static void increment(run_total& inst)
   {
      inst.accum++;  // this usage OK
   }
   void pr_total()
   {
      cout << "Accum: " << accum << "\n";
   }
};

int main()
{
   run_total total1, total2;

   total1.increment(total1);
   total1.pr_total();
   total2.increment(total2);
   total2.pr_total();
   return(0);
}
```

In the examples above, it should be noted that the static member function increment can be used without reference to instances of the class run_total:

```
int main()
{
  run_total total1, total2;

  run_total::increment();
  total1.pr_total();
  run_total::increment();
  total2.pr_total();
  return(0);
}
```

Here, only access to the non-static function pr_total must be controlled by the class instances total1 and total2.

BANK32: USING STATIC CLASS MEMBERS

As a more practical example of a case in which static class members might be used, here is the bank-account example reworked so that the account number is no longer prompted for in the setup function. Instead, each time an account object is created, the next available number is 'peeled off'. In summary, a variable global to all cust_acc class instances is needed to hold information logically common to them all.

```
class cust_acc
{
private:
  float bal;
  static int acc_num;
  int my_acc_num;
public:
  void setup();
  void lodge(float);
  void withdraw(float);
  void balance();
};

/*
 *
 * Program file 'accfunc.cpp' – defines
 * 'cust_acc' member functions.
 *
 */
```

```cpp
#include <iostream.h>
#include <string.h>
#include "accounts.h"

//
// Only setup function has changed
//
void cust_acc::setup()
{
  my_acc_num = acc_num++;
  cout << "Enter opening balance for account"
      << my_acc_num << ": ";
  cin >> bal;
  cout << "Customer account " << my_acc_num
            << " created with balance "
            << bal << endl;
}

#include <iostream.h>
#include "accounts.h"

int cust_acc::acc_num = 1000;

int main(void)
{
  cust_acc a1;

  a1.setup();
  a1.lodge(250.00);
  a1.balance();
  a1.withdraw(500.00);
  a1.balance();
  cust_acc a2;

  a2.setup();
  a2.lodge(1000.00);
  a2.balance();
  a2.withdraw(300.00);
  a2.balance();
  return(0);
}
```

3.3   Unions

The C++ union is a special case of the class construct. A
union is syntactically similar to a class (and a structure)
but the compiler only allocates space in memory sufficient
to accommodate the largest member of the union, along
with any additional space at the end needed by the
alignment requirements of the host computer system. At
any given time, an instance of only one union member
actually exists.

Like classes, unions can have data and function members.
They can also include constructor and destructor functions.
(These are dealt with in Chapter 4).

A union must not contain base classes or be itself a base
class. Unions must not contain members that are virtual
functions. Base and derived classes, along with virtual
functions, are covered in Chapter 6.

Classes may be union members, but classes that contain
constructor and/or destructor functions are not allowed
as union members.

Unions must not contain static members.

It is legal for unions to have members specified private,
protected or public. If none of these is specified, access
defaults to public, in the same way as for a structure.

Unions may be nested and may occur in arrays. Pointers
to unions may be defined and the pointers or the unions
themselves may be used as function arguments or return
values.

UNION33: A Spreadsheet Cell

Here is a complete example program that illustrates use
of a union. The program accepts input to a character array
and parses the contents as might an elementary spreadsheet
program. The array is analysed to determine if its contents
represent an integer, a double floating-point number or a
character string.

Depending on the type of the data, it is copied to the
appropriate member of the union, displayed then 'stored'.

```cpp
#include <iostream.h>
#include <stdlib.h>
#include <string.h>

//   Declare a union: it could be a simple
//   spreadsheet cell

union sp_cell
{
private:
  int       ival;
  double    dval;
  char      sval[20];
  char      instring[20];  // array for input
public:
  char      get_token();
  char      analyse();
  void      put_token(char);
};

char sp_cell::get_token()
{
  cout << "Enter a number, fraction or string: ";
  cin  >> instring;
  return(analyse());
}

char sp_cell::analyse()
{
  int i = 0;

  while ((instring[i] != '\0') && (i < 20))
  {
    if (instring[i] == '.')  // decimal point
            return ('d');
    if ((instring[i] < '0') >
                      (instring[i] > '9'))
            return ('s');
    i++;
  }
  return ('i');
}

void sp_cell::put_token(char token_type)
{
  switch (token_type)
  {
      case 'i':         ival = atoi(instring);
                        cout << "Integer " << ival
                               << "\n";
                        break;
```

```
    case 'd':      dval = atof(instring);
                   cout << "Double " << dval
                                  << "\n";
                   break;
    case 's':      strcpy(sval, instring);
                   cout << "String " << sval
                                  << "\n";
                   break;
    default:       cout << "Invalid data\n";
                   break;
  }
  cout << "Data has been stored\n";
}
int main()
{
  sp_cell cell;

  cell.put_token(cell.get_token());
  return(0);
}
```

This program is an example of the remarkable brevity that can be achieved in the calling function by use of classes with encapsulated data and function members.

The union **sp_cell** is declared with three data members representing a spreadsheet cell: an integer, a **double** and a character array. A further character array, **instring**, is defined to take input data.

The **main** function defines an instance, **cell**, of the union **sp_cell**. This is used to call the member function **put_token**. The call to **put_token** uses as its argument the return value of **get_token**, which prompts the user for input and accepts it into **instring**.

get_token in turn calls the function **analyse**, which does the string parsing and returns to **get_token** a character representing the type of data input. **get_token** returns the same character, which is used as a parameter by **put_token**, to determine the nature of conversion and storage required by the input data.

Note that only one data member of the union exists at any instant; the final one that exists is one of **ival**, **dval** or **sval**. Use of a union is suitable where space needs to be saved and, as in this case, where the classifications of data to be stored are mutually exclusive. No trace is kept by the compiler of which data member is currently 'live'; it is up to the programmer to know this.

A simple union – one without constructor or destructor functions – may have its first data member initialised with an initialiser list in curly braces. It may also be initialised by an assignment of a variable of the same type:

```
sp_cell cell  = { 5 };

sp_cell cell1 = cell;
```

A union declared without a name is an *anonymous union*. After declaration its members may be used without the normal member-access syntax:

```
int main()
{
    union { int ival; double dval; char sval;};

    ival=5;
    dval=2.23605;
    strcpy(sval,"abc");
    return(0);
}
```

Care should be taken that the names of other variables in the same scope do not clash with the union variable member names. Anonymous unions must not have function members or any members that are private or protected.

3.4   Bit Fields

Bit fields may be defined as member data objects of a class. Bit fields specify the length in bits of the data object they define.

The general form of a class containing bit fields is the same as that of an ordinary class except that the length in bits of some or all of its data members is given after a colon following the data member name. Here is the general form:

```
class [<class name>]
{
  [ private: I public: I protected: ]

  <type specifier1> <identifier1> : <length1>;
  <type specifier2> <fn_name2>;
  <type specifier3> <identifier2> : <length2>;
  <type specifier4> <identifier4>;

      .
      .

  <type specifierN> <identifierN> : <lengthN>;

}[<variable list>];
```

The items in square brackets are optional. The class members may also include functions and ordinary (non-bit) data members in any order. As with ordinary classes, the private, protected and public specifiers may also occur in any order and may be repeated.

BITF34: COMMUNICATIONS

Here is a communications-oriented example program that uses bit fields defined as part of the class comm_states:

```
volatile class comm_states
{
private:
  unsigned int dev_tx    : 1;
  unsigned int dev_rx    : 1;
  unsigned int dev_wait  : 1;
  unsigned int buf_full  : 1;
  unsigned int perms     : 3;
public:
  int transmit()         { return(dev_tx); }
  int reading()          { return(dev_rx); }
  void disable_tx()      { dev_tx = 0; }
  void disable_rx()      { dev_rx = 0; }
};

int main()
{
  comm_states line;

  if (line.reading())
  {
    cout << "Device receiving data\n";
    line.disable_tx();
  }
```

```
    if (line.transmit())
    {
        cout << "Device transmitting data\n";
        line.disable_rx();
    }
    return(0);
}
```

There are five member data items of the class **comm_states**, which are specified as bit members. All are of one bit in length, except the permissions field, which is three bits long.

All the data items are specified as being of type unsigned integer. Use of unsigned is desirable to avoid the leftmost (sometimes the only) bit in a bit field being used as a sign-bit.

ISO C requires that the type of bit field data items must be one of int, signed int or unsigned int. C++ additionally allows char, short and long in any of their signed or unsigned forms to be used.

The address of a bit field must not be taken:

    &line.dev_rx

is illegal. Equally, pointers and references to bit fields are disallowed.

The member functions of the class specify transmit and receive operations that are possible on the member data and on the communications device that the data represents. All the functions are implicitly inline and are very short. It is assumed that the flag values of **comm_states** are somehow changed in response to interrupts from the communications device; for example, when there is incoming data on the line to receive, the resulting interrupt causes **dev_rx** to be set to 1.

The transmit/receive status of the device is tested by calling either of two access functions, **transmit** and **reading**. All they do is return the values of the **dev_rx** and **dev_tx** fields. Depending on those return values, the functions **disable_rx** and **disable_tx** may be called. These simply set **dev_rx** and **dev_tx** respectively to zero.

This is a highly simplified example but is a good
illustration of an application where bit fields are actually
useful. The main justification for using bit fields is one of
saving space. Space is often at a premium in device-
driver code. Because of restrictions that bit fields impose
on program portability, however, use of the bit-level
operators on integer types may be preferable.

The manner in which memory is allocated for bit fields is
not specified by the C++ language definition and is
completely system-dependent. It is not possible to
generalise about how any given C++ implementation
will allocate space for this class:

```
volatile class comm_states
{
private:
  unsigned int dev_tx    : 1;
  unsigned int dev_rx    : 1;
  double x;
  unsigned int dev_wait : 1;
public:
  int transmit()              { return(dev_tx); }
  unsigned int buf_full   : 1;
  unsigned int perms      : 3;
  int reading()               { return(dev_rx); }
  void disable_tx()           { dev_tx = 0; }
  void disable_rx()           { dev_rx = 0; }
};
```

The syntax of this class is legal. Depending, however, on
how the local system allocates memory space for the
intermixed bit-field, function and other data members, it
may not give the same results as the comm_states class
used in the full example above. Tested on the author's
system using three different C++ development
environments, the program behaved differently with
each. Because of the portability limitations they place on
C++ code, bit fields should be used sparingly.

3.5 Class Scope

Every C++ data object has local, function, file or class
scope. Scope defines the visibility of a data object. If it
has *file* scope, it is visible throughout the program file in
which it is defined and is said to be global. If a data object
has *function* scope, it is visible only within the function
in which it is defined. Only goto labels have function
scope. If a data object has *local* scope, its visibility is
confined to the local enclosing compound statement.

Each of file, function and local scope are part of the C
language and have been incorporated in C++. *Class*
scope is added by C++.

A C++ class has its own scope. This means that a class
member is directly visible only to member functions of
the same class. Access to the class member is otherwise
limited to cases where the member-of (.), pointer (->) and
scope-resolution (::) operators are used with either the
base class or a derived class. A data object declared as a
friend of a class belongs to that class's scope.

Here is a modified example of the date class, which
illustrates the different aspects of class scope:

```
class date
{
private:
  int dd;
  int mm;
  int yy;
public:
  void get_data()
    { cin >> dd >> mm >> yy; }  // inline
  int  validate();
  int  find_day();
  void disp_day(int);
};
```

In client code, such as the main function, we define an
instance of the class and a pointer to it:

```
date day;

date *dptr = &day;
```

For all of the four member functions, all other class members are in scope. Thus, the code of the validate function might, if necessary, call the function disp_day, even though disp_day is declared later in the class than validate. Member function code may access other class members – data and function – directly, without using any prefixes to resolve scope.

To access function members from client code, the member-of and pointer operators must be used:

```
day.dd
```

is equivalent to:

```
dptr->dd
```

Likewise:

```
day.validate()
```

is the same in effect as:

```
dptr->validate()
```

If these prefixes are not used, the members are out of scope for the client code and compilation errors result. The private class members are always out of scope for client code; they must be accessed indirectly by means of the member functions, for which they are in scope.

Definitions of class members, and classes themselves, may be hidden (masked) by subsequent declarations:

```cpp
#include <iostream.h>

int dd = 999;

int main()
{
  class date
  {
  private:
    int dd;
    int mm;
    int yy;
  public:
    void pr_inscope()
           { cout << dd << "\n"; }
    void pr_outscope()
           { cout << ::dd << "\n"; }
  }sd;
```

```
    sd.pr_inscope();
    sd.pr_outscope();
    return(0);
}
```

Here, the global (file scope) variable **dd** is masked within the scope of the class **date** by the definition of the member data object **dd**. Within the class, the contents of the externally-defined instance of **dd** may be accessed using the unary scope resolution operator as shown. The output of this program is simply:

```
0
999
```

In the next example, a class is masked:

```
#include <iostream.h>

int dd = 999;

class date
{
private:
    int dd;
    int mm;
    int yy;
public:
    void pr_inscope()
        { cout << dd << "\n"; }
    void pr_outscope()
        { cout << ::dd << "\n"; }
}sd;

int main()
{
    int sd;

    ::sd.pr_inscope();
    ::sd.pr_outscope();
    return(0);
}
```

Again, the unary scope resolution operator is used so that the correct instance of **sd** may be employed to call the member functions of **date**. The result of the program is the same as the last example:

```
0
999
```

The function calls in the last example may be modified to
an equivalent form:

```
::sd.date::pr_inscope();
::sd.date::pr_outscope();
```

These calls explicitly (date::) resolve the scope of the
functions as members of the class date and further
resolve the particular instance (sd) of date in use.

Here is a modified version of the run_total example from
Section 3.2:

```
#include <iostream.h>
class run_total
{
private:
  static int accum;
public:
  static void increment() { accum++; }
  void pr_total()
  {
     cout << "Accum: " << accum << "\n";
  }
};
int run_total::accum = 0;
int main()
{
  run_total total1, total2;

  int run_total = 11;

  run_total::increment();
  total1.pr_total();
  run_total::increment();
  total2.pr_total();
  cout << run_total << "\n";
  return(0);
}
```

Here, although the class name, run_total, is redefined as
an integer in main, class scope is resolved in the calls to
the static member function increment, by means of the
binary scope resolution operator. The result of the program
is:

```
Accum: 1
Accum: 2
11
```

With derived classes and nested classes, use of the scope

resolution operator is at times necessary to avoid ambiguity when accessing class members. Otherwise, it is best to avoid masking declarations in the ways shown in the preceding examples. Such masking does not help program reliability or readability.

A class may be declared in file, local or class scope. Only goto labels have function scope. If declared in file scope, the class has global visibility; if in local scope, access to the class is restricted to code within the compound statement enclosing the declaration.

NESTED CLASS DECLARATIONS

Where a class is declared in class scope, the declaration is said to be nested – one class is declared within another. Declarations made in the nested class are not in scope for functions in the enclosing class and must be accessed according to the normal procedures. Equally, declarations in the enclosing class are not in scope for functions declared in the nested class.

Here are the relevant parts of an example program, again based on the date class, that shows use of nested classes:

```
// file 'dates.h', contains
// nested classes 'date' and 'curr_time'
class date
{
private:
  int dd;
  int mm;
  int yy;
public:
  class curr_time
  {
  private:
    int hr;
    int min;
    int sec;
  public:
    void correct_time();
  }t;
  void get_data();
  int  validate();
  int  find_day();
  void disp_day(int);
};
```

The nested class curr_time is added to the date class. curr_time is declared and an instance of it defined within date.

In this case, the function correct_time is used to reset the data members of class curr_time, probably by calling library functions declared in the standard header file time.h.

The calling sequence for this function is:

```
date day;
    .
    .
day.t.correct_time();    // set correct time
```

The header of the correct_time function, in order to conform with the C++ scope rules, must be written thus:

```
void date::curr_time::correct_time()
```

The definition of an instance of the class date also defines an instance of curr_time because of the definition of t embedded in date. The members of curr_time are accessed by double use of the member-of operator:

```
sd.t.correct_time();
```

The members of a nested class are not in scope for those of the enclosing class; to qualify the function header of correct_time only with the scope resolution date would cause the function correct_time to be out of scope even though it is a member of a class nested within date.

The definition of the curr_time class object t makes it a public member of date. If it were private, the function correct_time could not be called with the syntax:

```
sd.t.correct_time();
```

because t would now be a private member of date. Instead, a further member function of date would have to be defined to call correct_time.

Member functions of a nested class must not directly access members of the enclosing class, unless those members are static, or type names, or enumerators. Thus, for the function correct_time directly to access dd, which is a member of date, is illegal.

The ANSI C++ standard has introduced an extension

allowing forward declaration of nested classes. In the example above showing the time class nested within date, a forward declaration of time can instead be used with ANSI C++ implementations:

```
class date
{
private:
  int dd;
  int mm;
  int yy;
public:
  class curr_time;
  curr_time t;
  void get_data();
  int  validate();
  int  find_day();
  void disp_day(int);
};

class curr_time
{
private:
  int hr;
  int min;
  int sec;
public:
  void correct_time();
};
```

3.6 Classes and Pointers

Pointers to classes may be defined and used in C++ in much the same way as structure pointers are in C. C++ adds the reference notation and a special set of operators for use with pointers to class members. Consider this simple class declaration:

```
#include <iostream.h>

class fraction
{
public:
  double f;
  double g;
};
```

The main function following defines two instances of the class, x and y, and a pointer to a double floating-point type. The pointer is used in the conventional way to access and display the members of both instances of the class.

```
int main()
{
   fraction x, y;
   double *dptr;

   x.f = 1.1;
   y.f = 2.2;
   x.g = 3.3;
   y.g = 4.4;

   dptr = &x.f;
   cout << *dptr << "\n";

   dptr = &y.f;
   cout << *dptr << "\n";

   dptr = &x.g;
   cout << *dptr << "\n";

   dptr = &y.g;
   cout << *dptr << "\n";
   return(0);
}
```

The displayed results of the program are:

```
1.1
2.2
3.3
4.4
```

CLASS MEMBER POINTERS

It is quite legal to use pointers to class members in the way shown above. C++ provides an alternative type of pointer, the pointer to a class member, specially for accessing class members. Here is the same example reworked to illustrate it:

```
#include <iostream.h>

class fraction
{
public:
   double f;
   double g;
};
```

```
int main()
{
  fraction x, y;
  double fraction::*dptr;

  x.f = 1.1;
  y.f = 2.2;
  x.g = 3.3;
  y.g = 4.4;

  dptr = &fraction::f;
  cout << x.*dptr << " " << y.*dptr << "\n";

  dptr = &fraction::g;
  cout << x.*dptr << " " << y.*dptr << "\n";
  return(0);
}
```

The line:

```
double fraction::*dptr;
```

defines **dptr** not just as a pointer to an object of type **double**, but specifically as a pointer to **double** members of **fraction** objects. The member pointer **dptr** cannot subsequently be used to point to a simple **double** data object. The pointer is then assigned the address of the member variable f in class **fraction**. The notation:

```
x.*dptr
```

is used to access **x.f**. The operator '.*', introduced in C++, can be read 'x-dot-pointer-to-f' and returns the same value as **x.f**. Unlike the use of conventional pointers, the pointer **dptr** is used without change to access the member f of the **y** instance of the class; the notation used is **y.*dptr**.

This time, the displayed results are:

```
1.1 2.2
3.3 4.4
```

The '.*' operator may be substituted with the '->*' operator. Suppose that pointers to the class instance, rather than the class instance itself, are used:

```
fraction *xptr = &x;
fraction *yptr = &y;
```

The first display command reads:

```
cout << xptr->*dptr << " " << yptr->*dptr << "\n";
```

MEMBER FUNCTION POINTERS

Use of the specialised pointer-to-class-member syntax
may be desirable in all cases where class members are to
accessed using pointers but it is necessary where a
member function is to be called with a pointer. Member
functions of a class cannot legally be accessed using
conventional function pointers. For example, a
conventional pointer to function returning integer:

```
int (*fptr)();
```

cannot be used to point to a member function of a class,
even if that function exactly matches the pointer definition
in signature.

Consider the coord class with a function member:

```
class coord
{
private:
  int x_coord;
  int y_coord;
public:
  int locate_coords();
};
```

A conventional function pointer cannot be used to point
to the function locate_coords. Instead, we define a
pointer to member function:

```
int (coord::*mem_fn_ptr)();
```

assign a function address to it like this:

```
mem_fn_ptr = coord::locate_coords;
```

and call it:

```
mem_fn_ptr();
```

Use of the member-pointer operators provides better
control than using ordinary pointers to point to members
and less likelihood of pointers being used for unintended
purposes. Unfortunately, the syntax is somewhat
complicated. This may encourage programmers to stick
where they can with traditional pointers and (as even C
programmers are inclined to do) avoid function pointers
altogether.

CLASSES AS FUNCTION ARGUMENTS

Pointers to classes are sometimes used where classes are being passed as arguments to functions:

```cpp
#include <iostream.h>

class fraction
{
public:
  double f;
  double g;
};
void change_class(fraction *);

int main()
{
  fraction x, y;
  double fraction::*dptr;

  x.f = 1.1;
  y.f = 2.2;
  x.g = 3.3;
  y.g = 4.4;

  change_class(&x);

  dptr = &fraction::f;
  cout << x.*dptr << " " << y.*dptr << "\n";

  dptr = &fraction::g;
  cout << x.*dptr << " " << y.*dptr << "\n";
  return(0);
}

void change_class(fraction *xptr)
{
  xptr->f = 5.5;
  xptr->g = 6.6;
}
```

The program results are affected by the call to change_class:

```
5.5 2.2
6.6 4.4
```

By passing the address of the class instance **x** to the function change_class, the assignments in change_class are reflected in the calling function. Reference declarations are usually used instead to achieve the same purpose:

```
// function prototype
void change_class(fraction&);
// 'main' function otherwise unchanged to here
change_class(x);

dptr = &fraction::f;
cout << x.*dptr << " " << y.*dptr << "\n";

dptr = &fraction::g;
cout << x.*dptr << " " << y.*dptr << "\n";
return(0);
}
void change_class(fraction& xptr)
{
   xptr.f = 5.5;
   xptr.g = 6.6;
}
```

Depending on how it implements the C++ language, the compiler may replace the reference code with pointer referencing and de-referencing syntax. In any event, the programmer is saved from having to do it. The reference (trailing &) is only referred to in the change_class prototype and function header; in change_class, the class members are accessed as if the function had been called by value with the argument x.

The results of execution of this program are the same as those of the example using pointers.

Reference declarations qualified const are strongly recommended if it is not intended that the called function should change the value of its parameter:

```
void dont_change_class(const fraction& xptr)
{
   // compile error if x members changed
}
```

A function itself can be suffixed const:

```
class fraction
{
   //
public:
   dont_change_members() const
   {
      //
   }
};
```

A const function generates compilation errors if it attempts to change the value of members of the class object with which the function has been called. The const suffix only has meaning for class member functions.

THIS36: THE THIS POINTER

Every member function of a class has an implicitly defined constant pointer called this. The type of this is the type of the class of which the function is member. It is initialised, when a member function is called, to the address of the class instance for which the function was called.

Here is a representative example of the use of this:

```
#include <iostream.h>

class coord
{
private:
  int x_coord, y_coord;
public:
  void set_coords(int x_init, int y_init)
  {
     x_coord = x_init;
     y_coord = y_init;
  }
  void change_coords(int, int);
  void display_coords()
  {
     cout << "Coordinates: " << x_coord
         << " " << y_coord << "\n";
  }
};

int main()
{
  coord c1;

  c1.set_coords(5, 10);
  cout << "Original C1" << "\n";
  c1.display_coords();
  c1.change_coords(15, 20);

  cout << "Changed C1" << "\n";
  c1.display_coords();

  return(0);
}
```

```
void coord::
  change_coords(int x_chg, int y_chg)
{
  coord c2;

  c2.set_coords(x_chg, y_chg);

  cout << "Display C2" << "\n";
  c2.display_coords();

  *this = c2;
}
```

The this pointer is useful when it is needed during
execution of a class member function to get a 'handle' on
the class object used to call the function. Because, in a
member function, the class variable with which the
function was called is out of scope, the this pointer is
provided as that 'handle'.

Whether in class member functions the this pointer is
explicitly used or not, the C++ compiler accesses all class
members by means of an implicit this pointer.

Static member functions do not have this pointers. There
is only one instance of a static member function for a
class, so use of this does not make much sense. Any
attempt to use this in a static member function causes a
compilation error. Static member functions may otherwise
be accessed by means of pointers using the same syntax
as non-static member functions.

4 Constructors and Destructors

4.1 Basic Constructors and Destructors

One of the major weaknesses of C is that it provides no
mechanism for ensuring that newly defined data objects
are initialised to some reasonable value before they are
used. Neither is there a mechanism in C for cleaning up
after the data objects have been used and, perhaps,
returning the storage used by them to the operating
system's free storage list.

Constructor and destructor functions are introduced in
C++ to address this shortcoming. We have seen, in
Chapter 2, brief usage of a simple constructor and
destructor. This chapter describes them in more detail.

Constructors and destructors are (and must be) class
member functions that have the same name as the class of
which they are a part. In the case of the destructor, the
name is prefixed with a tilde '~'.

Consider a class called newclass:

```
class newclass
{
private:
  .
  //   private data members defined here
  .
public:
  newclass()          // constructor function
  {
    // initialising statements here
    cout << "Constructing....\n";
  }
  .
  //   other public members defined here
  .
  ~newclass()         //destructor function
  {
    // un-initialising statements here
    cout << "Destructing....\n";
  }
};
```

Here, the constructor function newclass is defined as a
public member function of the class of the same name. As
always, the public and private members may be in any
order; the ordering shown is merely conventional.

The constructor newclass need not be public; it can be
private or protected. Use of the protected keyword is
explained in Chapter 6. A constructor declared as a
public member function need not be the first public
member function in the list.

Similarly, the destructor function ~newclass need not
be declared public and may be declared anywhere among
other declarations. Putting the constructor declaration
first among the public members and the destructor
declaration last is no more than a common coding
convention.

```
class newclass
{
private:
  .
  //   private data members defined here
  .
  ~newclass()    // destructor function
  {
    // un-initialising statements here
    cout << "Destructing....\n";
  }
  .
public:
  .
  //   other public members defined here
  .
  newclass()       // constructor function
  {
    // initialising statements here
    cout << "Constructing....\n";
  }
  .
};
```

This is just as valid syntactically as the first example,
although a little more difficult to use because access to
the destructor function is restricted to member functions
of newclass.

In the case of the first declaration of newclass, the
definition:

```
newclass nc;
```

appearing anywhere in the program where newclass is
in scope causes an instance nc of the class newclass to
be defined and the initialising statements in the body of
the newclass constructor function to be executed.

When the class variable nc goes out of scope, the destructor
function ~newclass is implicitly called and its
uninitialising statements do suitable tidying-up
operations, which usually include returning storage to
the system's free list.

A destructor is almost always called implicitly in this
way. An explicit call to a destructor function is rare. An
example of such a call is given in Section 4.3.

You should note that constructor functions do not create
class objects, nor do destructor functions destroy them. A
class object is created by its definition; the creation is
immediately followed by execution of the body of the
constructor function. Conversely, when a class object
goes out of scope, its destructor function is executed *and
only then* is the object destroyed.

Here is an illustration, based on newclass, of how
constructor and destructor functions are called. First,
here is the declaration of newclass:

```
class newclass
{
private:
  int a, b, c;
public:
  newclass()
  {
     a = b = c = 0;
     cout << "Constructing....\n";
  }
  ~newclass()
  {
     cout << "Destructing....\n";
  }
};

void newfunc(void);
```

Next, here are the functions that use newclass:

```
int main()
{
  newfunc();
  return(0);
}

void newfunc()
{
  newclass nc1;
  {
    cout << "Defining nc2....\n";
    newclass nc2;

  }
  cout << "Out of scope of  nc2....\n";
}
```

newclass has three data members, all integers, and two member functions, its constructor and destructor. The constructor sets the three integers to zero and displays a message. The destructor simply displays a message. In the function newfunc, two instances, nc1 and nc2, of newclass are defined. The definitions call the constructor; when the definitions go out of scope, the destructor is implicitly called.

The displayed output of the program is this:

```
Constructing....
Defining  nc2....
Constructing....
Destructing....
Out of scope of  nc2....
Destructing....
```

Constructor and destructor functions must not have return types, not even void. They may contain return statements but when return is used in this way it must have no operands. Only

```
return;
```

is valid.

Constructors may take parameters; destructors must not, although void may be specified as a destructor argument list. Constructors taking parameters are shown in the next section.

BANK41: SIMPLE CONSTRUCTOR EXAMPLE

Here, once again using the bank-account class example, is a simple use of constructors. Up to now, the member function setup of the class cust_acc has been used to initialise the data members of the class.

After defining an instance of cust_acc, the programmer must remember to call setup to do the initialisation. In the following example, this two-step procedure is replaced with use of a constructor. A destructor is also included, in this case mainly for illustration. The reworked cust_acc class is declared in the accounts.h header file:

```
class cust_acc
{
private:
  float bal;
  int acc_num;
public:
  cust_acc();
  void lodge(float);
  void withdraw(float);
  void balance();
  ~cust_acc()
  {
  cout << "Account " << acc_num
    << " closed" << endl;
  }
};
```

The program file 'accfunc.cpp' contains the definitions of the class member functions other than the destructor. These definitions are unchanged from the examples shown in Chapter 3, except that setup is replaced by a constructor.

```
/*
 *
 * Program file 'accfunc.cpp'
 * defines 'cust_acc' member functions.
 *
 */

#include <iostream.h>
#include "accounts.h"

//
```

```
// customer_account member functions
//
cust_acc::cust_acc()
{
   cout <<
      "Enter number of account to be opened: ";
   cin >> acc_num;
   cout << "Enter initial balance: ";
   cin >> bal;
   cout << "Customer account " << acc_num
                  << " created with balance "
                  << bal << endl;
}
void cust_acc::lodge(float lodgement)
{
   bal += lodgement;
   cout << "Lodgement of " << lodgement
      << " accepted" << endl;
}
void cust_acc::withdraw(float with)
{
   if (bal > with)
   {
      bal -= with;
      cout << "Withdrawal of " << with
               << " granted" << endl;
      return;
   }
   cout <<
      "Insufficient balance for withdrawal of "
      << with << endl;
   cout << "Withdrawal of " << bal
      << " granted" << endl;
   bal      = (float)0;
}
void cust_acc::balance()
{
   cout << "Balance of account is " << bal << endl;
}
```

Immediately following creation in memory of the
cust_acc instance, a1, the constructor function
cust_acc::cust_acc() is automatically called to perform
initialising operations on a1. The creation of the a1
object:

```
cust_acc a1;
```

is therefore also an implicit function call that replaces the previous explicit call to setup. At the end of main, when the object a1 goes out of scope, the destructor function cust_acc::~cust_acc is implicitly called and, for the sake of completeness, 'closes' the account a1.

```
/*
 * Program file 'accounts.cpp'
 * drives the 'cust_acc' class
 */

#include <iostream.h>
#include "accounts.h"

int main()
{
   cust_acc a1;

   a1.lodge(250.00);
   a1.balance();
   a1.withdraw(500.00);
   a1.balance();
   return(0);
}
```

The constructor is declared in the class definition and defined later in the 'accfunc.cpp' program file with this header:

```
cust_acc::cust_acc()
```

Other functions that are not constructors must specify a return type at the start of the function header. Constructors and destructors must not contain a return type in either their declaration or definition.

Often, a constructor is defined as an implicitly inline function, as is, in this case, the destructor.

It can be seen from this example that constructors and destructors are in almost all respects ordinary functions. The statements they contain are not restricted to initialisation and destruction of data objects recently defined. They could, if required, be used for graphic screen display or to calculate the value of PI to 14 places. It is good practice, however, to use constructors and destructors for their intended purpose and to put extraneous code in other functions.

4.2   Constructors Taking Parameters

Constructors are functions and may take parameters like any other function. Here is a simple example of a class that uses a constructor function taking parameters:

```
#include <iostream.h>

class coord
{
private:
  int x_coord, y_coord;
public:
  coord(int x, int y)
  {
     x_coord = x;
     y_coord = y;
  }
  void print()
  {
     cout << x_coord << "\n";
     cout << y_coord << "\n";
  }
};

int main()
{
   coord point1 = coord(5,10);

   point1.print();

   //   coord point2;        // illegal

   coord point3(15,20);   // abbreviation

   point3.print();
   return(0);
}
```

This program does very little but it illustrates several aspects of constructor parameter syntax.

The implicitly inline constructor function **coord** has a header with an argument list declared in the same way as those of other functions. It is missing – and must not have – a return type specifier. The function takes two integer parameters. The code in **main** shows two ways of calling **coord**. The first:

```
coord point1 = coord(5,10);
```

is the full version; the function **coord** is called with the arguments 5 and 10 and the result of this function – the variables **x_coord** and **y_coord** set to 5 and 10 respectively – are assigned to **point1**, which is an instance of **coord**. The second constructor calling sequence:

```
coord point3(15,20);
```

is an abbreviation equivalent in syntax to the definition and initialisation of **point1** above. This abbreviated form of definition and constructor call is much more frequently used than the full version.

The simple definition in the last section:

```
cust_acc a1;
```

invokes the constructor **cust_acc::cust_acc**, which does not take parameters. This is also an abbreviated form of constructor syntax. Its full form is analogous to that shown above:

```
cust_acc a1 = cust_acc();
```

The definition of **point2** is commented out because it is illegal: a constructor that takes parameters cannot be called using a function name followed by an empty argument list.

The result of the program is simple:

```
5
10
15
20
```

The program defines two instances of the class **coord**. As part of their definition, they are initialised by the constructor to the parameter values supplied. The member function **print** of both instances is used to display the values of the data members.

There is no destructor function in the class **coord**. Use of destructors is most common when a member function – usually the constructor – performs dynamic allocation of memory, which should be freed at or before the end of program execution. In this case, no memory is dynamically allocated. Examples of dynamic allocation are shown later in this chapter.

BANK42: CONSTRUCTORS TAKING PARAMETERS

Here is a more substantial example of use of constructors – with and without parameters – in the familiar cust_acc class. The whole program is shown.

```
/*
 * Program 'accounts.cpp'
 * -- implements bank-account class with
 * overloaded constructors, one taking
 * parameters.
 *
 * Class declaration in 'accounts.h'
 */
class cust_acc
{
private:
  float bal;
  int acc_num;
public:
  cust_acc();
  cust_acc(int, float); // overloaded constructor
  void lodge(float);
  void withdraw(float);
  void balance();
};

/*
 *
 * Program file 'accfunc.cpp'
 * -- defines 'cust_acc' member functions.
 * Only constructors have changed
 * from the original program
 *
 */
#include <iostream.h>
#include "accounts.h"

cust_acc::cust_acc()
{
  cout <<
      "Enter number of account to be opened: ";
  cin >> acc_num;
  cout << "Enter initial balance: ";
  cin >> bal;
  cout << "Customer account " << acc_num
          << " created with balance "
              << bal << endl;
}
```

```cpp
cust_acc::cust_acc(int num_init, float bal_init)
{
  acc_num = num_init;
  bal = bal_init;
  cout << "Customer account " << acc_num
            << " created with balance "
                   << bal << endl;
}

void cust_acc::lodge(float lodgement)
{
  bal += lodgement;
  cout << "Lodgement of " << lodgement
       << " accepted" << endl;
}

void cust_acc::withdraw(float with)
{
  if (bal > with)
  {
    bal -= with;
    cout << "Withdrawal of " << with
              << " granted" << endl;
    return;
  }
  cout << "Insufficient balance for withdrawal of "
            << with << endl;
  cout << "Withdrawal of " << bal
            << " granted" << endl;
  bal      = (float)0;
}

void cust_acc::balance()
{
  cout << "Balance of account is "
            << bal << endl;
}
/*
 * 'accounts.cpp'
 * Create and initialise two accounts
 */
#include <iostream.h>
#include "accounts.h"

int main()
{
  cust_acc a1;
```

```
    a1.lodge(250.00);
    a1.balance();
    a1.withdraw(500.00);
    a1.balance();

    cust_acc a2(12345, 1000.00);
    a2.balance();
    a2.withdraw(750.00);
    a2.balance();
    return(0);
}
```

The cust_acc class declaration now contains two constructor functions. The first is to initialise objects of the cust_acc class in the way already shown. The second cust_acc constructor is an overloaded constructor. This is a special case of an overloaded function. Overloaded functions are covered in full in Chapter 5.

The overloaded constructor:

```
    cust_acc::cust_acc(int num_init, float bal_init)
```

causes a new instance of the class cust_acc to be assigned the values specified by the two variables in the argument list.

Consider the main function. An object, a1, of type cust_acc is created and is then initialised by the constructor function cust_acc::cust_acc(), the *default constructor*. This prompts the user for input of the account number and opening balance, confirming that the account has been successfully opened.

Most non-trivial classes in C++ programs will contain overloaded constructors. A class can be considered as a data type that, when instantiated, provides a range of services to end-user programmers. A real bank-account class of the type shown might provide as part of its set of services the facility for creating accounts in many different ways. For each method of creation, there would be a matching constructor.

4.3   Syntax Rules

This section gives further rules on the syntax and usage of constructors and destructors. Some of these rules are specially relevant in the context of inheritance and derived classes and are dealt with fully in Chapter 6.

In Section 3.1, it is stated that a class may be unnamed, with the name omitted like this:

```
class
{
private:

  .
  .
public:

  .
  .
}inst;
```

The variable inst is the class variable – an instance of the unnamed class. This class cannot be used as a function argument or return value. Neither is it legal for such a class to have constructor or destructor functions.

It is legal for both structures and unions to have either constructors or destructors or both as members.

Constructors may be overloaded in the way shown in the last section, but it is illegal to have two or more identically-declared constructors in the one class:

```
class coord
{
private:
  int x_coord, y_coord;
public:
  coord(int x, int y)
    { x_coord = x; y_coord = y; }
  coord(int x, int y) // illegal!
  {
    x_coord = x;
    y_coord = y;
    cout << "Constructing....\n";
  }
```

```
   void print()
   {
       cout << x_coord << "\n";
       cout << y_coord << "\n";
   }
};
```

The compiler judges the constructors to be identical if their headers are the same and then generates a compilation error. It does not matter if the functions contain different code, as they do in this example.

Destructors must not be overloaded:

```
class coord
{
private:
   int x_coord, y_coord;
public:
   .
   .
   .
   ~coord() { /* do something */ }
   ~coord() { /* do something else */ }
};
```

Constructor functions must not be declared const, static, virtual or volatile. The example showing an illegal const constructor declaration is representative:

```
class coord
{
private:
   int x_coord, y_coord;
public:
   const coord(int x, int y)
   {
       x_coord = x;
       y_coord = y;
   }
   .
   .
};
```

Destructors must not be declared const, static or volatile, but may be declared virtual. Virtual destructors, like other virtual functions, are used in classes derived from a base class and are examined in Chapter 6.

Constructors and destructors must be member functions of a class of the same name. They must not be declared outside class scope or as friend functions.

ADDRESSES OF MEMBER FUNCTIONS

It is illegal to take the address of a constructor or destructor:

```
#include <iostream.h>

class coord
{
public:
  coord(){};
  void myfunc(){ cout << "Called myfunc\n"; }
};

int main()
{
  //   Take constructor address, illegal
  &coord::coord;

  //   Take member function address, OK
  &coord::myfunc;

  //   Define member function pointer
  void (coord::* p)();

  //   Assign constructor address, illegal
  p = &coord::coord;

  //   Assign member function address, OK
  p = &coord::myfunc;

  //   Define 'coord' variable and use the
  //   function pointer to call 'myfunc'

  coord point;

  (point.*p)();
  return(0);
}
```

The operator ::*, which is used to define pointers to class members and was first shown in Section 3.6, is used to define a pointer p to member functions of the class coord.

The assignment of the address of coord::myfunc to this pointer is valid, but not that of the constructor coord.

The pointer p, now containing the address of coord::myfunc, is used to call the function. This must be done using the *. pointer-to-member operator, also first encountered in Section 3.6.

CALL43: CALLING MEMBER FUNCTIONS

Both constructors and destructors may call member functions of the same class. Both constructors and destructors may be called by member functions of the same class.

The following compact example shows all four possible operations:

```
#include <iostream.h>

class coord
{
private:
  int x_coord, y_coord;
public:
  coord(int x, int y);
  void const_call();
  void call_const();
  ~coord();
  void destr_call();
  void call_destr();
};

int main()
{
  coord point1 = coord(5,10);

  point1.call_const();

  point1.call_destr();
  return(0);
}

// Constructor and constructor-call functions

coord::coord(int x, int y)
{
  x_coord = x;
  y_coord = y;
  const_call();
}
void coord::const_call()
{
  cout << x_coord << "\n";
  cout << y_coord << "\n";
}
```

```
void coord::call_const()
{
   coord point2(15,20);
}

//   Destructor and destructor-call functions

coord::~coord()
{
   destr_call();
   cout << "Destructing....\n";
}

void coord::destr_call()
{
cout << "Coordinates: " << x_coord
     << " " << y_coord << "\n";
}

void coord::call_destr()
{
   this->~coord();
}
```

The example is complex and is easiest to explain using its
output, which is:

```
5
10
15
20
Coordinates: 15 20
Destructing....
Coordinates: 5 10
Destructing....
Coordinates: 5 10
Destructing....
```

Consider the main function. The first statement is a
declaration, which is also a call to the constructor of class
coord:

```
coord point1 = coord(5,10);
```

This calls the coord constructor function, which assigns
the values 5 and 10 to the data members and then calls the
member function const_call to display the values 5 and
10.

The next line in main:

```
point1.call_const();
```

calls the function call_const, which then defines a local instance, point2, of the class coord. The resulting constructor call assigns the values 15 and 20 to the data members of point2. The constructor calls const_call, which displays those values.

Immediately on exit from call_const, point2 goes out of scope and the destructor function, ~coord, is implicitly called. The destructor calls destr_call, which displays the values 15 and 20 followed by the message Destructing.....

The last line in main before the return:

```
point1.call_destr();
```

calls the function call_destr, which then does an explicit call to the destructor. The destructor displays the values of the data members of point1, 5 and 10, followed by the Destructing.... message.

Finally, when the main function is exited, point1 goes out of scope, the destructor is implicitly called, and the messages:

```
Coordinates: 5 10
Destructing....
```

are displayed for the second and final time.

A notable feature of this program is the explicit call to the destructor:

```
this->~coord();
```

Calling destructors explicitly is rare and only used for specialised applications. The most typical case is where a C++ program must implement its own memory management, a task more commonly left to the operating system.

CONSTRUCTORS AND DYNAMIC MEMORY ALLOCATION

Constructors may be used to initialise class objects for which memory has been dynamically allocated by the new operator:

```cpp
#include <iostream.h>
class coord
{
private:
  int x_coord, y_coord;
public:
  coord(int x, int y)
  {
    x_coord = x;
    y_coord = y;
  }
  void print()
  {
    cout << x_coord << "\n";
    cout << y_coord << "\n";
  }
};
int main()
{
  coord *p_coord;

  p_coord = new coord(5,10);

  p_coord->print();
  return(0);
}
```

Here, a new instance of the class type **coord** is allocated and its memory address assigned to the pointer **p_coord**. Also, the class's constructor function is called, initialising the data members of the class to the values **5** and **10**.

A class object represented by an automatic variable is destroyed when that variable goes out of scope. On the other hand, a class object for which memory is dynamically allocated:

```cpp
class coord
{
  //
};
ptr = new coord;
```

is persistent. When **ptr** goes out of scope, its destructor is not called and the memory associated with **ptr** remains allocated. For the destructor to be invoked, the memory must be explicitly deallocated:

```cpp
delete ptr;
```

This causes the destructor to be implicitly called.

CONSTRUCTORS WITH PRIVATE ACCESS

In all the examples shown so far in this section, the constructor functions have been declared public. If a constructor is declared private, access to it is restricted in the same way as for all other private member functions. The coord class is used again to illustrate this:

```
class coord
{
private:
  int x_coord, y_coord;
  coord(int x, int y)
  {
     x_coord = x;
     y_coord = y;
  }
public:
  void print()
  {
     cout << x_coord << "\n";
     cout << y_coord << "\n";
  }
};
```

The following statements written in client code cause compilation errors, because the constructor function coord is now accessible only from member functions of its class.

```
coord point1 = coord(5,10);      // illegal
point1.print();                  // call fails
```

If all the constructors of a class are made private, only static member functions, friends and members of existing objects of that class type may create new class objects. This restriction can be useful, especially if dynamic memory allocation is involved.

It is legal to make destructor functions private, but at the risk of never deallocating an object allocated earlier by a constructor:

```
class coord
{
private:
  int x_coord, y_coord;
  ~coord() { cout << "Destructing\n"; }
```

```
public:
   coord(int x, int y)
   {
      x_coord = x;
      y_coord = y;
   }
   void print()
   {
      cout << x_coord << "\n";
      cout << y_coord << "\n";
   }
   void destroy() { delete this; }
};
int main()
{
   coord *p_coord;
   p_coord = new coord(5,10);
   p_coord->print();
// delete p_coord;                    // error!
   p_coord->destroy();
   return(0);
}
```

In this example, the constructor is public and the destructor private. The statement:

```
delete p_coord;
```

is intended to delete the class object referred to by p_coord. Use of the delete operator causes the destructor to be called. In this case, the call to the destructor is out of scope because the main function is not a member of the class coord and does not have access to the private destructor. The member function destroy, on the other hand, has access to the destructor and calls it successfully.

A class containing either constructors or destructors or both may also contain data or function members or both declared with storage class static.

There are further syntax rules that apply to constructors and destructors as used with derived classes. These are explained fully in Chapter 6.

4.4   Initialisation and Assignment

GENERAL RULES

C++ makes a sharp distinction between the operations of
initialisation and assignment. The distinction is subtle,
but ignorance of it can lead to program errors.

Initialisation occurs when an object is created. In the case
of a class object, initialisation takes place when:

1. a class object is initialised as part of its definition

2. a function receives a class object as an argument

3. a function returns a class object

4. a class object containing a constructor is created

Assignment occurs when an assignment operator is used
in an expression to set a previously-defined object to a
value.

The left operand of an assignment is a previously-defined
object; that of an initialisation is not:

```
coord point1(5,10);
coord point2 = point1; // initialisation type 1 and 4
coord point3(point2);  // initialisation type 1 and 4
coord point4(10,15);
coord point4 =          // initialisation types 1 and 4
  f(point3);            // initialisation type 2
coord point5;
point5 = point4;       // assignment
coord f(coord point3_copy)
{
  return(point3_copy);   // initialisation type 3
}
```

A full program example, showing all four forms of
initialisation, as well as assignment, follows in Section 4.5.

In each case of initialisation, the compiler generates a
default copy mechanism (a *default copy constructor*) that
does a blind member-by-member copy, referred to as
memberwise initialisation.

If the class coord contains only simple (non-pointer)
data members, these default operations will work. Where

coord has pointer data members, the pointers themselves, not the data they point to, are copied between class objects. As a result, several copies of a pointer may be propagated among different class objects, all pointing at the same data. The first destructor function that deallocates the single copy of memory associated with all the copies of the pointer will work, but the second and subsequent will fail.

The class designer can resolve these problems by providing tailored copy constructors which perform 'smart assignment' of pointers which are class members. Copy constructors are dealt with in the next section.

The assignment:

```
point5 = point4;
```

is implemented by *memberwise assignment* using a compiler-generated instance of the assignment operator. It also fails when the two destructors are called. In this case, a specially overloaded assignment operator is needed. Overloaded operators are introduced in Chapter 5.

INITIALISATION WITH CONSTRUCTORS

A constructor is said to initialise a class object of which it is a member.

Programmers do not usually make a distinction between the terms 'initialisation' and 'assignment' as they apply to constructors. However, the execution of every constructor function takes place in two steps, those of initialisation and assignment, in that order.

If the body of a constructor function is null, there is no assignment phase:

```
class coord
{
private:
  int x_coord, y_coord;
public:
  coord(int x, int y)
  {
  }
};
```

In this example, only an initialisation takes place. The assignment step begins with execution of the body of the function coord which, in this case, is null. The next example is more meaningful:

```
class coord
{
private:
   int x_coord, y_coord;
public:
   coord(int x, int y)
   {
      x_coord = x;
      y_coord = y;
   }
};
         .
         .
   coord point(5, 10); //  define class instance
```

When the instance, point, of the class coord is defined, it is first initialised and then assignments are made to its members in the body of the constructor function. The need for the distinction becomes clear when a new facet of constructor syntax is introduced:

```
class coord
{
private:
   int x_coord, y_coord;
public:
   coord(int x, int y) : x_coord(x), y_coord(y)
   {
   }
};
```

The data member variables x_coord and y_coord are here set to the values of the constructor parameters x and y by means of the initialiser list that is supplied to the constructor after the colon following the function header. Note that the function body after the initialiser list is empty, although it does not have to be. Code, including reassignment of x_coord and y_coord, can be added to the constructor function body.

The constructor here behaves the same as the example with assignments in the function body. The difference is that the data members of the class now are initialised instead of being assigned to.

The items in the constructor initialiser list may be simple variables such as those shown above or more complex expressions such as class variables, arithmetic operations and function calls.

The constructor initialiser list is extensively used in Chapter 6 as the mechanism for calling constructors, and passing arguments among them, in class hierarchies.

Here is a case where constructor assignment is illegal and initialisation is required:

```
class coord
{
private:
   int x_coord;
   const int y_coord;
public:
   coord(int x, int y) : x_coord(x), y_coord(y)
   {
      x_coord = x;
      y_coord = y; // Error: 'const'
                   // assignment
   }
};
```

Assignment in the body of the constructor of the const data member, rather than initialisation within an initialiser list, causes a compilation error. There is nothing wrong, however, with making an assignment to the class member, x_coord, which has already been initialised.

4.5   Default and Copy Constructors

DEFAULT CONSTRUCTORS

The default constructor for a class is a constructor that takes no parameters. In the case of the coord class, the default constructor is:

```
coord()   { /* assignment code */ }
```

If a class declaration does not contain a constructor, the C++ compiler generates a default constructor in a manner transparent to the programmer. Every time an instance of a class is defined:

```
coord point;
```

the default constructor actually initialises the instance, point, of type coord.

Constructors can take default parameters; for example:

```
coord::coord(int x = 0)
```

allows the constructor to be called with no arguments or one argument; zero is used as the value of the parameter x within the constructor code. A constructor with only default arguments is also a default constructor. The constructor function header:

```
coord::coord(int x = 5, int y = 6)
```

allows the constructor to take zero, one or two parameters. If none is supplied, the values 5 and 6 are used as parameters within the code. If one is supplied, 6 is used as the second parameter. See Appendix A for a full description of the syntax of default arguments.

INITIALISING OBJECTS WITH COPY CONSTRUCTORS

A copy constructor is one that is called to initialise the class object of which it is a member to the value of another class object.

The prototype of a copy constructor is of the following general form:

```
<classname>::<classname>(const <classname>&);
```
In the case of the class coord, the prototype looks like this:

```
coord::coord(const coord&);
```

A copy constructor may be defined by the programmer. If this is not done, then initialising operations cause a default copy constructor to be called implicitly. The default copy constructor is not very refined, performing as it does simple memberwise initialisation.

Let us initialise a class object with the contents of a different object of the same class:

```
coord point1(5, 10);

coord point2 = point1;
```

Assume that coord has no copy constructor. The default copy constructor memberwise-initialises each member of point2 with the corresponding member of point1.

In memberwise initialisation such as that of point2 above, the default copy constructor is used. Ordinary constructors, if any, declared as part of the class coord, are not called.

CPCST451: Copy Constructors

Here is an example that demonstrates invocation a programmer-supplied copy constructor:

```
#include <iostream.h>

class coord
{
private:
  int x_coord, y_coord;
public:
  // default (non-copy) constructor
  coord() { x_coord = y_coord = 0; }
  coord(int x, int y)
  {
    x_coord = x;
    y_coord = y;
  }
  // Our copy constructor
  coord(const coord& copypoint)
  {
    x_coord = copypoint.x_coord;
    y_coord = copypoint.y_coord;
  }
  void print()
  {
    cout << x_coord << " "<< y_coord << "\n";
  }
};

int main()
{
  coord point1;    // use default constructor
  point1.print();

  // constructor coord(int, int)
  coord point2(5,10);
  point2.print();
```

```
   // initialise with our copy constructor
   coord point3 = point2;
   point3.print();

   // initialise with our copy constructor
   coord point4(point3);
   point4.print();
   return(0);
}
```

The class declaration contains three overloaded constructors: the first is the default constructor; the second assigns values to the class data members; and the third is our own copy constructor. The sequence of definitions in main shows how the constructors are used. The results of the four calls to the member function print are these:

```
0  0
5  10
5  10
5  10
```

In the example above, the definition:

```
coord point4(point3);
```

causes the data members of point4 to be initialised with the values 5 and 10 from point3.

The alternative initialising construct:

```
coord point4 = point3;
```

similarly uses our copy constructor.

In this case, the copy constructor explicitly specified behaves in the same way as the default copy constructor.

In cases such as this example, where the class data members are simple variables, memberwise initialisation is sufficient to create a new class object. However, where the data members are pointers or more-complex data objects, the memberwise initialisation carried out by the default copy constructor leads to errors.

CPCST452: MEMORY DEALLOCATION ERROR

Here is an example, again based on the coord class, of the kind of problem that arises:

```
#include <iostream.h>
class coord
{
private:
  int *x_coord, *y_coord;
public:
  coord(int x, int y)
  {
     cout << "Constructing....\n";
     x_coord  = new int;
     *x_coord = x;
     y_coord  = new int;
     *y_coord = y;
  }
  void print()
  {
     cout << *x_coord << " "<< *y_coord << "\n";
  }
  ~coord()
  {
     cout << "Destructing....\n";
     delete x_coord;
     delete y_coord;
  }
};
int main()
{
  coord point2(5,10);
  coord point3 = point2;
  point2.print();
  point3.print();
  return(0);
}
```

The private data members of **coord** are now pointers to integers. When the class object **point3** is defined and initialised:

```
coord point3 = point2;
```

the default copy constructor initialises the pointer values in **point3** with those stored in **point2**. The destructor, which is called twice, then attempts to deallocate the same memory twice. The results of doing this are undefined but are always an error and may cause the program to crash.

These are the output results of this program run on an 80486 PC with Borland Turbo C++:

```
Constructing....
5 10
5 10
Destructing....
Destructing....
Null pointer assignment
```

The last line is an error message indicating that the destructor tried to deallocate memory already freed.

The problem is resolved using a specially-written copy constructor, which is added to coord as a function member:

```
coord(const coord& copypoint)
{
  cout << "Copy constructing....\n";
  x_coord = new int;
  *x_coord = *(copypoint.x_coord);
  y_coord = new int;
  *y_coord = *(copypoint.y_coord);
}
```

The class object point3 in the main function is then initialised by the copy constructor. In the earlier example, the default copy constructor copied the pointer values x_coord and y_coord, leading to an attempted double memory deallocation. This time the *integer objects pointed to* by x_coord and y_coord are copied to newly-allocated memory in point3. When the destructor is eventually called twice, it each time deallocates different memory.

The class object point3 is initialised in main using the custom copy constructor:

```
int main()
{
  coord point2(5,10);

  // use the custom copy constructor to
  // initialise the data, not the pointers
  coord point3 = point2;
  point2.print();
  point3.print();
  return(0);
}
```

The output result is error-free.

CPCST453: ALL CASES OF INITIALISATION

The following program example attempts to summarise all possible cases of class-object initialisation and assignment. For the initialisations, a custom copy constructor is required; for the single case of assignment, overloading of the assignment operator is needed.

```
//
// Program cpcst3.cpp
// Illustrates initialisation and assignment
//
#include <iostream.h>
class coord
{
private:
   int *x_coord, *y_coord;
public:
   coord(int x, int y)
   {
      cout
      << "Constructing with 2 parameters....\n";
      x_coord  = new int;
      *x_coord = x;
      y_coord  = new int;
      *y_coord = y;
   }

   coord(const coord& copypoint)
   {
      cout << "Copy constructing....\n";
      x_coord = new int;
      *x_coord = *(copypoint.x_coord);
      y_coord = new int;
      *y_coord = *(copypoint.y_coord);
   }

   void print()
   {
      cout << *x_coord << " " <<
               *y_coord << "\n";
   }

   ~coord()
   {
      cout << "Destructing\n";
      delete x_coord;
      delete y_coord;
   }
};
```

```
// Prototype of function receiving class object
// as parameter and returning a class object

coord f(coord);

int main()
{
   coord  point1(5,10);
   coord  point4(0,0);

   // First case of initialisation
   coord point2 = point1;
   // Argument to copy constructor
   // has same effect
   // coord point2(point1);

   cout << "Calling function f\n";
   // Second (parameter copy) and third
   // (copy on return) cases
   coord point3 = f(point2);

   cout << "Returned from function f\n";

   // Ordinary assignment, shallow copy,
   // destructor called twice for same memory
   //  and fails
   point4 = point2;

   point1.print();
   point2.print();
   point3.print();
   point4.print();

   return(0);
}

coord f(coord copy)
{
   // Do nothing but return the class object
   cout << "Returning from function f\n";
   return(copy);
}
```

The program's output is this:

```
Constructing with 2 parameters....
Constructing with 2 parameters....
Copy constructing....
Calling function f
Copy constructing....
Returning from function f
Copy constructing....
```

```
Destructing
Returned from function f
5  10
5  10
5  10
5  10
Destructing
Destructing
Destructing
Destructing
Null pointer assignment
```

The custom copy constructor is called in all cases except that of the assignment. The memory-trashing problem described above in that case causes the destructor to be called twice for a single memory allocation. This explains the last line of the output.

To overcome this problem, we need to override the standard assignment operator to take on the meaning of the copy constructor function. The assignment:

```
point3 = point2;
```

would then call the copy constructor function. Techniques for overloading the assignment and other operators in this way are described in Chapter 5.

DEFAULT ARGUMENTS IN COPY CONSTRUCTORS

Finally, default arguments are allowed in copy constructors. The constructor declaration:

```
coord(const coord&, int n = 0);
```

specifies a custom copy constructor which may also take one or no parameters of type int. If there are no such parameters, n has the default value zero within the constructor function.

4.6   Constructors, Destructors and Arrays

Arrays of class objects may be defined in the same way as arrays of any other data object. Constructor and destructor functions may also be used with arrayed class objects. Here is an example of definition and initialisation

of a one-dimensional array of class objects. For this
example, we assume that the class coord has only one
data member:

```
#include <iostream.h>
class coord
{
private:
   int x_coord;
public:
   coord(int x) { x_coord = x; }
   void print()
      { cout << x_coord << "\n"; }
};
int main()
{
   coord point[5] = { 5, 10, 15, 20, 25 };

   for ( int i = 0; i < 5; i++ )
      point[i].print();
   return(0);
}
```

Initialisation of arrays of class objects is very much the
same as, for example, initialisation of arrays of simple C
structures. The elements of the initialiser list within curly
braces are assigned in turn by the constructor to the data
members of the coord class objects grouped in the array
point.

The print member function is invoked for each of the
arrayed class objects in turn and displays the contents of
x_coord for that object.

ARRAY461: 1D ARRAY OF CLASS OBJECTS

Let us now look at a one-dimensional class-object array
for the original declaration of the class coord, which had
two data members. Here is a full example program:

```
#include <iostream.h>

class coord
{
private:
   int x_coord, y_coord;
public:
   coord(int x, int y)
```

```
   {
      x_coord = x;
      y_coord = y;
   }
   void print()
   {
      cout << x_coord
           << " " << y_coord << "\n";
   }
};
int main()
{
   coord point[5] = {
                      coord(5, 10),
                      coord(15, 20),
                      coord(25, 30),
                      coord(35, 40),
                      coord(45, 50)
                      };
   for ( int i = 0; i < 5; i++ )
      point[i].print();
   return(0);
}
```

Again, a five-element array of class objects of type coord is defined, but the initialisation this time is more complex. The initialiser list within the curly braces is made up of five calls to the constructor, each with two integer arguments. The constructor function assigns each pair of parameters to the data members of the appropriate element of the class object array point. Once more, print is used to display the data members of the array of class objects. The result is this:

```
5  10
15  20
25  30
35  40
45  50
```

ARRAY462: 2D ARRAY OF CLASS OBJECTS

Now consider a two-dimensional class-object array.

```
class coord
{
private:
   int x_coord, y_coord;
```

```
public:
  coord(int x, int y)
  {
    x_coord = x;
    y_coord = y;
  }
  void print()
  {
    cout << x_coord << " " << y_coord << "\n";
  }
};
int main()
{
  coord point[3][2] =
          {
          coord(5, 10), coord(6, 11),
          coord(15, 20), coord(16, 21),
          coord(25, 30), coord(26, 31)
          };
  for ( int i = 0; i < 3; i++ )
    for ( int j = 0; j < 2; j++ )
          point[i][j].print();
  return(0);
}
```

Each element of the two-dimensional array **point** is an instance of the class **coord**. The data members of each of these elements are initialised by the constructor with the values shown in the calls to the constructor in the initialiser list. The order in which the elements are initialised is the same as that to be expected for any multi-dimensional array in C++: row-column, with the column subscript varying faster. Here are the displayed results:

```
5  10
6  11
15  20
16  21
25  30
26  31
```

An array of class objects can be dynamically allocated using the **new** operator and then deallocated using the special form of **delete** designed for arrays:

```
#include <iostream.h>

class coord
```

```
{
  coord() { x_coord = y_coord = 0; }
      .
      .
  ~coord() { cout << "Destructing....\n"; }
};

int main()
{
  coord *p_coord;

  p_coord = new coord[5];

  // Assign meaningful values to array members

  for ( int i = 0; i < 5; i++ )
    (p_coord + i)->print();

  delete [] p_coord;
  return(0);
}
```

In this example, a pointer – p_coord, of type coord – is
defined and used to point to a five-element array of class
objects allocated with new. For each array element
allocated, the constructor is called and assigns a value of
zero to the data members of that class object.

Code may be included at this point to assign to the data
members of the arrayed class objects initial values other
than zero.

The array is traversed with p_coord and the values of the
data members of each element are displayed. Finally,
each of the five elements of the array is deallocated using
delete. Each time an element is deleted, the destructor
function is called. In this case, the destructor simply
displays a message. Assuming the data members in all the
array elements are zero, the displayed result is this:

```
0  0
0  0
0  0
0  0
0  0
Destructing....
Destructing....
Destructing....
Destructing....
Destructing....
```

If the **delete** operation were made part of the destructor:

```
~coord()
{
  delete [] this;
  cout << "Destructing....\n";
}
```

the destructor would not be called. This is because objects created with **new** are persistent; they are not automatically deallocated when they go out of scope – in this case, when the **main** function terminates. Anyway, using delete...this in a destructor implies a recursive delete operation and results in unpredictable runtime errors.

We have seen that an array of class objects may be initialised using constructors. Where the array is allocated using the **new** operator, only a constructor with an empty argument list – a default constructor – is allowed. This was the case in the last example. The attempted initialisation in the following code segment is therefore illegal:

```
int main()
{
  coord *p_coord;

  p_coord = new coord[5];
  p_coord = {
            coord(5, 10),
            coord(15, 20),
            coord(25, 30),
            coord(35, 40),
            coord(45, 50)
            };
  for ( int i = 0; i < 5; i++ )
    (p_coord++)->print();
  return(0);
}
```

4.7 Example: A String Class

The character string – strictly, the null-terminated character array – is one of the data objects most commonly used in C and C++ programming. A large number of string operations are also defined, including those provided in the standard libraries. The ANSI C++ class library additionally defines a general purpose string class.

Because it illustrates well so many aspects of class implementation in C++, this section presents a string class example, in no way intended as an alternative to the standard string class. The program shown is used in Chapter 5 to illustrate the characteristics of C++ operator overloading facilities. It also demonstrates a typical usage of constructors and destructors.

STRING47: A String Class

First, the string class is declared as part of the header file str.h:

```
/*
 * str.h – defines string class
 */
class string
{
private:
  char *sptr;
  int  slen;
public:
  string();
  string(int);
  string(const char *);
  string(const string&);
  void set_str(const char *);
  char *substr(int, int);
  int strpos(const string&);
  char *access() { return(sptr); }
  ~string() { delete sptr; }
};
```

The class defines a character pointer as a private data member. The constructor functions in different ways allocate space for this pointer and initialise the resulting character array as a string. The other member functions of **string** define operations that are often carried out on strings.

The class **string** has four constructors and a destructor. It also defines an access function to retrieve the value of **sptr**. In between, two member functions are defined, each of which represents a discrete string operation.

Here are the member functions, including the constructors:

```cpp
/*
 *
 * strfunc.cpp -- defines string class functions
 *
 */
#include <iostream.h>
#include <string.h>
#include "str.h"

// string constructors

string::string()
{
  sptr = new char[50];
  *sptr = '\0';
  slen = 0;
}

string::string(int size)
{
  sptr = new char[size + 1];
  *sptr = '\0';
  slen = 0;
}

string::string(const char* s_in)
{
  int len_in = strlen(s_in);

  sptr = new char[len_in + 1];
  strcpy(sptr, s_in);
  slen = len_in;
}

string::string(const string& ob_in)
{
  int len_in = strlen(ob_in.sptr);

  sptr = new char[len_in + 1];
  strcpy(sptr, ob_in.sptr);
  slen = ob_in.slen;
}

void string::set_str(const char * s)
{
  strcpy(sptr, s);
  slen = strlen(s);
}
/*
```

```
 * function 'substr' − extracts from the string
 * sptr a substring specified by the substring's
 * start position and length. The substring is
 *  returned by the function
 */
char *string::substr(int start, int len)
{
  char *cp1,*cp2,*cp3,*sub;
  short displ;
  displ = strlen(sptr);
  cp1 = sptr;
  sub = cp2 = new char[20];
  if (start > displ)
  {
     cout << "start " << start << " string length "
                    << displ << " \n";
     *cp2 = '\0';
     return(cp2);
  }
  start -= 1;    // allow for zero start to array
  for (cp1+=start,cp3=cp1;
   (cp1<cp3+len)&&(*cp1); cp1++,cp2++)
     *cp2 = *cp1;
  *cp2 = '\0';
  return(sub);
}
/*
 * Function strpos − finds position of a search
 * string in sptr . Returns position if found,
 * negative value if not found.
 */
int string::strpos(const string& srch)
{
  int    len;
  char    *lptr; // local char pointer

  len  = strlen(srch.sptr);
  lptr = sptr;

  while (*lptr)
  {
     if ((strncmp(lptr, srch.sptr, len)) == 0)
             return(lptr - sptr + 1);
     lptr++;
  }
  return(-1);
}
```

Each constructor allocates a character array of the length specified by its parameter, null-terminates the array and sets its length counter.

substr works on the member string sptr of the class of which it is also a member. It returns an extracted part as a return value.

strpos finds the position of the string defined as a member of the class object srch in sptr. access allows member and non-member functions to retrieve the contents of sptr.

The main function calls all the functions described above, as well as a destructor which deallocates memory assigned by the constructor to sptr.

```cpp
/*
 * str.cpp – exercise string class
 */
#include <iostream.h>
#include "str.h"

int main()
{
    string s1("Now is the time");
    string s2("time");
    string s3(s1);
    char *sub;

    sub = s1.substr(5,6);
    cout << "Substring from 5 to 10 of  "
        << s1.access() << " is  " << sub << " \n";
    delete(sub);
    cout << "Position of  " << s2.access()
        << " in " <<
        s1.access() << " is  " << s1.strpos(s2)
            << " \n";
    cout << "Contents of s3: " << s3.access()
        << "\n";
    return(0);
}
```

The results output by this program are:

```
Substring from 5 to 10 of  Now is
the time  is  is the
Position of  time  in  Now is the
time  is  12
Contents of s3: Now is the time
```

4.8   Example: A List Class

Another data structure that can be well described using the C++ class construct is the linked list. This section presents an implementation of a singly-linked-forward list along with operations allowed on the list: addition, deletion and display of nodes. The example given below also uses almost all the C++ language constructs that we have so far encountered.

LIST48: A List Class

First, here is the declaration of the list classes, stored in the header file list.h:

```
class node
{
private:
  int    x;
  double y;
  node *next;
public:
  node(int, double);
  node * &Next() { return(next); }
  int    xval() { return(x); }
  double   yval() { return(y); }
};

class list
{
private:
  node *head, *tail, *curr, *tptr1, *tptr2;
public:
  list() { head = tail = curr = NULL; }
  void get_node_data(int&, double&);
  void add_node(int, double);
  void del_node(int, double);
  void dump_list();
  ~list() { destroy(); }
  void destroy();
};

class message
{
public:
```

```
void prompt()
{
    cout <<
    "Press 'a' and RETURN to add to list: \n";
    cout <<
    "Press 'd' and RETURN to delete from list:\n";
    cout <<
    "Press 'p' and RETURN to display list: \n";
    cout << "Press 'q' and RETURN to quit: \n";
}
};
```

The message class at the end is simple, representing a neat way to prompt the user. The declarations of the node and list classes are more interesting.

The list class defines the characteristics of the list and the possible operations on it. The list is made up of zero or more nodes that are in turn described by the class node. The list class contains in its private area a number of pointers that are used to point to list nodes. In its public area, list declares the functions that represent the operations possible on the list.

The list constructor does not allocate space in memory for the list nodes: that is left to the node constructor. It just sets the head, tail and current node pointers to null.

The destructor calls a function named destroy, which deallocates all the nodes in the list, effectively deleting it.

The declaration of get_node_data:

```
void get_node_data(int&, double&);
```

specifies as arguments references to two variables of type int and double. The function reads the data items from the standard input stream and the returned arguments reflect the change.

The list member functions add_node and del_node add nodes to and delete nodes from the list. In the case of del_node, the function arguments are used to search for a matching node, which is then deleted.

The node class has four member functions. One is a constructor; the others are access functions. The Next access function returns a reference-to-pointer to the next node in the list. The pointer is not copied when the function returns; instead, the function return value refers directly to the next pointer in the list node. It is thus possible to assign new pointer values to the Next function return value and thereby change next pointers in the list. The other access functions respectively return the values x and y of a node.

Let us now look at the definitions of the member functions of both classes, which are stored in the program file 'listfunc.cpp':

```cpp
#include <iostream.h>
#include "list.h"

void list::get_node_data(int& x, double& y)
{
  cout << "Enter Integer: ";
  cin >> x;
  cout << "Enter Double: ";
  cin >> y;
}

void list::add_node(int x, double y)
{
  // Create new list element

  curr = new node(x, y);

  //    Add the element to the end of the list
  if (head == NULL)
     head = curr;
  else
     tail->Next() = curr;
  tail = curr;
  tail->Next() = NULL;
}

void list::del_node(int x, double y)
{
  // Search for matching node
  tptr1 = tptr2 = head;
  while (tptr1)
  {
     if ((tptr1->xval() == x) && (tptr1->yval() == y))
             break;
     if (tptr1 != tptr2)
             tptr2 = tptr2->Next();
     tptr1 = tptr1->Next();
  }
```

```cpp
   if (!tptr1)
   {
      cout << "Node to be deleted not found\n";
      return;
   }

   if (tptr1 == head)
   {
      head = head->Next();
      delete tptr1;
      return;
   }

   if (tptr1 == tail)
   {
      tail = tptr2;
      tptr2->Next() = NULL;
      delete tptr1;
      return;
   }

   tptr2->Next() = tptr1->Next();
   tptr1->Next() = NULL;
   delete tptr1;
}
void list::dump_list()
{
   //    Display the current state of the list
   if (!head)
      cout << "List is empty\n";

   curr = head;
   while (curr)
   {
      cout << "Integer " << curr->xval()
           << " Double " << curr->yval() << "\n";
      curr = curr->Next();
   }
}
void list::destroy()
{
   while (head)
   {
      tptr1  = head;
      head   = head->Next();
      delete tptr1;
   }
}
```

```
node::node(int x_in, double y_in)
{
   x = x_in;
   y = y_in;
   next = NULL;
}
```

get_node_data takes int and double parameters, to which it assigns data input by the user. The changed parameters are returned to main.

add_node calls the node constructor using as arguments the int and double data parameters supplied to add_node. The call to the constructor allocates new memory space for the node and (in the constructor function body) assigns the data values to the node members.

Having allocated a node, add_node goes through the standard procedure of adding the node to the list. In all cases, the pointers that are data members of node are retrieved using access functions that are also members of node. Making extensive use of these access functions, del_node and dump_list respectively delete and display list nodes.

Now here is the main function, stored in the program file 'list.cpp', which drives all the member functions:

```
#include <iostream.h>
#include "list.h"

int main()
{
   int    c;
   int    x;
   double y;

   //    Call list constructor
   list l;
   message user;

   user.prompt();
   while (c = cin.get(), c != 'q' && c != EOF)
   {
      switch (c)
      {
      case 'a':
      case 'A':  l.get_node_data(x, y);
                 l.add_node(x, y);
                 break;
```

```
    case 'd':
    case 'D':    l.get_node_data(x, y);
                 l.del_node(x, y);
                 break;
    case 'p':
    case 'P':    l.dump_list();
                 break;
    default:
        cout << "Invalid option chosen\n";
                 break;
    }
    c = cin.get();
    user.prompt();
  }
  return(0);
}
```

This program exemplifies many of the characteristics of the object-oriented programming approach. Data and functions are encapsulated in distinct list and node classes. The data members of **node** cannot be accessed other than indirectly through its own member access functions; this data-hiding lessens the likelihood of the data member variables being corrupted. Constructor functions initialise objects of both classes automatically on their definition.

One major feature of the object-oriented approach, polymorphism, implemented by virtual functions and class inheritance, is missing. This is demonstrated in a development of the list program in Chapter 6.

5 Function and Operator Overloading

5.1 Function Overloading

This chapter deals with ambiguity. In natural language, ambiguity is common: *John painted a black picture* might mean either that John created a portrait using black paint or that he made a pessimistic prediction. The human mind is adept at accommodating such differences of meaning. Computers, formal language definitions and compilers are very much less so.

Both the C and C++ languages allow limited semantic ambiguity by means of *name overloading*. The name overloading facilities provided by C are much more limited than those of C++. Here is an example, common to both languages, where the meaning of a name depends on the context of its use:

```
void myfunc()
{
   int x = 5;
       .
      /* x == 5 here */
       .
   {
      int x = 6;
          .
             /* x == 6 here */
          .
   }
   /* x == 5 again */
}
```

Before the second definition of x in the nested compound statement, x refers to a location in computer memory containing the value 5. Within the nested compound statement after the second definition, x refers to a different location in memory containing the value 6. Finally, x reverts to the value 5 when its second definition goes out of scope.

C++ additionally introduces overloaded functions. A single function name may be used to refer to more than one instance of the function, with each instance of the function performing similar processing on different argument lists. The function instances are distinguished by the compiler on the basis of the different argument lists specified in their prototypes.

Overloaded constructors, introduced in Chapter 4, are a special case of overloaded functions. Another special case is the overloaded operator: the programmer may assign additional meanings to basic C++ operators.

For example, the + operator usually used for arithmetic addition may be assigned another meaning, such as concatenation of strings. The second meaning is used by the compiler depending on the context in which the operator is used.

Many of the basic C++ operators are in fact already overloaded. A good example is the modulus operator %. This can be used in more than one way:

```
printf("Remainder is %d\n",17%4);
```

The operator is treated in each case by the compiler in a manner appropriate to the context. Overloaded operators are examined starting at Section 5.4.

Function overloading promotes programming flexibility. It allows programmers to use the same function name to carry out operations on different data without having to be aware of how those operations are implemented.

As an example, suppose it is required to find the product of two numbers, either of which may be of type int or double. Four functions, all with the same name, are declared and defined to ensure a correct result regardless of the types of the arguments used in a call to the function.

```
// Overloaded function prototypes

int prod_func(int, int);
double prod_func(int, double);
double prod_func(double, int);
double prod_func(double, double);
```

The definitions of the functions are not shown; we can assume that the types and arithmetic operations are properly handled by them. The C++ compiler chooses the appropriate function instance depending on the syntax of the function call written by the programmer:

```
double prod;
 .
 .
 .
prod = prod_func(15, 2.718281828);
```

This code causes the function declared by the second prototype to be called.

FNOVL511: OVERLOADED FUNCTIONS

Here is a full-program example in which overloaded functions are used to find the squares of numbers.

```
#include <iostream.h>

// Function 'sqr_func' overloaded

float      sqr_func(float);
double     sqr_func(double);
double     sqr_func(float, float);

int main()
{
  float  f = 1.7320508;
  double d = 2.236068;

  cout << "Square of " << f << " is: "
            << sqr_func(f) << "\n";
  cout << "Square of " << d << " is: "
            << sqr_func(d) << "\n";
  cout << f << " multiplied by itself is "
            << sqr_func(f, f) << "\n";
  return(0);
}

float sqr_func(float f)
{
  return(f * f);
}

double sqr_func(double d)
{
  return(d * d);
}
```

```
double sqr_func(float f1, float f2)
{
   return(f1 * f2);
}
```

The results output by this program are:

```
Square of 1.732051 is: 3
Square of 2.236068 is: 5
1.732051 multiplied by itself is 3
```

There are three instances of sqr_func, all with different argument lists. The compiler selects the appropriate function depending on the arguments used in the function call. The criteria the compiler uses to make the selection are explained in the next section. Some basic selection rules follow.

- The compiler does not use the return type of the function to distinguish between function instances.

- The argument lists of each of the function instances must be different.

- Whether or not argument names supplied in a function call match the corresponding parameter names in the function definition does not affect the selection process.

Use of prototypes such as these, with matching function definitions later in the code, results in compilation errors:

```
float sqr_func(float);
double sqr_func(float);
```

The compiler regards the function sqr_func as having been defined identically twice, regardless of the different return types.

Two or more *identical* function prototypes may be used:

```
float sqr_func(float);
float sqr_func(float);
```

followed by definitions of different instances of the function:

```
float sqr_func(float f)
{
   cout <<
   "'sqr_func' called with float argument\n";
   return(f * f);
}
```

```
float sqr_func(double d)
{
   cout <<
   "'sqr_func' called with double argument\n";
   return(d * d);
}
```

The second of the two prototypes is effectively ignored:
a single function is declared as a result of the two
prototypes. The function calling code is this:

```
int main()
{
   float  f = 1.7320508;
   double d = 2.236068;

   cout << "Square of " << f << " is: "
              << sqr_func(f) << "\n";
   cout << "Square of " << d << " is: "
              << sqr_func(d) << "\n";
   return(0);
}
```

If the **sqr_func** function definitions are not seen by the
compiler before the point of their call in **main**, the **float**
instance of **sqr_func** is called twice, even if the function-
call argument is of type **double**:

```
'sqr_func' called with float argument
Square of 1.732051 is: 3
'sqr_func' called with float argument
Square of 2.236068 is: 5
```

Because the function prototypes governing the overloaded
function calls are identical, the argument used in any call
to the function is converted to **float**. If the **sqr_func**
function definitions precede **main** in the source code, the
function header:

```
float sqr_func(double d)
```

constitutes an overloading of the prototypes and this
program output results:

```
'sqr_func' called with float argument
Square of 1.732051 is: 3
'sqr_func' called with double argument
Square of 2.236068 is: 5
```

FNOVL512: OVERLOADED CLASS MEMBER

FUNCTIONS

Overloaded functions may be used in the definition of classes, while they may also be freely used in a procedural way, as in the previous examples. Here is a class implementation of the squares program:

```
#include <iostream.h>

class number
{
private:
  int num;
public:
  number() { num = 5; } // constructor
  int Num() { return(num); } // access function

  // Function 'sqr_func' overloaded

  int sqr_func(int);
  float sqr_func(float);
  double sqr_func(double);
};

int main()
{
  number n;
  int i = n.Num();

  cout << n.sqr_func(i) << "\n";
  cout << n.sqr_func( float(i) )  << "\n";
  cout << n.sqr_func( (double)i ) << "\n";
  return(0);
}
int number::sqr_func(int i)
{
  cout << "Returning int square: ";
  return(i * i);
}

float number::sqr_func(float f)
{
  cout << "Returning float square: ";
  return(f * f);
}
```

```
double number::sqr_func(double d)
{
  cout << "Returning double square: ";
  return(d * d);
}
```

The program uses a simple class, number, which defines one private integer member. This variable, num, is initialised by a simple constructor and its value retrieved in the function code using an access function. The value of num is assigned to the local variable i. The different instances of the overloaded function sqr_func are called depending on the type of i in the function calls.

The C (also C++) typecast notation is used in the double call; the C++ equivalent is used for the float call. The results output by the program are:

```
Returning int square: 25
Returning float square: 25
Returning double square: 25
```

5.2   FUNCTION CALL RESOLUTION

When an overloaded function is called there are three possible results:

- A single function instance is matched by the compiler to the function call and this instance is invoked.

- Multiple, ambiguous, matches are found by the compiler, which is unable to select between them. A compilation error results.

- No match can be found by the compiler and a compilation error results.

The following program illustrates all three cases.

```
#include <iostream.h>

float sqr_func(float);
double sqr_func(double);

int main()
{
  float  f = 1.7320508;
  double d = 2.236068;
  int    i = 5;
  int    *ip = &i;
```

```
  cout << "Square of " << f << " is: "
            << sqr_func(f) << "\n";
  cout << "Square of " << d << " is: "
            << sqr_func(d) << "\n";
  cout << "Square of " << i << " is: "
            << sqr_func(i) << "\n";
  cout << "Square of " << ip << " is: "
            << sqr_func(ip) << "\n";
  return(0);
}
float sqr_func(float f)
{
  return(f * f);
}
double sqr_func(double d)
{
  return(d * d);
}
```

The calls to the function **sqr_func** using **double** and
float arguments are successfully matched.

The call using the integer argument is matched by
promotion of the integer to either **float** or **double** type but
is ambiguous and causes a compilation error: the compiler
does not know which function instance to call as either
promotion is equally valid.

There is no matching function declaration or definition
for the call using the pointer argument. This causes a
compilation error.

Ambiguity arises in a number of other cases. First is the
case where the arguments of the overloaded function
instances are *not different enough*:

```
#include <iostream.h>
float sqr_func(float);
float sqr_func(float&);
int main()
{
  float  f = 1.7320508;
  cout << "Square of " << f << " is: "
            << sqr_func(f) << "\n";
  return(0);
}
```

```
float sqr_func(float f)
{
   return(f * f);
}
float sqr_func(float& d)
{
   return(d * d);
}
```

Here, the difference between a reference-to-float and a
float argument is not enough for the compiler to distinguish
between the function instances. A compilation error
results, reporting the ambiguity. In the same way, the
compiler does not distinguish between an argument
qualified const and one qualified volatile:

```
float sqr_func(const float);
float sqr_func(volatile float);
```

A call to sqr_func with either argument type is ambiguous
and causes a compilation error.

The compiler *does* distinguish between a pointer or
reference to a const argument and a pointer or reference
to a volatile argument:

```
float sqr_func(const float&);
float sqr_func(volatile float&);
float sqr_func(const float*);
float sqr_func(volatile float*);
```

A call to sqr_func with any of these argument types is
not ambiguous and is matched.

Overloaded member functions of a class which have the
same names and differ only in one being declared with
storage class static are not recognised by the compiler as
being different and a compilation error results.

Default arguments in calls to overloaded functions can
also cause ambiguity:

```
#include <iostream.h>

// function 'sqr_func' overloaded

int sqr_func(int);
int sqr_func(int, int = 1);
```

```
int main()
{
  int i = 9;
  int j = 9;
  cout << i << " multiplied by itself is "
            << sqr_func(i) << "\n";
  cout << i << " multiplied by " << j
            << " is " << sqr_func(i, j) << "\n";
  return(0);
}

int sqr_func(int i)
{
  return(i * i);
}

int sqr_func(int i, int j)
{
  return(i * j);
}
```

In this case, the first call to sqr_func is ambiguous. With only one argument in the call, both instances of sqr_func match because the default argument for the parameter j is set to the default value 1. When two arguments are explicitly supplied, only the second instance of sqr_func is matched, with the default argument unused.

A programmer defining an overloaded function should ensure that the order and type of arguments in any call to the function match the argument list in one (and only one) instance of the overloaded function. If the match is not exact, the C++ compiler will try very hard to resolve the function call to a match, but it is better that the programmer should avoid this altogether.

SUMMARY OF CALL RESOLUTION PROCEDURE

In summary, if a call to an overloaded function is not a mismatch and not ambiguous, the compiler resolves the match in one of four ways, in decreasing order of precedence.

First, an exact match:

```
// Overloaded function prototypes, definitions
// assumed to be later in the program
```

```
int sqr_func(int);
double sqr_func(double);

  .
  .
double e = 2.71828;
double esqr;

  .
  .
esqr = sqr_func(e);        // exact match
```

Second, by type promotion:

```
// Overloaded function prototypes, definitions
// assumed to be later in the program

int sqr_func(int);
double sqr_func(double);

  .
  .
float e = 2.71828;
double esqr;

  .
  .
esqr = sqr_func(e);        // promoted to 'double'
```

Third, by type-conversion according to the standard rules:

```
// Overloaded function prototypes, definitions
// assumed to be later in the program

short sqr_func(short);
double sqr_func(double *);

  .
  .
short ssqr;

  .
  .
// 10 is of type 'int', cannot be promoted or
// converted to 'double pointer', so converted
// instead to 'short'.

ssqr = sqr_func(10);       // 10 is of type 'int',
                           // converted to 'short'
```

Fourth, by user-defined type-conversion functions defined by means of operator overloading. These conversions are dealt with later in this chapter.

5.3   Formal Rules for Resolution

BEST VIABLE FUNCTION

If a call to an overloaded function contains multiple
arguments, the instance of the function that is actually
called is selected by the compiler according to a best-fit
algorithm. The parameters of the chosen function instance
will match the arguments in the function call better than
all the other function instances.

In specifying the rules for resolution of calls to overloaded
functions, the ANSI C++ standard formalises the notions
of *viable function* and *candidate function*. A viable
function, in the context a call to an overloaded function,
meets one of the following criteria:

- All candidate functions (those matching the function
  name used in the call) having exactly the same
  number of parameters as the number of arguments
  used in the call, are viable functions.

- Candidate functions with fewer parameters than the
  number of arguments used in the call are viable
  functions where their parameter lists are followed
  by an ellipsis (...) denoting a variable argument list.

- Candidate functions with more parameters than the
  number of arguments used in the call are viable
  functions if the surplus parameters have default
  arguments.

Where candidate functions are viable according to the
criteria listed above, it must also be possible to convert all
the arguments used in the function call to the
corresponding parameter types specified in the candidate
function's parameter list.

In a call to an overloaded function, the *best viable*
function is selected. If two or more functions are equally
viable, ambiguity and a compilation error result. If no
viable function is found, there is similarly a compilation
error. A viable function F1 is defined to be a better viable
function than a viable function F2 if no argument-
parameter conversion for F1 is worse than its counterpart
for F2 and:

- some argument-parameter conversion for F1 is better than its counterpart for F2, or else:

- F1 is a non-template function and F2 is a template function, or else:

- F1 is a more-specialised template function than F2.

The remaining issue is what constitutes a better or worse argument-parameter conversion. As stated in the last section, exact type match is best; followed in order, descending toward 'worst', by type promotion, type conversion and user-defined conversion.

- Exact type match is encountered when no conversions at all are required between argument and parameter. Cases of array-to-pointer conversion, function-to-pointer conversion and qualifier conversion also qualify as exact matches.

- Type promotion covers the cases of integral promotions (e.g. char to int) and floating-point promotions (e.g. float to double).

- Type conversion means all conversion, as opposed to promotion, operations. Conversions include floating-point conversions (e.g. double to float), floating-integral conversions (e.g. double to int), integral conversions and pointer conversions.

Here is an example, based on code shown in Section 5.1, of selection by the compiler among similar function instances. The function call and prototypes are given; we assume that the function definitions are properly made elsewhere in the program.

```
// Overloaded function prototypes

int prod_func(int, int);
double prod_func(int, double);
double prod_func(short, double);
double prod_func(double, int);
double prod_func(double, double);

// function call

double prod;

  .
  .

prod = prod_func(10, 3.1415927);
```

In this case, the compiler chooses for execution the function instance declared by the second prototype because its argument list is an exact match of the argument list supplied in the function call. If that function instance were missing, the instances:

```
int prod_func(int, int);
double prod_func(double, double);
```

would result in an ambiguous best viable function, according to the rules given above, and a compilation error would result.

OVERLOADED FUNCTION POINTERS

A mechanism is needed for the compiler to set up unique pointers to instances of overloaded functions that are inherently ambiguous. The problem is solved using the same argument-parameter matching rules described above. Depending on the definition of the function pointer and the types specified in its argument list, the function pointer is assigned the address of the exactly-matching or nearest-matching function instance.

The following example presents a series of declarations of overloaded functions. Because its argument types are int and double, the function pointer fptr is automatically assigned the address of the second instance of prod_func:

```
// Overloaded function prototypes

int prod_func(int, int);
double prod_func(int, double);
double prod_func(short, double);
double prod_func(double, int);
double prod_func(double, double);
    .
    .
// function pointer definition
    .
double (*fptr)(int i, double d);
    .
    .
    .
// A valid function pointer assignment,
// address of second function instance is
// assigned

fptr = prod_func;
    .
```

```
// A valid function call using pointer
  .
fptr(10, 3.1415927);
  .
  .
```

TYPE-SAFE LINKAGE

An overloaded function definition will probably comprise several instances of the function, all with the same name. Multiple occurrences of the same function name pose a problem for the linkage editor, which must resolve all name references in an unambiguous way and produce as its output an executable program derived from the source-code program files generated by the programmer.

It is possible for the compiler, as we have seen, to distinguish between function instances based on their different argument lists. At the link stage, however, this distinguishing information is normally lost. Multiple matching function names would then cause linkage-editor errors.

To get around this problem, the C++ compiler implements *name mangling*: it internally appends to the name of each function instance coded information about its parameters. This information is passed on to the linkage editor which is then able to carry out type-safe linkage of the mangled function name for each overloaded instance.

The details of the encoding that is done as part of the name-mangling process are dependent on the local C++ implementation. They are not part of the C++ language definition and are not described further here.

5.4 Operator Overloading Basics

Operator overloading is a special case of function overloading. The C++ programmer is allowed to assign additional meanings to most of the standard C++ operators (referred to for the remainder of this chapter as *basic operators*). This means that operators can be defined to do special processing not defined as part of the C++ language.

Operator overloading gives extra flexibility and power to the programmer. Operator overloading also allows classes to provide certain services; recall the requirement, illustrated in Chapter 4, for overloading the assignment operator to allow correct assignment of class objects.

In Chapter 2, an example is given in which the equality operator== is overloaded in meaning so that two class objects may be compared directly using that operator. C++ syntax does not allow the basic equality operator to be used to compare structures and classes, but provides the overloading mechanism that allows the programmer to customise operators.

The C++ basic operators that may be overloaded are:

!	~	+	-	*	&	/	%
<<	>>	<	<=	>	>=	==	!=
^	|	&&	>	+=	-=	*=	/=
%=	&=	^=	!=	<<=	>>=	,	->*
->	()	{}	=	++	--	new	delete

The operators on the last row in this table have some special characteristics when overloaded and are dealt with separately in Section 5.8.

There are unary (e.g. +5) and binary (e.g. a - b) forms of some operators. Both the unary and binary forms of the following operators may be overloaded:

+   -   *   &

The following C++ operators cannot be overloaded:

.   .*   ::   ?:

C++ does not allow new operators to be introduced by means of operator overloading. All operators to be overloaded must be taken from the set of overloadable operators given above.

It might be thought a good idea to introduce an operator := to denote explicit assignment, as in Pascal, and to overload the equality operator== with the C++ assignment operator =. The introduction of := is illegal; the overloading of == with = is legal but confusing and undesirable.

The set of operations that overloads a C++ basic operator is defined as a function. This function has as its name the operator to be overloaded prefixed with the keyword **operator**. The general form of the definition of an overloaded-operator function is:

```
<return type> [<class name>::]
    operator <op>(<arg list>)
{
   // set of operations implementing overload
}
```

Angle-brackets indicate that the enclosed item is replaced by a literal string. Items in square brackets are optional. Here is an example of how the + operator might appear when overloaded:

```
char add_char::operator+(add_char& c2)
{
   // operator function code
}
```

This definition means that the overloaded-operator function named by **operator+**, which has a single class-object parameter **c2**, carries out on **c2** and the class of which **operator+** is a member a set of operations specified by the function code.

The function name **operator+** need not be a contiguous string. Any number of spaces may surround the operator symbol+.

OPOVL54: OVERLOADING ADDITION

Here is a full example program, called 'add_char.cpp', which uses the class **add_char** and illustrates important aspects of operator overloading. Otherwise, the program is trivial, but the objective here is to provide a short complete working program that shows how to overload operators, rather than a long useful one that might obscure the issue.

```
#include <iostream.h>

class add_char
{
private:
  char c;
```

```
public:
  // constructor
  add_char(char c_in) { c = c_in; }
  // overloaded '+'
  char operator+(add_char& c2);
  char c_pr()              // access function
  {
      return(c);
  }
};

int main()
{
  add_char c1('g');
  add_char c2('h');
  char sum;

  sum = c1 + c2;

  cout << "'Sum' of " << c1.c_pr() << " and "
          << c2.c_pr() << " is " << sum << "\n";
  return(0);
}

char add_char::operator+(add_char& c2)
{
  // add to the c1 character the alphabetic
  // displacement of the c2 character. This
  // gives the 'sum' of the two characters.

  return(c + (c2.c - ('a' - 1)));
}
```

The purpose of the program is to perform alphabetic
addition of characters using a + operator overloaded to do
that special kind of addition. In the convention used by
the program, c added to a is d; and h added to g is o. The
program relies on the ASCII collating sequence and there
is a mixed-type expression in the operator function that
does the actual alphabetic addition.

The declaration of class add_char contains one private
data member, c, of type char. It has three member
functions: a constructor to initialise c to an alphabetic
value; an access function to retrieve the value of c; and an
overloaded-operator function giving a new meaning to
the operator +.

In the main function, two instances of add_char, c1 and c2, are defined and their data members initialised by the constructor to g and h respectively. A local variable, sum, is assigned the result of the overloaded-operator function call:

```
c1 + c2
```

The last statement in main displays that result:

```
'Sum' of g and h is o
```

Now we look at the overloaded-operator function operator+. Here is its header:

```
char add_char::operator+(add_char& c2)
```

This specifies one parameter, which is a reference to the class object c2 corresponding to the operand on the right-hand side of the overloaded addition c1 + c2. In this addition, the operand c2 is the argument to the overloaded-operator function operator+. The operand being used as an argument in the operator+ function call does not have to have the same name as the function parameter.

If the following class objects are defined and initialised:

```
add_char x1('c');
add_char x2('d');
```

it is legal to make x1 and x2 operands of the overloaded operator:

```
sum = x1 + x2;
```

The operand x2 is then copied *through the reference* to the operator+ parameter c2. Use of the reference declaration add_char& c2 in the case of a simple class like add_char is unnecessary, although it improves efficiency. In any case where the class object used as a parameter contains pointer data, use of the reference becomes necessary. Its use, and consequent elimination of the full class-object copy, means that the default copy constructor, with attendant memberwise initialisation, is not called. This in turn removes the double-memory-deallocation problem explained in Sections 4.4 and 4.5.

The overloaded-operator function operator+ is also passed an implicit this pointer to c1. The function can therefore directly access the data member c of c1.

In the return statement:

```
return(c + (c2.c - ('a' - 1)));
```

c is the private data member of c1, accessed using the implicit this pointer. Its contents are added arithmetically to those of c2.c, offset from the start of the alphabet. This last is an ordinary, not an overloaded, addition. The return statement could be written with the this pointer explicitly included:

```
return(this->c + (c2.c - ('a' - 1)));
```

Also, the assignment to sum can be written:

```
sum = c1.operator+(c2);
```

which may aid understanding of how the operator+ function receives an implicit this pointer referring to class object c1.

The syntax of overloaded operators, with the implicit this pointer, can be confusing. Some care should be taken at this point to understand it fully. Examples in the next sections of binary and unary operator overloading will illuminate the notation further.

A few important general rules for use of overloaded-operator functions are given next.

Functions that overload the operators =, [], () and -> must be class members. Overloading of these operators is dealt with further in Section 5.8.

Functions overloading other operators do not have to be class members but must take at least one argument that is a class object. This stipulation is designed to prevent a C++ basic operator being redefined unreasonably to operate on two non-class data objects. An example of unreasonable use would be to redefine the multiplication operator * to mean division when used with two integers.

Even with operator overloading, normal precedence and associativity of operators is unchanged. Thus, no matter how + and * might be overloaded, the expression:

```
a + b * c
```

will always be evaluated as:

```
a + (b * c)
```

A basic operator that is strictly unary or binary cannot be overloaded to mean the opposite:

```
!x        // '!' is always unary
17 % 6    // '%' is always binary
```

Operator overloading cannot, for example, produce a unary % operator or a binary ! operator.

An overloaded operator does not have to mimic the purpose of the equivalent basic operator but it should, in order not to be confusing. The overloading of + in the program 'add_char.cpp' in this section is quite appropriate; + being overloaded to cause subtraction of characters would not be.

5.5   Binary Operator Overloading

The example program 'add_char.cpp' in the last section defines as a member of class add_char an overloaded-operator function operator+, which redefines the action of the + binary operator to perform alphabetic addition of characters.

This is an example of binary operator overloading, which is a typical use of operator overloading and is examined further in this section. A function that overloads a binary operator may be a member of a class, a friend of a class, or neither a friend nor a member of a class. Overloaded-operator functions qualified as friends are covered in Section 5.7. For now, we will consider the differences in syntax and usage between member and non-member binary operator overloading functions.

If an operator function is a class member, it always has one item less in its argument list than there are operands of the overloaded operator. In the case of binary operator overloading, this means that the definition of a member operator function contains an argument list with one item. An example is taken from 'add_char.cpp':

```
// 'call' to overloaded operator '+'
// contains two operands

sum = c1 + c2;
```

```
// Header of operator function definition
// contains one parameter, corresponding
// to the second operand above

char add_char::operator+(add_char& c2)
```

The left operand is passed implicitly to the operator function by means of a **this** pointer and the right operand is copied explicitly through the reference to the function parameter **c2**.

The **operator+** function is a class member; in this case a member of the **c1** class object on the left side of the operator in the assignment. A member operator function such as **operator+** requires that its left operand be an object of its class. Such a member function cannot have an object of basic (non-class) type on the left side of the expression in which it is called. This code is illegal:

```
int i1;
    .
    .
sum = i1 + c2;
```

This assignment is legal if the code in **operator+** is changed so that its second parameter is of integral type:

```
int i2;
    .
    .
sum = c1 + i2;
```

If an operator function is not a class member, it always has the same number of items in its argument list as there are operands of the overloaded operator. In the case of binary operator overloading, this means that the definition of a non-member operator function contains an argument list with two items.

OPOVL55: NON-MEMBER OVERLOADED BINARY OPERATOR

Here is 'add_char.cpp' reworked so that **operator+** is no longer a member of the class **add_char**:

```
#include <iostream.h>

class add_char
{
private:
  char c;
```

```
public:
  // constructor
  add_char(char c_in) { c = c_in; }
  char c_pr()                 // access function
  {
    return(c);
  }
};
// overloaded '+'
char operator+(add_char&, add_char&);
int main()
{
  add_char c1('g');
  add_char c2('h');
  char sum;

  sum = c1 + c2;

  cout << "'Sum' of " << c1.c_pr() << " and "
       << c2.c_pr() << " is " << sum << "\n";
}
char operator+(add_char& c1, add_char& c2)
{
  // add to the  c1  character the alphabetic
  // displacement of the  c2  character. This
  // gives the 'sum' of the two characters.

  return(c1.c_pr() + (c2.c_pr() - ('a' - 1)));
}
```

The program gives the same output result as before. The
main change is that **operator+** is now declared and
defined as a function in file scope, outside the scope of the
class **add_char**. It also takes two arguments: references
to both the class objects **c1** and **c2** are now explicitly
specified.

A non-member operator function such as **operator+**
does not require that its left operand be a class object. It
is only necessary that one of its operands be a class object.

If the left operand of a binary overloaded-operator function
is not a class object, the function must not be a class
member.

With **operator+** being of file scope, the assignment to
sum may alternatively be written:

```
sum = operator+(c1, c2);
```

This is useful in showing that operator+ is a true function although it also overloads an operator.

In the return statement within the operator+ function, the data member c of class object c1 is now retrieved with an access function. Use of the access function is necessary because operator+ is no longer a member function of c1 and is no longer passed an implicit this pointer to c1.

When operator+ is declared and defined outside the scope of class add_char, it cannot directly access any private members of add_char. In the example shown, this is not a problem, but this access is sometimes required. To achieve it, friend operator-overloading functions are often used. This use of friend in this context is explained in Section 5.7.

Another practical example of use of binary operator overloading is given below. It is a modified version of the string class introduced in Chapter 4, which defines member functions to do such things as find substrings and the position of one string in another.

The example makes the obvious extension of encapsulating in the string class an overloaded operator for string concatenation, implemented using the standard library function strcat. A comprehensive string class might well include all the library functions but, for the example, one is enough.

The example implements strcat as an overloaded binary operator, +=. Here is the reworked declaration of the string class:

```
/*
 * str.h – defines string class
 */
class string
{
private:
  char *sptr;
  int  slen;
public:
  string();
  string(int);
  string(const char *);
  string(const string&);
```

```
    void set_str(const char *);
    char *substr(int, int);
    int  strpos(const string&);
    char *access() { return(sptr); }

    // new member binary operator-overload
    // function for string concatenation

    void operator+=(string&);

    ~string() { delete sptr; }
};
```

The declaration is the same as in Chapter 4 except for the addition of the overloaded-function declaration.

The program file 'strfunc.cpp' contains definitions for the member functions of **string**. As the only change to this file is the addition of the definition of **operator+=**, that is all that is shown.

```
/*
 *
 * strfunc.cpp – defines string class functions
 *
 */
#include <iostream.h>
#include <string.h>
#include "str.h"

// string constructor

    .
    .
//   Other member functions unchanged
    .
    .
    .
/*
 *   'operator+=' – does string concatenation
 */
void string::operator+=(string& s2)
{
    strcat(sptr, s2.sptr);
}
```

operator+= has one parameter, a reference to the class object **s2**, which corresponds to the expression operand to the right of the overloaded operator when it is used in main. As we have already seen, operator+= is passed an implicit this pointer to the operand on the left of the operator, which must be a class object.

The implementation of the overloaded += for string concatenation is rudimentary: no provision is made for the receiving string length being sufficient. The intention here is not to show bulletproof string concatenation but to concentrate on using overloaded operators.

Here is the main function, again with unchanged code omitted:

```
/*
 * str.cpp – exercise string class
 */
#include <iostream.h>
#include "str.h"

int main()
{
   string s1(50);
   string s2("time");

   // Code here is unchanged
   .
   .
   // Call to overloaded '+=' operator to
   // concatenate s1 and s2

   s1.set_str("Now is the ");
   s1 += s2;
   // Display concatenated string
   cout << "Joined strings: "
            << s1.access() << "\n";
   return(0);
}
```

Two class objects, s1 and s2, are defined and initialised. The extent of the member string sptr of class object s1 is increased to 50 to ensure that it is large enough to hold the two strings concatenated. The statement:

```
s1 += s2;
```

calls the operator function +=, which uses strcat to join the contents of the member strings of the operands s1 and s2. Finally, the concatenated strings are displayed:

```
Now is the time
```

5.6 Unary Operator Overloading

If an operator function is a class member, it always has one item less in its argument list than there are operands of the overloaded operator. In the case of unary operator overloading, this means that the definition of a member operator function contains an empty argument list.

OPOVL561: OVERLOADED UNARY OPERATOR

To demonstrate unary overloading, a modified version of 'add_char.cpp' from Section 5.4 is used:

```cpp
#include <iostream.h>
class add_char
{
private:
  char c;
public:
  // constructor
  add_char(char c_in) { c = c_in; }
  char operator++();      // overloaded '++'
  char c_pr()             // access function
  {
     return(c);
  }
};
int main()
{
  add_char c1('g');

  cout << "Initial value: " << c1.c_pr() << "\n";
  c1++;    // increment class 'char' member
           // with overloaded unary operator

  cout << "Incremented value: "
          << c1.c_pr() << "\n";
  return(0);
}
char add_char::operator++()
{
  //  increment the alphabetic value of c
  //  and return
  c++;      // '++' is not overloaded here
  return(c);
}
```

The operator function is declared like this:

```
char operator++();
```

This causes the ++ operator to carry out the actions defined in operator++ on a single operand which is a member of the same class as operator++. In the program, the operator function is called like this:

```
c1++;
```

operator++ is implicitly passed a this pointer to the class object c1. The function can therefore access the data member c and increment it. This increment is not overloaded, because the operand is not a class type. Finally, the value of the incremented data member of c1 is displayed:

```
Initial value: g
Incremented value: h
```

If an operator function that overloads a unary operator is not a class member, its definition contains an argument list with one item.

OPOVL562: Non-Member Overloaded Unary Operator

Here is the previous version of 'add_char.cpp' (OPOVL561) reworked so that operator++ is no longer a member of the class add_char:

```
#include <iostream.h>
class add_char
{
private: char c;
public:
  // constructor
  add_char(char c_in) { c = c_in; }
  char c_pr()              // access function
  {
     return(c);
  }
};

char operator++(add_char&); // overloaded '++'
int main()
{
  add_char c1('g');
  cout << "Initial value: "
             << c1.c_pr() << "\n";
```

```
    //   increment class 'char' member with
    //   overloaded unary operator

  cout << "Incremented value: "
           << c1++ << "\n";
  return(0);
}

char operator++(add_char& c1)
{
  //   increment the alphabetic value of c
  //   and return

  return((c1.c_pr()) + 1);
}
```

The main change in the program is that **operator++** is no longer a member of add_char. This means that **operator++** has one parameter, a class object of type add_char. The operator function is called in the same way as before:

```
  c1++;
```

There are also some subtle changes in this version of the program, made necessary by the facts that **operator++** is no longer a class member and its code does not have access to the class data member.

In the return statement, an access function must be used to get the value of c1.c, which is then incremented by 1. The increment-by-1 is done with explicit addition of 1, not with the basic ++ operator. Overloading the unary ++ and -- operators is complicated by their prefix and postfix uses. Rules for these uses are given in Section 5.8.

The returned value is transient: it is not stored in the class object c1. The call to the operator function is therefore embedded in the cout statement for immediate display.

5.7   Friend Operator Functions

C++ classes can have friends, which are introduced in Section 2.6. A friend function is not a member of the class within which it is declared but it has right of access to the non-public members of the class.

In general, use of friend functions in C++ is frowned upon slightly. One of their best uses, however, is in the area of operator overloading. In general, friend overloaded-operator functions are more readable than their class-member equivalents, because the number of the operator's operands becomes equal to the number of arguments supplied to the overloading function. In certain cases, as we shall see in Section 8.5, overloaded-operator functions *cannot* be class members and qualification of their declaration with friend becomes necessary.

The string class presented in Section 5.5 incorporating the overloaded operator += is now shown with the operator function modified to be a friend of the members of class string.

```
/*
  * str.h – defines string class
  */
class string
{
private:
  char *sptr;
  int slen;
public:
  string();
  string(int);
  string(const char *);
  string(const string&);
  void set_str(const char *);
  char *substr(int, int);
  int strpos(const string&);
  char *access() { return(sptr); }

  // new member binary operator-overload
  // function for string concatenation

  // operator function is now also a 'friend'

  friend void operator+=(string&, string&);

  ~string() { delete sptr; }
};
```

operator+= now has the same access privileges as if it were a member of string, while having all the other characteristics of a non-member function.

In particular, its left operand does not have to be an object of its own class, as it does when the operator function is a class member. The general rule remains in force that at least one operand of an overloaded operator must be a class object.

The definition of operator+= is in the program file 'strfunc.cpp', which defines the member functions of string. operator+= is the only function that changes:

```
void operator+=(string& s1, string& s2)
{
   strcat(s1.sptr, s2.sptr);
}
```

Because operator++ is no longer a member of string, it is defined with two parameters in its argument list, one corresponding to each of the operands of the overloaded operator when it is called in main:

```
s1 += s2;
```

operator++ is a friend of string. This allows direct access to private members of the class in a way that is illegal without declaration of the operator++ function as a friend. The main function is unchanged.

Using friend in the declaration of operator functions has the advantages of clarity and flexibility. For normal binary operator overloading, the operator function is a member of the same class as the object being modified. In this case, the overloaded operator has two operands, but the operator function has only one parameter, corresponding to the second operand:

```
void operator+=(string&);
```

If the operator function is declared as being not a member of the class, the declaration syntax is clearer:

```
void operator+=(string&, string&);
```

but the function now does not have access to the private members of string. The best of both worlds is obtained using a friend declaration:

```
friend void operator+=(string&, string&);
```

This has relative clarity of syntax and the flexibility to allow access to all class data.

5.8 Advanced Operator Overloading

Overloading the following operators involves some special rules:

[]	array bounds
()	function
=	assignment
->	pointer
++	increment
--	decrement
new	memory allocation
delete	memory deallocation

These and other rules governing advanced use of overloaded operators are described in this section.

OPERATOR []

The [] notation used to specify array bounds is a binary operator that may be overloaded. Its operands are a class name and a subscript value. When the [] operator is overloaded, the code defined in the operator[] function is executed every time a subscripted reference is made to an object of the class of which operator[] is a member.

When a non-class object is subscripted the compiler automatically uses the basic C++ [] operator instead of the overloaded operator.

A function overloading [] must be a non-static member of a class object.

One of the major uses of the overloaded [] is in gaining subscripted access to the array members of a class object. This access can be made *safe* by including code in the operator[] function to do execution-time checking for array subscripts being out of bounds.

To illustrate use of the overloaded [] operator in implementing *safe arrays*, here again is the string class program:

```
/*
 * str.h – defines string class
 */
class string
{
private:
  char *sptr;
  int  slen;
public:
  string();
  string(int);
  string(const char *);
  string(string &);
  void set_str(const char *);
  char *access() { return(sptr); }
  int getSlen() { return(slen); }

  // binary operator-overload function for
  // string concatenation

  void operator+=(string&);

  // overloaded array-bounds function
  //  to implement safe array
  char &operator[](int);

  ~string() { delete sptr; }
};

  extern const int MAX;
```

There are several changes from the string class declaration used in Section 5.7. The member functions substr and strpos are removed. The overloaded function operator[] is declared, as is the access function getSlen. The latter is defined inline, while operator[] is defined along with the other member functions in the program file 'strfunc.cpp':

```
/*
 *
 * strfunc.cpp – defines string class functions
 *
 */
#include <iostream.h>
#include <stdlib.h>          // added for 'exit'
                             // function call
#include <string.h>
#include "str.h"
```

```
.
//   Other member functions unchanged
.
.
// 'operator[]' – implements safe array
// with class subscripting
char &string::operator[](int i)
{
   if ((i < 0) || (i > (MAX - 1)))
   {
      cout << "Illegal array index used\n";
      exit(1);
   }
   return(sptr[i]);
}
```

operator[] takes as a parameter the subscript value used
and checks that it is within the defined array bounds. If it
is not, the program terminates with an error message; if
it is, the required element of the member string of the
class object is returned. Here is the code that uses
operator[]:

```
string s1(MAX);
string s2(MAX);

s1.set_str("");
s2.set_str(" for all good men");

// Call to overloaded '[]' operator to do
// safe-array copy within class objects s1and s2

for (int i = 0; i < s2.getSlen(); i++)
   s1[i] = s2[i];
```

Two string class objects, s1 and s2, are defined. Their
character-array members are assigned literal strings. The
overloaded [] operator is used to subscript s1 and s2.
Each time [] is used, the operator[] function is called,
which does array-bound checking and returns a character
from the array.

Each iteration causes two calls to be made to operator[].
The first is to the operator[] member of s2. This is an
implicit function call equivalent to the following:

```
s2.operator[](i)
```

operator[] returns a reference to a character extracted
from the member array, sptr2, of s2. In the same way,

s1[i] returns a reference to a character extracted from its member array. The character assignment is then made.

The return value of **operator[]** must be a reference to, rather than the value of, an array element. Because the return value of **s1[i]** is a reference, it is an lvalue and can legally be assigned the return value of **s2[i]**. If it were not a reference, but rather the actual value of an array element, it would not be an lvalue and the assignment would cause compilation errors.

The loop that copies the array elements is controlled by the return value of the access function **getSlen**. This value is the number of characters stored at the pointer **s2.sptr** and may be quite different from the extent of memory allocated to that pointer. If the length value were wrong – say an arbitrarily large number – and the value of MAX is 50, the safe-array mechanism implemented by the function operator[] would report an out-of-bounds reference like this:

```
Illegal array index used
```

and cause program termination.

Neither the C nor the C++ languages has any inherent array-bound checking. If a traditional program overflows array bounds, it may well crash. C++ makes it possible, with the overloaded [] operator, for the programmer to implement array-bound checking and code to handle overflow.

OPERATOR ()

The function-call binary operator () can be overloaded and is often used as an *iterator* – a function that returns the next element of a collection each time it is called. The operands of the overloaded () are a class object and an optional argument list.

A function overloading () must be a non-static member of a class object. To implement an iterator in the **string** class, a prototype for the overloaded-operator function **operator()** is added to the declaration of **string**:

```
class string
{
private:      //existing private members
              // unchanged
```

```
    int ssub; // added to keep iterator
              // subscript count
public:
  // public members unchanged

  // overloaded function-call operator,
  // iterates over string

  char operator()();

  ~string() { delete sptr; }
};
```

The overloaded function **operator()** is defined:

```
  // 'operator()' - implements string iterator

  char string::operator()()
  {
    return(sptr[ssub++]);
  }
```

Now, when a **string** class object is used with the function-call operator (), the next character is returned from the member array of that object. The **main** function contains the code that *iterates over* the array.

```
  int main()
  {
    string s2(MAX);

    s2.set_str(" for all good men");

    // Call to overloaded '()' operator to
    // retrieve all a string's characters
    // individually by iteration

    char c;
    cout <<
    "String s2  output character-by-character:";
    while (c = s2())    // iterate
      cout << c;
    return(0);
  }
```

Implementing iterators is not the only purpose of overloading the () operator. An argument list may also be supplied and used as parameters by the code of the **operator()** function. The function might, for example, each time it is called retrieve a character specified by position:

```
char string::operator()(int pos)
{
  return(sptr[pos]);
}
    .
    .
// Iterator call retrieves element 5
c = s1(5);
```

OPERATOR =

In Section 4.4 it is pointed out that a class object may be assigned to another of the same type. By default, member-wise assignment – a blind bitwise copy – is used. If the class objects contain pointer members, memory will become corrupted when those pointers are deallocated. This effect is similar to that which copy constructors are used to avoid during initialisation of class objects.

The code

```
s1 = s2;
```

performs memberwise assignment of s2 to s1. The memory allocated for s1.sptr is lost; and, after the assignment, calls to the destructor for both s1 and s2 will attempt to deallocate the same memory. Memberwise copy of class objects is a blunt instrument that can be refined by overloading the assignment operator. The overloaded assignment operator is binary and its operands are two class objects.

Here again is the string class declaration, with unchanged members omitted and an overloaded assignment operator added.

```
class string
{
private:
  //   private members unchanged
public:
  //   public members unchanged

  // overloaded assignment operator,
  // copies strings

  string& operator=(string&);

  ~string() { delete sptr; }
};
```

The operator= function takes as its parameter a reference
to the class object on the right side of the overloaded
assignment. When called, it is also implicitly passed a
this pointer to the class object on the left side of the
assignment. It modifies that class object and returns a
reference to it as the result of the assignment. Here is the
code of the operator= function:

```
// 'operator=' - assigns strings

string& string::operator=(string& s2)
{
    //   deallocate string space in class
    //   object (this) being copied to, then
    //   reallocate enough space for the
    //   object being copied

    delete sptr;
    sptr = new char [s2.slen];

    //   copy the string and its length

    slen = s2.slen;
    strcpy(sptr, s2.sptr);
    //   return this class object to the
    //   assignment

    return(*this);
}
```

The overloaded class assignment is done in main like this:

```
s1 = s2;
```

The operator= function is called with a reference to s2
as an argument. A this pointer to s1 is implicitly passed
to operator=. The memory pointed to by s1.sptr is
deallocated and then reallocated to the same pointer with
memory sufficient for the copy from s2.sptr. The length
of the member string of s2 is also copied. Finally, a
reference to the changed contents of s1 is returned to the
assignment. In this way the contents of s2 are copied to
s1 without the unwanted side-effects referred to above.

Both the parameter and return value of operator= must
be references to the operands of the overloaded
assignment. If a full rather than a reference copy is made
of the parameter s2, the member character pointers sptr
of both copies still point at one string in memory. Then
the destructor is called twice for s2, once when it goes out

of scope on exit from **operator=** and once when it goes out of scope on exit from **main**. The destructor tries to deallocate the same instance of **sptr** on both occasions. The result is a runtime memory error. Using references stops a full class-object copy being made and prevents the error.

The final statement in the function:

```
return(*this);
```

often causes puzzlement. It is rarely well explained; most textbooks confine themselves to the observation that it allows chaining of the overloaded assignment, in the form:

```
s3 = s2 = s1;
```

Without the **return** statement as shown, the simple overloaded assignment **s2 = s1;** works, but the chained assignment does not. The simple assignment has the equivalent explicit function-call form:

```
s2.operator=(s1);
```

which has the effect of changing the contents of **s2**, including proper copy of the data at its member pointer, to those of **s1**.

By extension, the chained assignment has the equivalent form:

```
s3.operator=(s2.operator=(s1));
```

from which it can be seen that the nested function call **s2.operator=(s1);** must return ***this** to provide an argument for the outer function call **s3.operator=(.....** In short, without the **return(*this)**, the contents of **s3** after the chained assignment would not be those of **s1**.

STRING58: THE FINAL STRING CLASS

We can now show the **string** class in the final form that it reaches in this book. The class contains four constructors, a destructor, four overloaded-operator functions and three other member functions. The **set_str** and the **operator+=** functions are now bulletproof, where in previous examples they are deliberately simplified. To keep the code to a reasonable length, functions such as **substr** and **strpos** are again omitted.

```cpp
// str.h -- defines string class

class string
{
private:
  char *sptr;
  int slen;
  int ssize;
  int ssub;
public:
  string();
  string(int);
  string(const char *);
  string(const string &);
  void set_str(const char *);
  char *access() { return(sptr); }
  int getSlen() {return(slen); }

  // binary operator-overload function for
  // string concatenation

  void operator+=(string&);
  // overloaded array-bounds function
  // to implement safe array

  char &operator[](int);

  // overloaded function-call operator,
  // iterates over string

  char operator()();

  // overloaded assignment operator
  // copies strings

  string& operator=(string&);

  ~string() { delete sptr; }
};

extern const int MAX;
```

The code implementing the four constructors and the
other member functions is in the program file
'strfunc.cpp':

```cpp
// strfunc.cpp – defines string class functions

#include <iostream.h>
#include <stdlib.h>      // for 'exit' function call
#include <string.h>
#include "str.h"
```

```
// string constructors
string::string()
{
  sptr = new char[MAX];
  ssize = MAX;
  *sptr = '\0';
  ssub  = slen = 0;
}
string::string(int size)
{
  sptr = new char[size];
  ssize = size;
  *sptr = '\0';
  ssub  = slen = 0;
}
string::string(const char *s_in)
{
  slen = ssize = strlen(s_in) + 1;
  sptr = new char[slen];
  strcpy(sptr, s_in);
  ssub = 0;
}
string::string(const string& ob_in)
{
  slen = ssize = strlen(ob_in.sptr) + 1;
  sptr = new char[slen];
  strcpy(sptr, ob_in.sptr);
  ssub = 0;
}
void string::set_str(const char *s_in)
{
  delete sptr;
  slen = ssize = strlen(s_in) + 1;
  sptr = new char[slen];
  strcpy(sptr, s_in);
  ssub = 0;
}
void string::operator+=(string& s2)
{
  char *ap;

  slen += (s2.slen + 1);
  ap = new char[slen];
  strcpy(ap, sptr);
```

```
   strcat(ap, s2.sptr);
   delete sptr;
   ssize = slen;

   sptr = new char[slen];
   strcpy(sptr, ap);
}

// 'operator[]' – implements safe array
// with class subscripting

char &string::operator[](int i)
{
   if ((i < 0) || (i > MAX))
   {
      cout << "Illegal array index used\n";
      exit(1);
   }
   return(sptr[i]);
}

// 'operator()' – implements string iterator
char string::operator()()
{
   return(sptr[ssub++]);
}

// 'operator=' – assigns strings

string& string::operator=(string& s2)
{
   // watch for the case of assignment of
   //   the same class! (e.g: s1 = s1 would
   //   mean losing the string)

   if (this == &s2)
      return(*this);

   //   deallocate string space in class object
   //   (this) being copied to, then re-allocate
   //   enough space for the object being copied

   delete sptr;
   sptr = new char[s2.slen];

   // copy the string and its length

   slen = ssize = s2.slen;
   strcpy(sptr, s2.sptr);

   // return this class object to the assignment

   return(*this);
}
```

The code that calls the member functions of **string** is in the **main** function in the program file 'str.cpp'.

```cpp
// program file 'str.cpp'

#include <iostream.h>
#include "str.h"

const int MAX = 256;

int main()
  {
  string s1;
  string s2(MAX);
  string s3("and into Mary's bread and jam ");
  string s4("his sooty foot he put");
  s1.set_str("Mary had a little lamb ");
  s2.set_str("whose feet were black as soot ");

  s1 += s2;// overloaded '+='
  s1 += s3;
  s1 += s4;

  string s5;

  s5 = s1;          // overloaded assignment

  cout << "s5: " << s5.access() << endl;

  string s6(s5);    // copy constructor
  cout << "s6: " << s6.access() << endl;

  string s7 = s6;   // copy constructor
  cout << "s7: " << s7.access() << endl;

  string s8;
  for (int i = 0; i < s7.getSlen(); i++)
     s8[i] = s7[i];    // subscript overloading
  cout << "s8: " << s8.access() << endl;

  char c;
  cout << "Iterated s8: ";
  while (c = s8())          // iterate over s8
     cout << c;
  return(0);
  }
```

Essentially, the program initialises the **string** objects **s1**, **s2**, **s3** and **s4** and, with these, sets up **s5**, **s6**, **s7** and **s8** using the various constructor and overloaded-operator facilities implemented by the class. When the program is run, the nursery rhyme is each time displayed in full by sending to the output stream the contents of the string objects **s5** through **s8**.

OPERATOR ->

The basic unary pointer operator may be overloaded. Its operand is a class object. If a class object **ob** is defined that has a data member **x**, use of an overloaded -> operator:

```
ob->x
```

is equivalent to:

```
(ob.operator->())->x
```

The function **operator->** may be thought of as a *smart pointer* that allows the programmer to use the simple notation **ob->x** without having to be concerned about the internal class representation.

Here is an example of the smart pointer operator in use. The example is based on the **list** class introduced in Chapter 2.

```
// list.h – include file for elementary
// list-handling program

class list
{
private:
  struct element
  {
  int        x;
  double     y;
  };
  element* instance;
public:
  list() { instance = new element; }

  //  Overloaded smart pointer operator
  //  function
  element* operator->();

  ~list() { delete instance; }
};

//  'assign' and 'display' declarations are
//  non-members

void assign(node&);
void display(node&);
```

The list class declares a structure and structure pointer, as well as constructor, destructor and **operator->** functions. For purposes of the example, the functions **assign** and **display** are made non-members of list. The functions are defined thus:

```cpp
//   listfunc.cpp

#include <iostream.h>
#include "list.h"

void display(list& list_in)
{
   cout << "Integer: " << list_in->x << " Double: "
            << list_in->y << " \n";
}

void assign(list& list_in)
{
   int x;
   double y;

   cout << "Enter an integer: ";
   cin  >> x;
   cout << "Enter a double: ";
   cin  >> y;

   list_in->x = x;   // conventional use:
                     // list_in.instance->x
   list_in->y = y;
}

element* list::operator->()
{
   if (!instance)
      cout << "Memory allocation error\n";
   return(instance);
}
```

operator-> is a smart pointer function. It returns a pointer of type **element *** so that subsequent (overloaded) use of:

```cpp
list_in->x
```

is expanded to:

```cpp
list_in.instance->x
```

A test is also done to ensure that instance is not null. Finally, the class member functions are called from client code:

```
list list1;
assign(list1);
display(list1);
```

INCREMENT AND DECREMENT OPERATORS

Unary operator overloading with the ++ and -- operators is introduced in Section 5.6. We now look at the question of how C++ handles prefix and postfix uses of these operators when they are overloaded.

The declaration of the overloaded-operator function is made with a dummy argument of type int for the postfix form, and with no such dummy argument for the prefix form.

For member functions of a class, the declarations are made like this:

```
void operator++();// prefix

void operator++(int);      // postfix
```

Class-member operator functions for unary operators specify no parameters. Non-member operator functions for unary operators specify one parameter and their prefix and postfix declarations are of the form:

```
void operator++(arg);      // prefix

void operator++(arg,int); // postfix
```

The dummy int may be specified alone or with an identifier or a default value:

```
void operator++(int x);

void operator++(int = 0);
```

In any case, the argument is ignored and zero automatically substituted for it by the compiler.

Multiple overloading of an operator in this way also, of course, shows that overloading of overloaded operators that are members of the same class is legal in C++.

OPOVL581: OVERLOADED PREFIX AND POSTFIX INCREMENT

Here is an example, using the add_char class, of overloading the ++ operator with prefix and postfix usages.

```
#include <iostream.h>

class add_char
{
private:
  char c;
public:
  // constructor
  add_char(char c_in) { c = c_in; }

  // Overloaded prefix and postfix
  // overloaded-operator functions.

  char operator++(); // overloaded '++' (prefix)
  char operator++(int); // overloaded '++' (postfix)
  char c_pr()            // access function
  {
     return(c);
  }
};

int main()
{
  add_char c1('g');
  char c_temp;

  cout << "Initial value: "
     << c1.c_pr() << "\n";

  c_temp = c1++;

  cout << "Assigned value: "
     << c_temp << "\n";
  cout << "Postfix increment value: "
          << c1.c_pr() << "\n";

  c_temp = ++c1;

  cout << "Assigned value: "
     << c_temp << "\n";
  cout << "Prefix increment value: "
     << c1.c_pr() << "\n";
  return(0);
}
```

```
char add_char::operator++()
{
  //   increment the alphabetic value of  c
  //   and return

  cout << "Prefix 'operator++' called\n";
  return(++c);
}
char add_char::operator++(int = 0)
{
  //   increment the alphabetic value of  c
  //   and return

  cout << "Postfix 'operator++' called\n";
  return(c++);
}
```

The appropriate operator++ function is called depending
on whether the usage in main is c1++ or ++c1. The
program displays these results:

```
Initial value: g
Postfix 'operator++' called
Assigned value: g
Postfix increment value: h
Prefix 'operator++' called
Assigned value: i
Prefix increment value: i
```

OPERATORS new AND delete

Like all the other overloadable operators we have seen,
new and delete may be overloaded and thereby given
extra capabilities. When overloaded, new and delete
differ from the other operators in these ways:

- Their return types are strictly specified.

- When defined as class members, they are treated as
  static member functions of that class.

- They need not be class members or take any class
  arguments.

new and delete can be overloaded in two ways:

- They can be overloaded globally, in which case they
  override the basic new and delete operators for the
  program in which the overloading is done.

- They can be overloaded locally for a class, in which case the overloaded uses of new and delete allocate and deallocate memory of objects of that class type. The basic new and delete operators remain in force for all other uses.

Class overloading of new and delete is more common than global overloading.

The primary purpose of overloading the new and delete operators is in taking control of memory management for a class. Ordinarily, the programmer makes new and delete (or malloc/free) calls and relies on runtime system and operating system services to manage the allocation and deallocation of memory in a transparent manner.

Depending on the kind of data objects defined by a class, the programmer may need extra control over the memory management strategy for that class. For example, the basic new and delete operators may be less efficient than overloaded versions of the operators for classes defining small data objects. In such a situation, the programmer uses a class to allocate a large contiguous block of memory. new and delete, overloaded with respect to that class, then make allocations of memory from the block and mark memory free within the block when it is deallocated by the application program.

In most cases however, the basic new and delete operators suffice and programmers do not often find it necessary to take direct control of memory management by overloading them.

Overloaded new must return a void pointer and its first argument must be an object of type size_t, representing the size of the memory area to be allocated. It can have multiple arguments after that first argument.

Overloaded delete must have a void return type and a first argument of type void *, pointing to the memory to be deallocated. It may additionally have a second argument of type size_t, representing a size of memory area to deallocate.

In the example that follows, a class number is defined with assignment to and display of the int member num.

new and delete are overloaded so that they actually use the C Library functions malloc and free to allocate and deallocate memory.

The argument size of the overloaded new function is automatically initialised by the compiler to the size of memory required for allocation of an instance of the class number.

OPOVL582: OVERLOADED new AND delete

```
// newdelov.cpp

#include <iostream.h>
#include <stdlib.h>

class number
{
private:
  int num;
public:
  number()
  {
    cout << "Enter an integer: ";
    cin >> num;
  }
  ~number() { cout << "num is " << num << "\n"; }

  void *operator new(size_t); // overloaded 'new'

  void operator delete(void *, size_t);
  // overloaded 'delete'
};

void* number::operator new(size_t size)
{
  void *mptr;

  cout << "In overloaded 'new' function\n";
  if ((mptr = malloc(size)) == NULL)
  {
    cout << "memory allocation error\n";
    return(NULL);
  }

    return(mptr);
}

void number::operator delete(void *mptr, size_t)
{
  cout << "In overloaded 'delete' function\n";
```

```
      free(mptr);
  }
  int main()
  {
    number *n1;
    int *iptr = new int;      // default 'new'
    n1 = new number;          // overloaded 'new'
    delete iptr;              // default 'delete'
    delete n1;                // overloaded 'delete'
    return(0);
  }
```

The main function uses both the overloaded and basic forms of the new and delete operators. This is a sample of user interaction with the program:

```
In overloaded 'new' function
Enter an integer: 12
num is 12
In overloaded 'delete' function
```

OPOVL583: INITIALISING ALLOCATED MEMORY

A modification of 'newdelov.cpp' overloads the new operator to initialise number::num to a specific value.

```
// newdelov.cpp
#include <iostream.h>
#include <stdlib.h>

class number
{
private:
  int num;
public:
  number()
  {
     cout << "Constructing...";
  }
  ~number()
  {
  cout << "Destructing, num is " << num << "\n";
  }
  void *operator new(size_t, int);
  // overloaded 'new'

  void operator delete(void *, size_t);
  // overloaded 'delete'
};
```

```
void* number::
  operator new(size_t size, int init_num)
{
  number *mptr;

  cout << "In overloaded 'new' function\n";
  if ((mptr = (number *)malloc(size)) == NULL)
  {
    cout << "memory allocation error\n";
    return(NULL);
  }

  mptr->num = init_num;
  return(mptr);
}
void number::operator delete(void *mptr, size_t)
{
  cout << "In overloaded 'delete' function\n";

  free(mptr);
}
int main()
{
  number *n1;

  n1 = new(14) number; // overloaded 'new'

  delete n1;             // overloaded 'delete'
  return(0);
}
```

USER-DEFINED CONVERSIONS

It is possible in C++ to convert the data types of objects using typecasts or overloaded-operator functions. The language also provides a variant of the overloaded operator, called the *conversion function*, which is intended specially for type-conversion operations.

Its declaration is of the following general form:

```
operator <type>() { return(<value>); }
```

Neither a return type nor parameters are allowed. The data object represented by <value> is automatically converted to <type> when it is assigned to a variable of that type.

OPOVL584: User Defined Type Conversion

In the following example, an object of the class type
complex is converted to floating-point using an
overloaded float converter that ignores the imaginary
part of the complex number.

```
/*
 * complex.cpp: program with 'float'
 * conversion operator to convert
 * objects of type 'complex' to floating-point
 */
#include <iostream.h>

class complex
{
private:
  float real, imag;
public:
  complex(float r = 0.0, float i = 0.0)
  {
    real = r;
    imag = i;
  }

  // overloaded inserter operator!!
  friend ostream&
    operator<<(ostream& s, complex c)
  {
    s << c.real << "," << c.imag;

    return(s);
  }

  // overloaded 'float' operator function
  operator float() { return(real); }
};

int main()
{
  complex c(4.6, 5.7);

  float f = c;

  cout << "Complex number " << c
    << " converted to float is " << f << endl;

  return(0);
}
```

In main, the constructor is used to initialise a complex class object. The variable f is defined of the overloaded type float. f is initialised to the fractional part of the complex number. To send an object of type complex to the output stream, an overloaded insertion operator << is defined. See Section 7.5 for explanation of the mechanisms involved in this overloading.

In a real development environment complex might be a standard class available in a library. It is good practice not to introduce many conversion functions in library classes. Doing so both clutters the classes and compromises data hiding. It is better to make a general-purpose class for numeric conversion, such as number, and to use its constructor function to do the conversion.

OPOVL585: A TYPE CONVERSION CLASS

```cpp
/*
 * convert.cpp: program with 'number' class
 * containing conversion constructor
 */
#include <iostream.h>

class complex
{
private:
   float real, imag;
public:
   complex(float r = 0.0, float i = 0.0)
   {
      real = r;
      imag = i;
   }

   friend ostream&
      operator<<(ostream& s, complex c)
   {
      s << c.real << "," << c.imag;

      return(s);
   }

   float getReal() const { return(real); }
};
```

```
class number
{
private:
  float f;
public:
  number(const complex& c)
  {
    f = c.getReal();
  }
  friend ostream&
    operator<<(ostream& s, number n)
  {
    s << n.f;

    return(s);
  }
};

int main()
{
  complex c(4.6, 5.7);

  number f(c);

  cout << "Complex number " << c
    << " converted to float is " << f << endl;

  return(0);
}
```

OTHER RULES FOR OPERATOR OVERLOADING

Some further rules governing less-common uses of overloaded operators are now given.

- Operator functions cannot take default arguments.

- Operator functions can be private or protected members of a class, as well as public.

- It is illegal to define an operator function that uses only pointer operands.

- If an overloaded-operator function is defined twice, as both class-member and non-member functions, the definitions will necessarily have different argument lists.

- Calls to the function name are resolved using the rules for selection of overloaded functions given earlier in the chapter.

- The preprocessing symbols '#' and '##' cannot be overloaded.

6 Derived Classes and Inheritance

6.1 Introduction

The object-oriented programming approach is characterised by use of derived classes with virtual functions.

All the topics dealt with in the preceding five chapters are essentially groundwork that anyone learning C++ must cover to be able to take advantage of the programming power offered by classes, containing virtual functions, organised in hierarchies. This chapter explains how to:

- Derive classes from existing base classes.

- Control access to the data members of derived and base classes.

- Use constructors and destructors to initialise and destroy instances of derived and base classes.

- Derive classes from multiple base classes.

- Use virtual base classes to resolve circularity of inheritance – the so-called Directed Acyclic Graph (DAG).

- Use the C++ implementation of polymorphism: the hierarchy of base and derived classes combined with virtual functions.

Classes often have much in common with other classes. Where classes are similar, it is desirable to define them in terms of characteristics they have in common, rather than fully and separately defining classes with much duplication.

The mechanism provided by C++ to allow classes to reuse declarations made in other classes is class derivation. Derived classes are said to inherit the declarations made in existing base classes.

We can draw an intuitive example of this process from the **employee** class example presented throughout this chapter. All employees share certain characteristics.

Minimally, they have a name, date of birth, employee number and grade; all employees are also hired, paid and (perhaps) fired.

For specific employee types, other data and behaviour are required. A Manager will probably have a salary and bonus, as opposed to the hourly-pay regime of the generic employee. A Supervisor may have a union number. A Line Manager may share some of the characteristics of both the Manager and Supervisor. For example, they may both be entitled to use secretarial services. A director, on the other hand, may have exclusive access to a Personal Assistant. Vice-Presidential attributes may include a company-paid yacht in the Caribbean or Mediterranean.

It is possible to define for each employee a separate class that describes it and its behaviour. It is better to look for commonality and to reduce the effort required for many separate definitions. A good approach is to look for what is the basic object, or lowest common denominator, to define a class which describes that object and to derive other class definitions from it.

In the employee example, it makes sense to define a generic class called **employee**, holding basic information on the characteristics and behaviour of all employees. Class definitions for **supervisor**, **manager** and the others may then be derived from the **employee** class.

This design process, when well implemented in C++, allows extensive reuse of code and gives considerable software development cost and time savings over more traditional languages such as C.

Classes may inherit characteristics from one or more base classes. Single inheritance means that the derived class inherits only one base class. Multiple inheritance means that the derived class inherits more than one base class. In either single or multiple inheritance, the base class may in turn be a derived class of one or more base classes. In this way, class hierarchies of arbitrary depth may be built.

When classes **supervisor** and **manager** are derived from class **employee**, they have much in common. There are, however, differences of detail in the ways in which similar operations are carried out. For example, all the employees are paid but on different terms and schedules. Displaying the status and qualifications of a director will differ in detail from the equivalent operation for a janitor.

To deal elegantly with implementing these differences, C++ implements polymorphism – the ability to define many different operations that use the same name and present the same interface to the programmer. The word *polymorphous*, according to Webster's, means *assuming many forms* and is derived from the Greek *polus* (many) and *morphe* (form).

In cases such as paying an employee or reporting her status, the necessary operations are related but different and do indeed require processing of *many forms* using the same programmer interface.

C++ implements polymorphism using virtual functions declared in a base class and inherited by one or more derived classes. The same function call may be used to carry out a similar (but different) operation for any of the classes in the hierarchy. Different instances of the function must be defined for each of the possible operations; the appropriate instance is selected at runtime depending on the class object used in the function call.

For example, a virtual function called **pay** remunerates the employee object of which it a member. The payment operation is carried out on the appropriate basis (hourly, salaried and so on) depending on whether the class object referenced in the function call is, say, an instance of **technician** or **manager**.

When the function **displayStatus** is called, the runtime system calls the version of **displayStatus** that is a member of the class referenced in the function call and, by a process of selection transparent to the programmer, either a full resumé or a short statement of qualification is given.

Virtual functions provide a further level of abstraction: the detailed implementations of the different virtual-function instances are hidden and need not interest the programmer making the function call. The programmer does not even have to discriminate between the instances: one function call does the job for all class objects in the hierarchy. In this way, the internal implementation of classes and their functions can remain a black box to the programmer. This improves modularity and flexibility and reduces the incidence of error.

In Chapter 5, it is pointed out that the compiler resolves the problem of selecting between different instances of functions having one overloaded name. Overloaded function calls are resolved at compilation time, and the process of including the appropriate function instance is referred to as *early binding*.

Use of virtual functions is a form of function overloading. However, calls to virtual functions are resolved at runtime and the process by which the appropriate instance is included is referred to as *late binding* or *dynamic binding*.

As is explained later in this chapter, late binding of virtual functions gives the programmer flexibility not approached by C or other traditional languages in responding efficiently to random data input.

Their provision of class hierarchies and polymorphism makes object-oriented languages, and C++ in particular, very useful for use in several kinds of application development. Good examples include database, communications and implementation of graphic user interfaces (GUIs).

Consider the GUI example. Various objects are displayed on the screen presenting a GUI. All the objects can be generalised as 'windows' of more or less specialised type. While there is no immutable rule governing the design of class hierarchies for GUIs, a common approach is to categorise all windows as either Controls (buttons, check boxes and others) or entry/display Windows (for example, frame windows, list boxes and combo boxes).

Using virtual functions, the single operation **ShowWindow** might be used to cause correct display of *any* window according to the characteristics defined by its class instance. The important thing is that the programmer does not have to be aware of the internal implementation details of the different types of windows. The simple **ShowWindow** command carries out that operation for all of them.

Additionally using virtual functions, generic operations (click on a button, click on a dialog box) are possible on different objects, without the programmer having to be aware of how the responses to the clicks are internally implemented.

Traditional procedural languages such as C and Pascal cater well for situations where processing starts at the beginning, proceeds sequentially through a series of operations, and finishes.

Object-oriented programs, written with languages such as C++, can be regarded as *simulations*: they closely mimic the operations and interactions of objects in the real world. Objects displayed as part of a GUI can interact in many ways. Clicking on a button may require a pop-up menu to appear. A member function of the Button class calls (*sends a message* to) a member function of the Popup class to make this happen.

Depending on the selection made from the menu, other GUI objects may be manipulated, or some kind of internal processing, such as file processing, may be needed. By representing all the GUI objects as members of a class hierarchy, C++ can, better and more reliably than traditional languages, handle the event-driven nature of their interaction.

6.2   Class Inheritance

The general syntax form that specifies a derived class is this:

```
class <derived class>:[<access>]<base class name>
{
  .
  .
  // derived class declaration
  .
};
```

Items in square brackets are optional and those within angle-brackets denote mandatory items that are replaced by a literal string.

To illustrate the syntax with an example, here is a first look at the employee class hierarchy. This class hierarchy is used for much of this chapter to show by example the different aspects of inheritance and simple implementations of virtual functions.

Here are the declarations of the employee base class and of three derived classes, technician, supervisor and manager. We need not be concerned about their full contents yet.

```
class employee
{
  // no private members, but could be
protected:
  // members hidden from rest of world
public:
  int grade;
  // public class members
};

class technician : public employee
{
private:
  // class members specific to 'technician'
public:
  int unionNo;
  // public member functions can access
  // private members of this class as well
  // as protected members of 'employee'
};

class supervisor : public employee
{
private:
  //
public:
  //
};

class manager : public employee
{
private:
  //
public:
  //
};
```

After the employee class is declared, the declaration:

```
class supervisor : public employee
```

```
{
//
};
```

announces a new type, supervisor, which inherits all non-private characteristics of employee and, between the curly braces, adds zero or more declarations of its own. The class keyword must be specified, as must the names of the two class types, separated by a colon.

The access specifier public is optional but usually necessary. When a class is derived from one or more other classes, and when the access specifier public is used in the derived class declaration, public members of the base class become public members of the derived class. If public is not specified in this way, the members of the derived class are by default private.

It is also possible to declare a structure and to use it as a base class from which other structures or classes are derived. Public members of a base structure by default become public members of structures or classes derived from it. In the case of base structures (but not base classes), the access specifier public, as used above, can be omitted. Class member access control is explained fully in the next section.

Each of technician, supervisor and manager are declared as derived classes of the base class employee. Using an object of any of the derived types, all non-private members of the inherited employee object may be accessed as if those members were also members of the derived classes. A few lines of code illustrate this:

```
// define 'technician' and 'employee' class objects

employee  e1;
technician t1;

// illustrate basic access rules, assuming
// 'public' access specifier in derived-class
// declarations

e1.grade = 1; // OK,  grade is 'employee'
              // member

t1.grade = 1; //OK,  grade is 'technician'
              // member derived from 'employee'
```

```
t1.unionNo = 53;  // OK, unionNo is
                  // 'technician' member not
                  // derived from 'employee'

e1.unionNo = 7;   // Error, unionNo is not in
                  // scope for 'employee' object
```

This shows that a derived class inherits all non-private members of a base class and that those members are in scope for the derived class. The converse is not true: new members declared in a derived class are not in scope for the base class.

EMPLOY62: A SIMPLE EMPLOYEE CLASS HIERARCHY

Here is a full-program example that illustrates single class inheritance and the C++ syntax used to access the members of the classes in a hierarchy. It is the first example in this chapter based on the **employee** model.

The program is organised in three program files. employee.h contains the class declarations. The program file 'empfunc.cpp' defines the member functions of the class hierarchy and 'emp.cpp' the small amount of code needed to define class objects and use their members.

```
/*****************************************************
 *
 * employee.h
 *
 *****************************************************/
enum qualification {NONE, CERT, DIPLOMA,
DEGREE, POSTGRAD};

class employee
{
protected:
  char *name;
  char *dateOfBirth;
  int individualEmployeeNo;
  static int employeeNo;
  int grade;
  qualification employeeQual;
  float accumPay;
public:
  // constructor
  employee();
```

```
  // destructor
  ~employee();

  void pay();
  void promote(int);     // scale increment
  void displayStatus();
};

class technician : public employee
{
private:
  float hourlyRate;
  int   unionNo;
public:
  // constructor
  technician();

  // destructor
  ~technician();

  void pay();
  void displayStatus();
};

class supervisor : public employee
{
private:
  float monthlyPay;
public:
  // constructor
  supervisor();

  // destructor
  ~supervisor();

  void pay();
  void displayStatus();
};

class manager : public employee
{
private:
  float monthlyPay;
  float bonus;
public:
  // constructor
  manager();
```

```
    // destructor
    ~manager();

    void pay();
    void displayStatus();
};
```

The classes technician, supervisor and manager are derived from the base class employee. All non-private members of employee are inherited by and are common to the derived classes.

All the classes have a constructor and a destructor. The constructors do not yet take parameters. Each class defines its own pay and displayStatus functions. The existence of multiple definitions of these functions among the classes does not cause ambiguity. Any call to, say, the pay function for a given class must, in client code, be qualified with a class object:

```
//   illustrate 'pay' function call

supervisor   s1;
   .
   .
s1.pay();    //   not ambiguous
```

The function pay could be called without qualification from within a member function of technician. In that case, the pay function that is a member of technician is called.

The base class employee, uniquely, contains a declaration for the function promote. The employee instance of this function is called no matter which object type –employee, technician, supervisor or manager – is used to qualify the promote call.

The program file 'empfunc.cpp' contains the code that implements the member functions of the four classes.

```
/****************************************************
 *
 *  empfunc.cpp
 *
 ****************************************************/
#include <iostream.h>
#include <string.h>
#include "employee.h"
```

```cpp
//    define and initialise static member
int employee::employeeNo = 1000;
//    define 'employee' member functions first
employee::employee()
{
  char nameIn[50];

  cout << "Enter new employee name ";
  cin >> nameIn;

  name = new char[strlen(nameIn) + 1];
  strcpy(name, nameIn);
  dateOfBirth = NULL;
  individualEmployeeNo = employeeNo++;
  grade = 1;
  employeeQual = NONE;
  accumPay = 0.0;
}

employee::~employee()
{
  delete name;
  delete dateOfBirth;
}

void employee::pay()
{
}

void employee::promote(int increment)
{
  grade += increment;
}

void employee::displayStatus()
{
}

//    define 'technician' member functions
technician::technician()
{
  hourlyRate = 5.4;
  unionNo   = 0;
  cout << "Hourly employee " << name
     << " is hired" << endl;
}

technician::~technician()
```

```
{
  cout << "Hourly employee " << name
    << " is fired!" << endl;
}

void technician::pay()
{
  float paycheck;

  paycheck = hourlyRate * 40;
  accumPay += paycheck;
  cout << "Hourly employee "
    << individualEmployeeNo
    << " paid " << paycheck << endl;
}

void technician::displayStatus()
{
  cout << "Hourly employee "
    << individualEmployeeNo << " is of grade "
    << grade << " and has been paid "
    << accumPay << " so far this year"
  << endl;
}

//    define 'supervisor' member functions

supervisor::supervisor()
{
  monthlyPay = 1700.00;
  cout << "Supervisor " << name << " is hired"
  << endl;
}

supervisor::~supervisor()
{
  cout << "Supervisor " << name << " is fired!"
  << endl;
}

void supervisor::pay()
{
  accumPay += monthlyPay;
  cout << "Supervisor " << individualEmployeeNo
    << " paid " << monthlyPay << endl;
}

void supervisor::displayStatus()
{
  cout << "Supervisor " << individualEmployeeNo
    << " is of grade " << grade
```

```
      << " and has been paid " << accumPay
      << " so far this year" << endl;
}

//     define 'manager' member functions

manager::manager()
{
  monthlyPay = 2100.00;
  bonus     = 210.0;
  cout << "Manager " << name << " is hired"
    << endl;
}

manager::~manager()
{
  cout << "Manager " << name << " is fired!"
    << endl;
}

void manager::pay()
{
  accumPay += monthlyPay;
  cout << "Manager " << individualEmployeeNo
    << " paid " << monthlyPay << endl;
}

void manager::displayStatus()
{
  cout << "Manager " << individualEmployeeNo
    << " is of grade " << grade
    << " and has been paid " << accumPay
    << " so far this year" << endl;
}
```

None of the constructor functions takes any parameters, so
employee::employee() must prompt the user for input of
employee names. In the typical case, no instances of the
base class, employee, will be explicitly defined. Two of
its member functions, pay and displayStatus, therefore
have no purpose and are empty.

Here is the main function:

```
/***************************************************
 *
 * emp.cpp
 *
 ***************************************************/
#include <iostream.h>
#include "employee.h"
```

```
int main()
{
  technician t1;
  supervisor s1;
  manager   m1;

  t1.pay();
  t1.displayStatus();

  s1.pay();
  s1.displayStatus();

  m1.pay();
  m1.displayStatus();

  return(0);
}
```

Three class objects are defined, one each for technician, supervisor and manager. In each case, an underlying employee object is implicitly defined also. This can be seen from the fact that, in each case, the employee constructor is called before the constructor for the derived class. The constructors used in this example are as simple as they possibly can be. Full rules for the use of constructors (with and without parameters) and destructors in class hierarchies are given in Section 6.4.

The program produces the following output. Text in bold type is that entered by the user.

```
Enter new employee name john
Hourly employee john is hired
Enter new employee name chris
Supervisor chris is hired
Enter new employee name marilyn
Manager marilyn is hired
Hourly employee 1000 paid 216
Hourly employee 1000 is of grade 1
    and has been paid 216 so far
    this year
Supervisor 1001 paid 1700
Supervisor 1001 is of grade 1
    and has been paid 1700 so far
    this year
Manager 1002 paid 2100
Manager 1002 is of grade 1
    and has been paid 2100 so far
    this year
Manager marilyn is fired!
```

```
Supervisor chris is fired!
Hourly employee john is fired!
```

The function call m1.displayStatus() causes the status of the manager class object to be displayed. The call:

```
m1.employee::displayStatus();
```

could be made; this uses the scope resolution operator to force selection of employee::displayStatus(). Using the ordinary syntax:

```
m1.displayStatus();
```

causes selection of the displayStatus function redefinition in the derived class object m1. This syntax is possible because employee is the base class of manager. The inverted usage:

```
employee e1;
    .
    .
e1.manager::displayStatus();
```

is illegal, because manager is not a base class of employee. A compilation error results. Using e1, the direct call to employee::displayStatus could be made like this:

```
e1.displayStatus();
```

but gives no result, since employee::displayStatus is an empty function.

An arbitrary number of classes may be derived from any legal class: we could, for example, derive the class secretary from employee, or director from manager. A derived class may have more than one base class. This is multiple inheritance, which is covered in Section 6.5.

Objects of a derived class may be assigned to objects of a public base class, but not the other way round:

```
// derived class object assignment

employee e1;
technician t1;
supervisor s1;

        .
        .
e1 = t1;    // OK, assignment to base class
s1 = e1;    // Error: s1 is not base class of e1
s1 = t1;    // Error:  invalid typecast
```

A union must not contain a base class or be itself a base class.

All overloaded-operator functions declared in a base class, except an overloaded assignment, may be inherited by derived classes.

friend declarations that are part (but not members) of a class are not inherited:

```
class employee
{
private:
  int grade;
public:
  .
  .
  friend class contractor;
};

class contractor { /*...*/ };

class consultant : public contractor
{
  // cannot access  grade  here
};
```

6.3   Access Control

The effect of the access-specifier keywords private and public has already been explained. This section additionally deals with the protected keyword, as well as the levels of access to members of derived classes that are allowed by various combinations of private, protected and public.

BASE CLASS ACCESS

Base class access for a derived class is defined by use of any of the access-specifiers private, protected or public.

In public derivation:

```
class manager : public employee
```

manager inherits protected and public members of employee and retains those access levels.

In protected derivation:

```
class manager : protected employee
```

manager inherits **protected** and **public** members of **employee**, but forces all the inherited public members to be protected: they cannot be accessed from client code using an **employee** object.

In private derivation:

```
class manager : private employee
```

all non-private members of **employee** are inherited by **manager** but are now private members of **manager**, regardless of whether they are specified with protected or public access in **employee**.

Public derivation is the default for structures and unions; class derivation defaults to private. Here is an example that illustrates many of the possibilities of base class access:

```
class a
{
protected:
  int x;
public:
  int y;
  int z;
};

class b : private a    // members of a
                       // private in b
{
protected:
  a::x;                // x converted to protected
public:
  a::y;                // y converted to public

  void myfunc()
  {
    x = 5; // OK, protected
  }
};

int main()
{
  b b_inst;

  b_inst.y = 6;    //   OK, public
```

```
    b_inst.z = 7;    //   Error, still private
    return(0);
}
```

Class a has three data members. Class b inherits class a,
but with private base class access. Unless their access
levels are specifically converted, b::x, b::y and b::z are
private members of class b only accessible by member
functions of b.

Two explicit conversions are done: a::x is converted to a
protected member and a::y to a public member of b.
a::z remains a private member of b. Conversions such as
these can only reinstate the access level of a derived
member to exactly that specified in the base class in
which it was defined. In this example, a::x can only be
converted in class b to protected, not to private or
public.

After the conversions, a::x can be accessed by the function
b::myfunc(). Because a::x is protected, it cannot be
directly accessed in main. On the other hand, a::y has
been reinstated to public and is the subject of an
assignment in main.

Any access to a::z using the class variable b_inst causes
a compilation error.

Although the practice is discouraged, friend declarations
can be used to circumvent many access restrictions:

```
    class a
    {
    private:
      int z;
      friend class b;
    };
    class b : private a    // members of a
                           // private in b
    {
    public:
      void myfunc()
      {
        z = 7; //  OK, now a 'friend'
      }
    };
```

In this example, z is a private member of class a and is not inherited by b. The friend declaration in class a overrides this access restriction.

CLASS MEMBER ACCESS

A class member declared with public access is visible to all code wherever that class is in scope. A class member declared with private access is visible wherever that class is in scope, but only to member functions of the class. A class member declared with protected access is visible wherever that class is in scope, but only to member functions of the class and to member functions of classes derived from it.

All three access levels are used within the employee class hierarchy shown in Section 6.2.

Structure members are by default public; those of classes are by default private. Either may have members that are protected. Declaring members protected is only useful if the structure or class in which the declaration is made is to serve as a base class from which others will be derived.

Unions may have their members declared public, private or protected. Some compilers reject the keywords private and protected in union declarations. Since unions cannot be base classes, using protected access in union declarations does not serve a useful purpose.

6.4   Constructors and Destructors

Base and derived classes can have as members constructors or destructors or both. Constructors declared in base or derived classes may take parameters.

This section considers the order in which constructor and destructor members of a class hierarchy are called and the means by which arguments are passed to constructors in the hierarchy.

In a class hierarchy formed of a base class and zero or more derived classes, constructor functions are executed starting with the base class in order of class derivation.

Destructor functions are called in reverse order of derivation. Here is a trivial example that shows the calling order of constructors and destructors:

```cpp
#include <iostream.h>

class a
{
public:
  a()
  {
     cout << "Constructing base class\n";
  }
  ~a()
  {
     cout << "Destructing base class\n";
  }
};

class b : public a
{
public:
  b()
  {
     cout << "Constructing derived class\n";
  }
  ~b()
  {
     cout << "Destructing derived class\n";
  }
};

int main()
{
  // define derived-class instance and
  // call the derived and base constructors
  b b_inst;

  // call the destructors when b_inst goes
  // out of scope
  return(0);
}
```

The calling order can be traced through the program output:

```
Constructing base class
Constructing derived class
Destructing derived class
Destructing base class
```

Constructor and destructor functions are never inherited. Therefore, in a class hierarchy, the constructor of a derived class does not take on any of the characteristics of the constructor (if any) declared in its base class.

If a base class constructor takes parameters, the initialisation can be done in the normal way. Here is the employee base class reworked to declare constructor and destructor functions taking parameters:

```
class employee
{
protected:
  char *name;
  char *dateOfBirth;
  int individualEmployeeNo;
  static int employeeNo;
  int grade;
  qualification employeeQual;
  float accumPay;
public:
  // constructor: name and grade
  employee(char *, int);
  // constructor: name, birthdate, grade,
  // qualification
  employee(char *, char *, int, qualification);

  // destructor
  ~employee();

  void pay();
  void promote(int);        // scale increment
  void displayStatus();
};
```

Class objects of type employee are initialised with definitions like this:

```
employee e1("Karen", 4);
employee e2("John", "580525", 4, DEGREE);
```

The first definition creates a class object e1 of type employee and calls the matching constructor function (the one declaring two parameters in its argument list) to initialise the object with the arguments "Karen" and 4.

In a class hierarchy, what is usually required is to initialise a derived class object using a constructor of that derived class. When a derived class object is created, an object of the base class type is created also. A mechanism is

needed to call the derived constructor with arguments
and then to transmit some, all or none of those arguments
to the base class constructor so that the base member
variables may be initialised.

This mechanism is an extension to the syntax of the
constructor function header. Here is its general form:

```
<constr-name>([<arglist1>]):<base>([<arglist2>])
{
   //   code of derived-class constructor
}
```

The argument lists are optional; the names of the base
class and the derived class constructor are required.

Consider the case of creation of a derived-class object of
type technician. The constructors of both the employee
and technician classes take parameters. The technician
class declaration is this:

```
class technician : public employee
{
private:
   float hourlyRate;
   int   unionNo;
public:
   // name, grade, rate, union ID
   technician(char *, int, float, int);

   // name, birthdate, grade, qualification,
   // rate, union ID
   technician
      (char *, char *, int, qualification, float, int);

   // destructor
   ~technician();

   void pay();
   void displayStatus();
};
```

The header of the second constructor function of the
technician class is written as follows:

```
technician::technician(char *nameIn,
            char *birthIn,
            int gradeIn,
            qualification qualIn,
            float rateIn,
            int unionNoIn)
         : employee(nameIn, birthIn, gradeIn, qualIn)
```

Four of the six parameters received by the technician constructor arguments are passed on to the matching employee constructor. The technician constructor takes its own parameters, rateIn and unionNoIn, and assigns them to the member variables hourlyRate and unionNo of its class.

In general, the argument list of a derived class constructor must have an entry for every argument used in the constructor call, even if some of those arguments are simply passed on to a base class constructor, as is the case in this example.

EMPLOY64: CLASS HIERARCHY WITH CONSTRUCTORS TAKING PARAMETERS

The full employee class hierarchy, shown with constructors and destructors taking parameters, follows.

```
/*****************************************************
 *
 * employee.h
 *
 *****************************************************/
enum qualification {NONE, CERT, DIPLOMA,
DEGREE, POSTGRAD};

class employee
{
protected:
  char *name;
  char *dateOfBirth;
  int individualEmployeeNo;
  static int employeeNo;
  int grade;
  qualification employeeQual;
  float accumPay;
public:
  // constructor: name and grade
  employee(char *, int);

  // constructor: name, birthdate, grade,
  // qualification
  employee(char *, char *, int, qualification);

  // destructor
  ~employee();

  void pay();
  void promote(int);        // scale increment
```

```cpp
    void displayStatus();
};

class technician : public employee
{
private:
  float hourlyRate;
  int   unionNo;
public:
  // name, grade, rate, union ID
  technician(char *, int, float, int);

  // name, birthdate, grade, qualification,
  // rate, union ID
  technician
    (char *, char *, int, qualification, float, int);

  // destructor
  ~technician();

  void pay();
  void displayStatus();
};

class supervisor : public employee
{
private:
  float monthlyPay;
public:
  // name, grade, rate
  supervisor(char *, int, float);
  // name, birthdate, grade, qualification, rate
  supervisor(char *, char *, int, qualification, float);
  // destructor
  ~supervisor();

  void pay();
  void displayStatus();
};

class manager : public employee
{
private:
  float monthlyPay;
  float bonus;
public:
  // name, grade, rate, bonus
  manager(char *, int, float, float);

  // name, birthdate, grade, qualification,
  // rate, bonus
```

```
   manager(char *, char *, int, qualification,
     float, float);
   // destructor
   ~manager();

   void pay();
   void displayStatus();
};
```

The member functions of all four classes are implemented
in the program file 'empfunc.cpp':

```
/****************************************************
*
* empfunc.cpp
*
****************************************************/
#include <iostream.h>
#include <string.h>
#include "employee.h"

// define and initialise static member

int employee::employeeNo = 1000;

// define 'employee' member functions first

employee::employee(char *nameIn, int gradeIn)
{
   name = new char[strlen(nameIn) + 1];
   strcpy(name, nameIn);
   dateOfBirth = NULL;
   individualEmployeeNo = employeeNo++;
   grade = gradeIn;
   employeeQual = NONE;
   accumPay = 0.0;
}

employee::employee(char *nameIn,
        char *birthIn,
        int gradeIn,
        qualification qualIn)
{
   name = new char[strlen(nameIn) + 1];
   strcpy(name, nameIn);
   dateOfBirth = new char[strlen(birthIn) + 1];
   strcpy(dateOfBirth, birthIn);
   grade = gradeIn;
   employeeQual = qualIn;
   individualEmployeeNo = employeeNo++;
   accumPay = 0.0;
}
```

```cpp
employee::~employee()
{
  delete name;
  delete dateOfBirth;
}

void employee::pay()
{
}

void employee::promote(int increment)
{
  grade += increment;
}

void employee::displayStatus()
{
}

// define 'technician' member functions

technician::technician(char *nameIn,
          int gradeIn,
          float rateIn,
          int unionNoIn)
       : employee(nameIn, gradeIn)
{
  hourlyRate = rateIn;
  unionNo    = unionNoIn;
  cout << "Hourly employee " << name
     << " is hired" << endl;
}
technician::technician(char *nameIn,
          char *birthIn,
          int gradeIn,
          qualification qualIn,
          float rateIn,
          int unionNoIn)
 : employee(nameIn, birthIn, gradeIn, qualIn)
{
  hourlyRate = rateIn;
  unionNo    = unionNoIn;
  cout << "Hourly employee " << name
     << " is hired" << endl;
}

technician::~technician()
{
  cout << "Hourly employee " << name
     << " is fired!" << endl;
}
```

```
void technician::pay()
{
  float paycheck;

  paycheck = hourlyRate * 40;
  accumPay += paycheck;
  cout << "Hourly employee "
     << individualEmployeeNo
      << " paid " << paycheck << endl;
}

void technician::displayStatus()
{
  cout << "Hourly employee "
     << individualEmployeeNo << " is of grade "
     << grade << " and has been paid "
     << accumPay << " so far this year" << endl;
}

// define 'supervisor' member functions
supervisor::supervisor(char *nameIn,
          int gradeIn,
          float rateIn)
        : employee(nameIn, gradeIn)
{
  monthlyPay = rateIn;
  cout << "Supervisor " << name
     << " is hired" << endl;
}

supervisor::supervisor(char *nameIn,
          char *birthIn,
          int gradeIn,
          qualification qualIn,
          float rateIn)
 : employee(nameIn, birthIn, gradeIn, qualIn)
{
  monthlyPay = rateIn;
  cout << "Supervisor " << name
     << " is hired" << endl;
}

supervisor::~supervisor()
{
  cout << "Supervisor " << name
     << " is fired!" << endl;
}

void supervisor::pay()
```

```
{
  accumPay += monthlyPay;
  cout << "Supervisor " << individualEmployeeNo
     << " paid " << monthlyPay << endl;
}

void supervisor::displayStatus()
{
  cout << "Supervisor " << individualEmployeeNo
     << " is of grade " << grade
     << " and has been paid " << accumPay
     << " so far this year" << endl;
}

// define 'manager' member functions

manager::manager(char *nameIn,
        int gradeIn,
        float rateIn,
        float bonusIn)
 : employee(nameIn, gradeIn)
{
  monthlyPay = rateIn;
  bonus    = bonusIn;
  cout << "Manager " << name << " is hired"
     << endl;
}

manager::manager(char *nameIn,
        char *birthIn,
        int gradeIn,
        qualification qualIn,
        float rateIn,
        float bonusIn)
 : employee(nameIn, birthIn, gradeIn, qualIn)
{
  monthlyPay = rateIn;
  bonus    = bonusIn;
  cout << "Manager " << name << " is hired"
     << endl;
}

manager::~manager()
{
  cout << "Manager " << name << " is fired!"
     << endl;
}

void manager::pay()
{
  accumPay += monthlyPay;
```

```cpp
    cout << "Manager " << individualEmployeeNo
        << " paid " << monthlyPay << endl;
}

void manager::displayStatus()
{
    cout << "Manager " << individualEmployeeNo
        << " is of grade " << grade
        << " and has been paid " << accumPay
        << " so far this year" << endl;
}
```

The classes and their member functions are driven by the main function in the program file 'emp.cpp':

```cpp
/****************************************************
 *
 * emp.cpp
 *
 ****************************************************/
#include <iostream.h>
#include "employee.h"

int main()
{
    technician t1("Mary", 1, 5.40, 1234);
    technician t2
        ("Jane", "651029", 2, CERT, 5.40, 1235);
    supervisor s1("Karen", 4, 1350.00);
    supervisor s2
        ("John", "580525", 4, DEGREE, 1700.00);
    manager m1("Susan", 6, 1350.00, 150.00);
    manager m2 ("Martin", "580925", 5,
        POSTGRAD, 1700.00, 200.00);

    t1.pay();
    t1.displayStatus();

    t2.pay();
    t2.displayStatus();

    s1.pay();
    s1.displayStatus();

    s2.pay();
    s2.displayStatus();

    m1.pay();
    m1.displayStatus();

    m2.pay();
    m2.displayStatus();
```

```
   return(0);
 }
```

The output of this program when it is run is this:

```
Hourly employee Mary is hired
Hourly employee Jane is hired
Supervisor Karen is hired
Supervisor John is hired
Manager Susan is hired
Manager Martin is hired
Hourly employee 1000 paid 216
Hourly employee 1000 is of grade 1
     and has been paid 216 so far
     this year
Hourly employee 1001 paid 216
Hourly employee 1001 is of grade 2
     and has been paid 216 so far
     this year
Supervisor 1002 paid 1350
Supervisor 1002 is of grade 4
     and has been paid 1350 so far
     this year
Supervisor 1003 paid 1700
Supervisor 1003 is of grade 4
     and has been paid 1700 so far
     this year
Manager 1004 paid 1350
Manager 1004 is of grade 6
     and has been paid 1350 so far
     this year
Manager 1005 paid 1700
Manager 1005 is of grade 5
     and has been paid 1700 so far
     this year
Manager Martin is fired!
Manager Susan is fired!
Supervisor John is fired!
Supervisor Karen is fired!
Hourly employee Jane is fired!
Hourly employee Mary is fired!
```

Care should be taken to understand this output and the
order of events during the execution of the program.

Recall that neither constructor nor destructor functions
are inherited. If a derived class does not have a destructor
and its base class does, a default destructor is generated

automatically by the compiler for the derived class. This is to ensure that derived class objects are properly discarded when objects of the derived class go out of scope.

As can be seen from the program output above, a base class constructor executes before a constructor in a class derived from it. However, if the derived class constructor passes arguments to the base class constructor, those arguments are evaluated before either constructor is executed.

This means that members of the derived class cannot be passed as arguments to the constructor of the base class, because instances of neither the derived nor the base classes have yet been defined.

6.5   Multiple Inheritance

Up to now, we have considered inheritance by derived classes only of single base classes. A derived class can inherit the characteristics of more than one base class. This facility of C++ reflects and accommodates real-world objects that programmers may want to simulate.

The general syntax form that specifies a class derived from multiple base classes is this:

```
class <derived class>
  :[<access1>] <base name1>,
   [<access2>] <base name2>,

     .

   [<accessN>] <base nameN>
{
   .
   // derived class declaration
   .
};
```

For example, suppose a class d is to be declared that inherits the classes a, b and c. Classes a and c are to be inherited by d with public access, and b with private access. Here is the syntax for declaration, with multiple inheritance, of class d:

```
class d : public a, private b, public c
{
  //  'class d' declarations
};
```

A base class name must not be included more than once in a multiple-inheritance derivation list:

```
class d :    public a,
       public a, // illegal!
       public c
{
  //  'class d' declarations
};
```

However, the same class name may be used more than once if it is an indirect base class – if it in turn is derived from a base class. Here is an example:

```
class a     //  base class
{
  //  'class a' declarations
};

class b : public a  // 'b' indirect base class
{
  //  'class b' declarations
};

class c : public a  // 'c' indirect base class
{
  //  'class c' declarations
};

//   declaration of multiply-inherited class 'd'
//   OK: 'b' and 'c' are indirect base classes

class d : public b, public c
{
  //  'class d' declarations
}
```

The constructor functions of a singly-inherited hierarchy of classes are executed in order of class derivation. The same is true for hierarchies containing classes derived from multiple bases.

If the base classes have constructor functions, the constructors are executed, left to right, in the same order as that in which the base classes are specified. Destructors are invoked in the reverse order. This is a generalisation of the execution-order rules given in the last section, as a simple example will show:

```
#include <iostream.h>

class base
{
public:
  base() { cout << "Constructing 'base'\n"; }
  ~base() { cout << "Destructing 'base'\n"; }
};

class a : public base
{
public:
  a() { cout << "Constructing 'a'\n"; }
  ~a() { cout << "Destructing 'a'\n"; }
};

class b
{
public:
  b() { cout << "Constructing 'b'\n"; }
  ~b() { cout << "Destructing 'b'\n"; }
};

class c
{
public:
  c() { cout << "Constructing 'c'\n"; }
  ~c() { cout << "Destructing 'c'\n"; }
};

class d : public a, public b, public c
{
public:
  d() { cout << "Constructing 'd'\n"; }
  ~d() { cout << "Destructing 'd'\n"; }
};

int main()
{
  d d1;    // define instance of 'd'
  return(0);
}
```

Here we have a base class base, from which a is derived. Classes b and c are separately declared and a, b and c in turn are base classes of d. When an instance, d1, of class d is defined in the main function, the constructors are invoked in the order of derivation and the destructors are executed in reverse order. The order can be traced from the program's output:

```
Constructing 'base'
Constructing 'a'
Constructing 'b'
Constructing 'c'
Constructing 'd'
Destructing 'd'
Destructing 'c'
Destructing 'b'
Destructing 'a'
Destructing 'base'
```

Any or all of the constructor functions in a class hierarchy containing classes derived from multiple bases may require arguments. The order of execution of the constructors and destructors, as well as the passing of arguments among constructors, is best illustrated by an example.

EMPLOY65:

EMPLOYEE CLASS WITH MULTIPLE INHERITANCE

In the following example, the employee class hierarchy is reworked so that the derived classes manager and supervisor become the joint base classes of a new class, lineManager.

```
enum qualification {NONE, CERT, DIPLOMA,
DEGREE, POSTGRAD};
class employee
{
protected:
  char *name;
  char *dateOfBirth;
  int individualEmployeeNo;
  static int employeeNo;
  int grade;
  qualification employeeQual;
  float accumPay;
public:
  // constructor: name and grade
  employee(char *, int);

  // constructor: name, birthdate, grade,
  // qualification
  employee(char *, char *, int, qualification);
```

```cpp
  // destructor
  ~employee();

  void pay();
  void promote(int);        // scale increment
  void displayStatus();
};

class technician : public employee
{
private:
  float hourlyRate;
  int   unionNo;
public:
  // name, grade, rate, union ID
  technician(char *, int, float, int);

  // name, birthdate, grade, qualification,
  // rate, union ID
  technician
    (char *, char *, int, qualification, float, int);

  // destructor
  ~technician();

  void pay();
  void displayStatus();
};

class supervisor : public employee
{
protected:
  float monthlyPay;
public:
  // name, grade, rate
  supervisor(char *, int, float);

  // name, birthdate, grade, qualification, rate
  supervisor(char *, char *, int, qualification, float);

  // destructor
  ~supervisor();

  void pay();
  void displayStatus();
};

class manager : public employee
{
protected:
  float monthlyPay;
  float bonus;
```

```
public:
  // name, grade, rate, bonus
  manager(char *, int, float, float);

  // name, birthdate, grade, qualification,
  // rate, bonus
  manager(char *, char *,
    int, qualification, float, float);

  // destructor
  ~manager();

  void pay();
  void displayStatus();
};

class lineManager : public supervisor,
  public manager
{
public:
  // name, grade, rate, bonus
  lineManager(char *, int, float, float);
  // name, birthdate, grade, qualification,
  // rate, bonus
  lineManager(char *, char *, int,
    qualification, float, float);

  // destructor
  ~lineManager();

  void pay();
  void displayStatus();
};
```

Notice how the class lineManager is derived from both
supervisor and manager. The members of supervisor
and manager hitherto governed by private access
permissions are now protected, so that they can be
accessed by the member functions of lineManager. The
first lineManager constructor takes four parameters, of
which three are passed to the supervisor base class and
all four to the manager base class. The definition of the
first constructor in lineManager is as follows:

```
lineManager::lineManager(char *nameIn,
                  int gradeIn,
                  float rateIn,
                  float bonusIn)
  : supervisor(nameIn, gradeIn, rateIn),
  manager(nameIn, gradeIn, rateIn, bonusIn)
```

```
{
  cout << "Line Manager " << name
     << " is hired" << endl;
}
```

If an instance of lineManager is defined:

```
lineManager lm1("Eleanor", 5, 16.5, 250.0);
```

The first three arguments are passed to the matching supervisor constructor function so that the object of type supervisor that underlies the lineManager object can be initialised. All four arguments are similarly passed to the matching manager constructor function. The body of the lineManager constructor itself does nothing other than emit a message confirming the new hire.

The full code of this program is not given here but is included on the disk offered with this book. This is partly because it is quite long and partly because there is one vital component missing. When the code, in its current state, is compiled, the compiler produces a lot of error messages complaining about ambiguity in referencing class members. The reason is best explained with a diagram:

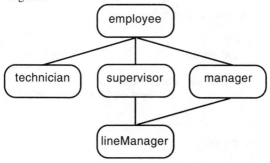

This is what our class hierarchy looks like. When an object of type lineManager is defined, two employee objects are first created. Then, one object each of type supervisor and manager is instantiated. Finally, the lineManager object is completed. The point is that there are two employee objects and any reference to a member of the employee class (for example name or grade) using a lineManager object is ambiguous and is rejected by the compiler. In the next section, we see how to avoid this problem.

6.6   Virtual Base Classes

Consider a very simplified, abstract illustration of the problem of ambiguity raised in the last section:

```
#include <iostream.h>

class a
{
public:
  int x;
};

class b : public a
{
public:
  int y;
};

class c : public a
{
public:
  int z;
};

class d : public b, public c
{
public:
  void print()
  {
    cout << "Values are " << x << " "
                    << y << " " << z << "\n";
  }
};

int main()
{
  d d_inst;

  d_inst.x = 5;
  d_inst.y = 6;
  d_inst.z = 7;

  d_inst.print();
  return(0);
}
```

The base class a is declared and is singly-inherited by each of classes b and c. These are used as multiple base classes by the derived class d. The problem is that the line:

```
d_inst.x = 5;
```

contains an ambiguous reference to the variable x. The definition of d_inst creates two instances of the class a, one each for b and c. The problem is resolved by declaring the base class a as virtual in each of the declarations of b and c:

```
class b : virtual public a
{
public:
  int y;
};
class c : virtual public a
{
public:
  int z;
};
```

This causes b and c to share a single instance of a rather then multiple, ambiguous instances.

EMPLOY66:

EMPLOYEE CLASS WITH VIRTUAL BASE CLASSES

The full implementation of the employee class hierarchy, with multiple inheritance and virtual base classes is now given. The program is long but different from its predecessor in only two major respects:

- It qualifies the manager and supervisor classes as virtual base classes. The effect of this is to resolve the two underlying instances of the employee class to a single, unambiguous, instance that can correctly be referenced using a derived lineManager object.

- The employee instance becomes an *immediate base class* of lineManager, requiring that it, along with the supervisor and manager objects, be initialised as part of the definition of the lineManager constructor functions.

Here is the program, organised in the familiar employee.h header file and the program files 'empfunc.cpp' and 'emp.cpp':

```
/****************************************************
 *
 * employee.h
 *
 ****************************************************/
enum qualification {NONE, CERT, DIPLOMA,
DEGREE, POSTGRAD};

class employee
{
protected:
  char *name;
  char *dateOfBirth;
  int individualEmployeeNo;
  static int employeeNo;
  int grade;
  qualification employeeQual;
  float accumPay;
public:
  // constructor: name and grade
  employee(char *, int);
  // constructor: name, birthdate, grade,
  // qualification
  employee(char *, char *, int, qualification);

  // destructor
  ~employee();

  void pay();
  void promote(int);      // scale increment
  void displayStatus();
};

class technician : public employee
{
private:
  float hourlyRate;
  int   unionNo;
public:
  // name, grade, rate, union ID
  technician(char *, int, float, int);

  // name, birthdate, grade, qualification,
  // rate, union ID
  technician
    (char *, char *, int, qualification, float, int);

  // destructor
  ~technician();

  void pay();
```

```cpp
  void displayStatus();
};

class supervisor : virtual public employee
{
protected:
  float monthlyPay;
public:
  // name, grade, rate
  supervisor(char *, int, float);

  // name, birthdate, grade, qualification, rate
  supervisor(char *, char *, int, qualification, float);

  // destructor
  ~supervisor();

  void pay();
  void displayStatus();
};

class manager : virtual public employee
{
protected:
  float monthlyPay;
  float bonus;
public:
  // name, grade, rate, bonus
  manager(char *, int, float, float);

  // name, birthdate, grade, qualification,
  // rate, bonus
  manager(char *, char *,
      int, qualification, float, float);

  // destructor
  ~manager();

  void pay();
  void displayStatus();
};

class lineManager : public supervisor, public
manager
{
public:
  // name, grade, rate, bonus
  lineManager(char *, int, float, float);

  // name, birthdate, grade, qualification,
  // rate, bonus
  lineManager(char *, char *, int, qualification,
float, float);
```

```
  // destructor
  ~lineManager();

  void pay();
  void displayStatus();
};
/******************************************************
*
*  empfunc.cpp
*
******************************************************/
#include <iostream.h>
#include <string.h>
#include "employee.h"

// define and initialise static member

int employee::employeeNo = 1000;

// define 'employee' member functions first

employee::employee(char *nameIn, int gradeIn)
{
  name = new char[strlen(nameIn) + 1];
  strcpy(name, nameIn);
  dateOfBirth = NULL;
  grade = gradeIn;
  individualEmployeeNo = employeeNo++;
  accumPay = 0.0;
}

employee::employee(char *nameIn,
        char *birthIn,
        int gradeIn,
        qualification qualIn)
{
  name = new char[strlen(nameIn) + 1];
  strcpy(name, nameIn);
  dateOfBirth = new char[strlen(birthIn) + 1];
  strcpy(dateOfBirth, birthIn);
  grade = gradeIn;
  employeeQual = qualIn;
  individualEmployeeNo = employeeNo++;
  accumPay = 0.0;
}

employee::~employee()
{
  delete name;
```

```
  delete dateOfBirth;
}

void employee::pay()
{
}

void employee::promote(int increment)
{
  grade += increment;
}

void employee::displayStatus()
{
}

// define 'technician' member functions

technician::technician(char *nameIn,
          int gradeIn,
          float rateIn,
          int unionNoIn)
        : employee(nameIn, gradeIn)
{
  hourlyRate = rateIn;
  unionNo    = unionNoIn;
  cout << "Hourly employee " << name
     << " is hired" << endl;
}

technician::technician(char *nameIn,
          char *birthIn,
          int gradeIn,
          qualification qualIn,
          float rateIn,
          int unionNoIn)
 : employee(nameIn, birthIn, gradeIn, qualIn)
{
  hourlyRate = rateIn;
  unionNo    = unionNoIn;
  cout << "Hourly employee " << name
  << " is hired" << endl;
}

technician::~technician()
{
  cout << "Hourly employee " << name
     << " is fired!" << endl;
}
```

```cpp
void technician::pay()
{
  float paycheck;

  paycheck = hourlyRate * 40;
  accumPay += paycheck;
  cout << "Hourly employee "
    << individualEmployeeNo
    << " paid " << paycheck << endl;
}

void technician::displayStatus()
{
  cout << "Hourly employee "
    << individualEmployeeNo << " is of grade "
    << grade << " and has been paid "
    << accumPay << " so far this year"
    << endl;
}

// define 'supervisor' member functions

supervisor::supervisor(char *nameIn,
          int gradeIn,
          float rateIn)
        : employee(nameIn, gradeIn)
{
  monthlyPay = rateIn;
  cout << "Supervisor " << name
    << " is hired" << endl;
}

supervisor::supervisor(char *nameIn,
          char *birthIn,
          int gradeIn,
          qualification qualIn,
          float rateIn)
        : employee(nameIn, birthIn, gradeIn, qualIn)
{
  monthlyPay = rateIn;
  cout << "Supervisor " << name
    << " is hired" << endl;
}

supervisor::~supervisor()
{
  cout << "Supervisor " << name
    << " is fired!" << endl;
}
```

```
void supervisor::pay()
{
  accumPay += monthlyPay;
  cout << "Supervisor " << individualEmployeeNo
     << " paid " << monthlyPay << endl;
}

void supervisor::displayStatus()
{
  cout << "Supervisor " << individualEmployeeNo
     << " is of grade " << grade
     << " and has been paid " << accumPay
     << " so far this year" << endl;
}

// define 'manager' member functions

manager::manager(char *nameIn,
           int gradeIn,
           float rateIn,
           float bonusIn)
      : employee(nameIn, gradeIn)
{
  monthlyPay = rateIn;
  bonus    = bonusIn;
  cout << "Manager " << name << " is hired"
     << endl;
}

manager::manager(char *nameIn,
           char *birthIn,
           int gradeIn,
           qualification qualIn,
           float rateIn,
           float bonusIn)
  : employee(nameIn, birthIn, gradeIn, qualIn)
{
  monthlyPay = rateIn;
  bonus    = bonusIn;
  cout << "Manager " << name << " is hired"
     << endl;
}

manager::~manager()
{
  cout << "Manager " << name << " is fired!"
     << endl;
}
```

```cpp
void manager::pay()
{
  accumPay += monthlyPay;
  cout << "Manager " << individualEmployeeNo
    << " paid " << monthlyPay << endl;
}

void manager::displayStatus()
{
  cout << "Manager " << individualEmployeeNo
    << " is of grade " << grade
    << " and has been paid " << accumPay
    << " so far this year" << endl;
}

// define 'lineManager' member functions

lineManager::lineManager(char *nameIn,
                   int gradeIn,
                   float rateIn,
                   float bonusIn)
    : supervisor(nameIn, gradeIn, rateIn),
    manager(nameIn, gradeIn, rateIn, bonusIn),
    employee(nameIn, gradeIn)
{
  cout << "Line Manager " << name
    << " is hired" << endl;
}

lineManager::lineManager(char *nameIn,
                   char *birthIn,
                   int gradeIn,
                   qualification qualIn,
                   float rateIn,
                   float bonusIn)
: supervisor(nameIn, birthIn, gradeIn,
  qualIn, rateIn),
manager(nameIn, birthIn, gradeIn,
  qualIn, rateIn, bonusIn),
employee(nameIn, birthIn, gradeIn, qualIn)
{
  manager::monthlyPay = rateIn;
  bonus      = bonusIn;
  cout << "Line Manager " << name
    << " is hired" << endl;
}

lineManager::~lineManager()
```

```
{
  cout << "Line Manager " << name
    << " is fired!" << endl;
}
void lineManager::pay()
{
  accumPay += manager::monthlyPay;
  cout << "Line Manager "
    << individualEmployeeNo << " paid "
    << manager::monthlyPay << endl;
}
void lineManager::displayStatus()
{
  cout << "Line Manager "
    << individualEmployeeNo << " is of grade "
    << grade << " and has been paid "
    << accumPay << " so far this year" << endl;
}
/****************************************************
*
* emp.cpp
*
****************************************************/
#include <iostream.h>
#include "employee.h"

int main()
{
  lineManager   m1
  ("Susan", 6, 1350.00, 150.00);
  lineManager   m2
  ("Martin", "580925", 5, POSTGRAD,
  1700.00, 200.00);

  m1.pay();
  m1.displayStatus();

  m2.pay();
  m2.displayStatus();

  return(0);
}
```

When run, the program's output is this:

```
Supervisor Susan is hired
Manager Susan is hired
Line Manager Susan is hired
```

```
Supervisor Martin is hired
Manager Martin is hired
Line Manager Martin is hired
Line Manager 1000 paid 1350
Line Manager 1000 is of grade 6
    and has been paid 1350 so far
    this year
Line Manager 1001 paid 1700
Line Manager 1001 is of grade 5
    and has been paid 1700 so far
    this year
Line Manager Martin is fired!
Manager Martin is fired!
Supervisor Martin is fired!
Line Manager Susan is fired!
Manager Susan is fired!
Supervisor Susan is fired!
```

Again, you should trace the output of this program carefully, noting the two crucial changes. First, **supervisor** and **manager** are now declared as being derived from a single unambiguous instance of the virtual base class **employee**:

```
class supervisor : virtual public employee
{
  .
  .
class manager : virtual public employee
{
```

Second, and consequently, the constructors of the derived class **lineManager** now reflect the fact that **employee**, like **supervisor** and **manager**, is now an immediate base class:

```
lineManager::lineManager(char *nameIn,
                  int gradeIn,
                  float rateIn,
                  float bonusIn)
    : supervisor(nameIn, gradeIn, rateIn),
    manager(nameIn, gradeIn, rateIn, bonusIn),
    employee(nameIn, gradeIn)
        // immediate base!
{
```

6.7   Pointers to Class Hierarchies

A pointer to a base class object may be used to point to any class derived from that object. This fact is critically important in the use of virtual functions and for the C++ implementation of polymorphism, both of which are explained in detail in the next section.

When a base class pointer is used to point to an object derived from that base type, it may only be used to access members derived from the base class.

A pointer to a derived class object cannot be used to point to an object of the base class without an explicit and unambiguous typecast operation. This is because derived classes are types that are distinct from those of their base class or classes.

EMPLOY67: POINTERS TO CLASSES IN A HIERARCHY

A highly-simplified **employee** class hierarchy is used to illustrate these rules for use of pointers to derived classes. The class declarations are in **employee.h**:

```
/*****************************************************
 *
 * employee.h
 *
 *****************************************************/
enum qualification {NONE, CERT, DIPLOMA,
DEGREE, POSTGRAD};
class employee
{
protected:
  char *name;
  char *dateOfBirth;
  int individualEmployeeNo;
  static int employeeNo;
  int grade;
  qualification employeeQual;
  float accumPay;
public:
  // constructor
  employee();
  void pay();
};
```

```
class technician : public employee
{
private:
  float hourlyRate;
  int   unionNo;
public:
  // constructor
  technician();
  void promote(int);      // scale increment
  void pay();
};
class supervisor : public employee
{
private:
  float monthlyPay;
public:
  // constructor
  supervisor();

    void pay();
};
class manager : public employee
{
private:
  float monthlyPay;
  float bonus;
public:
  // constructor
  manager();

  void pay();
};
```

The member functions of the classes are implemented in the program file 'empfunc.cpp':

```
/***************************************************
 *
 * empfunc.cpp
 *
 ***************************************************/
#include <iostream.h>
#include <string.h>
#include "employee.h"
//     define and initialise static member

int employee::employeeNo = 1000;

//     define 'employee' member functions first
```

```cpp
employee::employee()
{
  char nameIn[50];

  strcpy(nameIn, "Base Employee");

  name = new char[strlen(nameIn) + 1];
  strcpy(name, nameIn);
  dateOfBirth = NULL;
  individualEmployeeNo = employeeNo++;
  grade = 1;
  employeeQual = NONE;
  accumPay = 0.0;
}

void employee::pay()
{
  cout << "Base-class employee paid!" << endl;
}

//     define 'technician' member functions

technician::technician()
{
  strcpy(name, "Technician");
  hourlyRate = 5.4;
  unionNo   = 0;
}

void technician::promote(int increment)
{
  grade += increment;
}

void technician::pay()
{
  float paycheck;

  paycheck = hourlyRate * 40;
  accumPay += paycheck;
  cout << "Technician paid!" << endl;
}

//     define 'supervisor' member functions

supervisor::supervisor()
{
  strcpy(name, "Supervisor");
  monthlyPay = 1700.00;
}
```

```cpp
void supervisor::pay()
{
  accumPay += monthlyPay;
  cout << "Supervisor paid!" << endl;
}

//    define 'manager' member functions

manager::manager()
{
  strcpy(name, "Manager");
  monthlyPay = 2100.00;
  bonus      = 210.0;
}

void manager::pay()
{
  accumPay += monthlyPay;
  cout << "Manager paid!" << endl;
}
```

Code in the main function is used to exercise the classes:

```cpp
/***************************************************
 *
 * emp.cpp
 *
 ***************************************************/
#include <iostream.h>
#include "employee.h"

int main()
{
  employee     e1;
  technician   t1;
  supervisor   s1;

  employee     *eptr = &e1;
  technician   *tptr = &t1;
  supervisor   *sptr = &s1;
  eptr->pay();   // call base-class 'pay'

  eptr = &t1;
  eptr->pay();   // still call base-class 'pay'
  t1.pay();      // derived-class 'pay'

  eptr = &s1;
  eptr->pay();   // still call base-class 'pay'
  s1.pay();      // derived-class 'displayStatus'

  //tptr = &e1;  Illegal assignment
```

```
    tptr = (technician *)(&e1);
    tptr->pay();   // call technician 'pay'
    return(0);
}
```

The pointer **eptr** can only correctly be set to the address of **t1** by explicit assignment:

```
    eptr = &t1;
```

Now, although **eptr** points to an object of a class derived from **employee**, it can only be used to access objects derived from **employee**, for example, the base-class **pay** function.

Any member function of a derived class that is not inherited from **employee** must be accessed directly with the derived class object:

```
    t1.promote(5);
```

An attempt to do this:

```
    eptr->promote(5);
```

causes a compilation error.

Because the **pay** function is derived from **employee**, it may be called with the pointer of base-class type:

```
    eptr->pay();
```

Whenever it is so called, the function **employee::pay()** is called. If, on the other hand, a derived-class object is used to qualify the call:

```
    t1.pay();
```

the **pay** function defined for that derived class, in this case **technician::pay()**, is called.

Assigning the address of the base class object **e1** to a pointer of the derived class type **technician**:

```
    tptr = &e1;
```

is illegal; a derived class pointer cannot point to a base class object. The code is fixed with an explicit typecast operation:

```
    tptr = (technician *)(&e1);
```

and the pointer **tptr** can then be used to access **technician::pay()**, not **employee::pay()**.

The output of the program when it is run is this:

```
Base-class employee paid!
Base-class employee paid!
Technician paid!
Base-class employee paid!
Supervisor paid!
Technician paid!
```

To summarise: if a pointer of base class type is used to call a member function of a class hierarchy, the base class instance of the function is always called. Otherwise, to call a function for a particular class object, the type of that object must be known to the programmer.

It would be much more useful if this restriction were removed and a pointer could be used to access derived class objects independently of the base class. This would mean that one pointer could be used to point to objects of different types and allow generic processing to be done on objects of those types.

This is the essence of polymorphism as implemented by C++. Only one small change must be made to the program shown in this section to achieve polymorphism: the function employee::pay() must be specified virtual in the declaration of the class employee.

Virtual functions and polymorphism are the subject of the remainder of this chapter.

6.8   Virtual Functions

BASICS

If a pointer to a base class object is assigned the address of a derived class object, the pointer remains pointing at the base class members and can only be used to access the base class members.

If a member function of the base class is declared virtual, the pointer can be used to access the redefinition of the function that is found in the derived class, rather than always accessing the base class instance of the function.

A function declared **virtual** can be called in the same way as any other function. However, when the virtual function is accessed with a pointer or reference to a class object, the instance of the function called is the instance defined by that class object.

All redefinitions in derived classes of a virtual function must have argument lists identical to those of the base declaration of the virtual function. ANSI C++ newly allows the return types in *overriding* declarations of virtual functions in derived classes to differ from the return type specified in the base class.

Consider a **virtual** version of EMPLOY67, shown in the last section. In the base class **employee**, the **pay** function is prefixed with the keyword **virtual**:

```
class employee
{
protected:
   char *name;
   char *dateOfBirth;
   int individualEmployeeNo;
   static int employeeNo;
   int grade;
   qualification employeeQual;
   float accumPay;
public:
   // constructor
   employee();

   virtual void pay();      // virtual function!
};
```

The derived class declarations are unchanged. It is unnecessary but good practice also to prefix the **pay** function headers in the derived classes with **virtual**. If this is not done, the only way to identify virtual functions in a hierarchy is to examine the whole hierarchy. The **main** function is also unchanged. When the program is run, the results are these:

```
Base-class employee paid!
Technician paid!
Technician paid!
Supervisor paid!
Supervisor paid!
Base-class employee paid!
```

After the first line is output, the base class object pointer **eptr** is assigned the address of the technician class object t1:

```
eptr = &t1;
```

Because **eptr** has been assigned a pointer of type technician *, then, when the function call is made:

```
eptr->pay();
```

the redefinition of the **pay** function contained in the derived class technician is selected at runtime and executed. When **eptr** is assigned the address of the supervisor class object s1, the function call eptr->pay(); causes supervisor::pay() to be selected at runtime and executed.

The final line of output is interesting. In the main function of EMPLOY67 in the last section, the lines

```
tptr = (technician *)(&e1);

tptr->pay();// call technician 'pay'
```

cause the base-class pointer to be typecast to technician *, and technician::pay() is called. With the introduction of the virtual **pay** function, the contents of the pointer remain those of a base-class pointer, albeit typecast to technician *, and the virtual function table mechanism referred to below ensures that the function employee::pay() is called.

A redefinition of a virtual function in a derived class is said to override, rather than overload, the base class instance of the function. The difference is important because, unlike in the case of ordinary function overloading, the resolution of virtual function calls is done at runtime. The process is referred to as late, or dynamic, binding.

It is legal for a derived class not to override a virtual function defined in a base class: it contains no redefinition of the virtual function. In such a case, the base class instance of the function is called even if a pointer to the derived class is used in the function call.

Virtual functions are inherited through multiple levels in a derived class hierarchy. If a virtual function is defined only in a base class, that definition is inherited by all the derived classes.

Another difference between virtual and overloaded functions is that virtual functions must be class members, while overloaded functions do not have to be.

INTERNALS OF VIRTUAL FUNCTIONS

To enable different instances of a virtual function to be selected at runtime, a *virtual function table* (*vtbl*) is automatically stored in each derived class object concerning the type of that object. The *vtbl* is used to implement indirect calls to appropriate instances of virtual functions.

The virtual function table mechanism imposes an overhead of one extra pointer indirection in the function call. The flexibility afforded by virtual functions justifies the penalty.

While the precise implementation of virtual function tables is compiler- and implementation-dependent, the following example is representative.

```
class A
{
public:
  int a;
  virtual void f1(int);
  virtual void f2(int);
  virtual void f3(int);
};

class B: public A
{
public:
  int b;
  void f2(int);
};

class C: public B
{
public:
  int c;
  void f3(int);
};
```

An object in memory of the class C will look something like this:

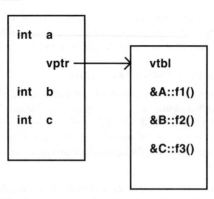

A call using a base-class pointer to a virtual function:

```
A *ap = new C;
ap->f3(14);
```

may be translated by the compiler to this:

```
(*(ap->vptr[2]))(ap, 14);
```

which, when deciphered, is a call to the function C::f3() with argument 14 and the pointer ap copied to the function's this pointer.

VIRTUAL DESTRUCTORS

In general, if a base class has a virtual function, it should also have a virtual destructor. Virtual destructors ensure that, when the destructors of a class hierarchy are called (in reverse order), they discard memory for the right class objects. The following program example shows what can happen if destructors are not virtual:

```
#include <iostream.h>

class base
{
public:
  base()
    { cout << "Constructing base" << endl; }
  ~base()
    { cout << "Destructing base" << endl; }
};
```

```
class derived : public base
{
public:
  derived()
    { cout << "Constructing derived" << endl; }
  ~derived()
    { cout << "Destructing derived" << endl; }
};

int main()
{
  base* bp = new derived;
                    // create a derived object
  delete bp;        // delete a base object

  return(0);
}
```

When run, the output of the program as shown is this:

```
Constructing base
Constructing derived
Destructing base
```

showing that the derived constructor is matched, wrongly, by a **base** destructor call. To correct the program, the **base** destructor is made virtual:

```
virtual ~base()
  { cout << "Destructing base" << endl; }
```

and the resulting program output shows that the constructors and destructors are called in the correct sequence:

```
Constructing base
Constructing derived
Destructing derived
Destructing base
```

6.9 Abstract Classes

As part of the process of designing a class hierarchy, it is often necessary to declare a base class that itself serves no useful purpose. Such a base class is usually the common denominator of more concrete classes derived from it.

The **employee** class is quite a good example of such a class. If you think about it, no-one has ever seen an *employee*. You have seen a *manager*, a *secretary*, a *supervisor* and so on, but never an abstract *employee*. Even the operation of paying the **employee** by calling the function **employee::pay()** does not mean very much — it being more common to pay real rather than generic employees. This is why **employee::pay()** is left empty in the first examples of this chapter. The class employee can be termed an *abstract class*.

The function **employee::pay()** does nothing and is defined only to serve as a base virtual function for the **pay** functions in the derived classes, which actually do some processing. Where there is a dummy virtual function like this, a different declaration can be used and the dummy definition discarded:

```
virtual void pay() = 0;
```

Now there is no instance of **employee::pay()** and the declaration is called a *pure virtual function*. The pure virtual function must be overridden by one or more functions in a derived class. The general form of declaration of a pure virtual function is this:

```
virtual <ret type> <name>([<arg list>]) = 0;
```

Formally, a class that contains at least one pure virtual function is called an abstract class.

EMPLOY69: MANY VIRTUAL FUNCTIONS

Here is the **employee** class hierarchy in its final form. It is the integration of the multiply-inherited model implemented by the example EMPLOY66 with virtual functions and abstract classes as explained over the last three sections.

```
/*****************************************************
 *
 * employee.h
 *
 *****************************************************/
enum qualification {NONE, CERT, DIPLOMA,
DEGREE, POSTGRAD};

class employee
{
protected:
  char *name;
  char *dateOfBirth;
  int individualEmployeeNo;
```

```
    static int employeeNo;
    int grade;
    qualification employeeQual;
    float accumPay;
public:
  // constructor: name and grade
  employee(char *, int);

  // constructor: name, birthdate, grade,
  // qualification
  employee(char *, char *, int, qualification);

  // virtual destructor
  virtual ~employee();

  virtual void pay() = 0;
  void promote(int);      // scale increment
  virtual void displayStatus() = 0;
};

class technician : public employee
{
private:
  float hourlyRate;
  int   unionNo;
public:
  // name, grade, rate, union ID
  technician(char *, int, float, int);

  // name, birthdate, grade, qualification,
  // rate, union ID
  technician(char *,char *,int,qualification,float,int);
  // destructor
  ~technician();

  void pay();
  void displayStatus();
};

class supervisor : virtual public employee
{
protected:
  float monthlyPay;
public:
  // name, grade, rate
  supervisor(char *, int, float);

  // name, birthdate, grade, qualification, rate
  supervisor (char *,char *, int, qualification, float);
  // destructor
  ~supervisor();

  void pay();
```

```cpp
    void displayStatus();
};

class manager : virtual public employee
{
protected:
  float monthlyPay;
  float bonus;
public:
  // name, grade, rate, bonus
  manager(char *, int, float, float);

  // name, birthdate, grade, qualification,
  // rate, bonus
  manager
    (char *, char *, int, qualification, float, float);
  // destructor
  ~manager();

  void pay();
  void displayStatus();
};

class lineManager : public supervisor,
                    public manager
{
public:
  // name, grade, rate, bonus
  lineManager(char *, int, float, float);

  // name, birthdate, grade, qualification,
  // rate, bonus
  lineManager
  (char *, char *, int, qualification, float, float);
  // destructor
  ~lineManager();
  void pay();
  void displayStatus();
};

/****************************************************
*
*  empfunc.cpp
*
****************************************************/
#include <iostream.h>
#include <string.h>
#include "employee.h"

// define and initialize static member
int employee::employeeNo = 1000;
```

```
// define 'employee' member functions first
employee::employee(char *nameIn, int gradeIn)

{
  name = new char[strlen(nameIn) + 1];
  strcpy(name, nameIn);
  dateOfBirth = NULL;
  grade = gradeIn;
  individualEmployeeNo = employeeNo++;
  accumPay = 0.0;
}

employee::employee(char *nameIn,
       char *birthIn,
       int gradeIn,
       qualification qualIn)

{
  name = new char[strlen(nameIn) + 1];
  strcpy(name, nameIn);
  dateOfBirth = new char[strlen(birthIn) + 1];
  strcpy(dateOfBirth, birthIn);
  grade = gradeIn;
  employeeQual = qualIn;
  individualEmployeeNo = employeeNo++;
  accumPay = 0.0;
}

employee::~employee()
{
  delete name;
  delete dateOfBirth;
}

void employee::promote(int increment)
{
  grade += increment;
}

// define 'technician' member functions

technician::technician(char *nameIn,
                  int gradeIn,
                  float rateIn,
                  int unionNoIn)
     : employee(nameIn, gradeIn)
{
  hourlyRate = rateIn;
  unionNo   = unionNoIn;
  cout << "Hourly employee " << name
          << " is hired" << endl;
}
```

```cpp
technician::technician(char *nameIn,
                  char *birthIn,
                  int  gradeIn,
                  qualification qualIn,
                  float rateIn,
                  int  unionNoIn)
  : employee(nameIn, birthIn, gradeIn, qualIn)
{
  hourlyRate = rateIn;
  unionNo    = unionNoIn;
  cout << "Hourly employee " << name
    << " is hired" << endl;
}

technician::~technician()
{
  cout << "Hourly employee " << name
    << " is fired!" << endl;
}

void technician::pay()
{
  float paycheck;

  paycheck = hourlyRate * 40;
  accumPay += paycheck;
  cout << "Hourly employee "
    << individualEmployeeNo
    << " paid " << paycheck << endl;
}

void technician::displayStatus()
{
  cout << "Hourly employee "
    << individualEmployeeNo << " is of grade "
    << grade << " and has been paid "
    << accumPay << " so far this year"
    << endl;
}

// define 'supervisor' member functions

supervisor::supervisor(char *nameIn,
                  int  gradeIn,
                  float rateIn)
          : employee(nameIn, gradeIn)
{
  monthlyPay = rateIn;
  cout << "Supervisor " << name
    << " is hired" << endl;
}
```

```cpp
supervisor::supervisor(char *nameIn,
                       char *birthIn,
                       int gradeIn,
                       qualification qualIn,
                       float rateIn)
 : employee(nameIn, birthIn, gradeIn, qualIn)
{
  monthlyPay = rateIn;
  cout << "Supervisor " << name
     << " is hired" << endl;
}

supervisor::~supervisor()
{
  cout << "Supervisor " << name
     << " is fired!" << endl;
}

void supervisor::pay()
{
  accumPay += monthlyPay;
  cout << "Supervisor " << individualEmployeeNo
     << " paid " << monthlyPay << endl;
}

void supervisor::displayStatus()
{
  cout << "Supervisor " << individualEmployeeNo
     << " is of grade " << grade
     << " and has been paid " << accumPay
     << " so far this year" << endl;
}

// define 'manager' member functions

manager::manager(char *nameIn,
            int gradeIn,
            float rateIn,
            float bonusIn)
 : employee(nameIn, gradeIn)
{
  monthlyPay = rateIn;
  bonus    = bonusIn;
  cout << "Manager " << name << " is hired"
     << endl;
}

manager::manager(char *nameIn,
            char *birthIn,
            int gradeIn,
            qualification qualIn,
```

```
                float rateIn,
                float bonusIn)
  : employee(nameIn, birthIn, gradeIn, qualIn)
{
   monthlyPay = rateIn;
   bonus      = bonusIn;
   cout << "Manager "
        << name << " is hired" << endl;
}

manager::~manager()
{
   cout << "Manager " << name << " is fired!"
        << endl;
}

void manager::pay()
{
   accumPay += monthlyPay;
   cout << "Manager " << individualEmployeeNo
        << " paid " << monthlyPay << endl;
}

void manager::displayStatus()
{
   cout << "Manager " << individualEmployeeNo
        << " is of grade " << grade
        << " and has been paid " << accumPay
        << " so far this year" << endl;
}

// define 'lineManager' member functions

lineManager::lineManager(char *nameIn,
                   int  gradeIn,
                   float rateIn,
                   float bonusIn)
    : supervisor(nameIn, gradeIn, rateIn),
      manager(nameIn, gradeIn, rateIn, bonusIn),
      employee(nameIn, gradeIn)
{
   cout << "Line Manager " << name
   << " is hired" << endl;
}

lineManager::lineManager(char *nameIn,
                   char *birthIn,
                   int  gradeIn,
                   qualification qualIn,
                   float rateIn,
                   float bonusIn)
```

```
: supervisor(nameIn, birthIn,
    gradeIn, qualIn, rateIn),
manager(nameIn, birthIn,
    gradeIn, qualIn, rateIn, bonusIn),
employee(nameIn, birthIn, gradeIn, qualIn)
{
  manager::monthlyPay = rateIn;
  bonus       = bonusIn;
  cout << "Line Manager " << name
    << " is hired" << endl;
}

lineManager::~lineManager()
{
  cout << "Line Manager " << name
    << " is fired!" << endl;
}

void lineManager::pay()
{
  accumPay += manager::monthlyPay;
  cout << "Line Manager "
    << individualEmployeeNo << " paid "
    << manager::monthlyPay << endl;
}

void lineManager::displayStatus()
{
  cout << "Line Manager "
    << individualEmployeeNo
    << " is of grade " << grade
    << " and has been paid " << accumPay
    << " so far this year" << endl;
}
/***************************************************
*
* emp.cpp
*
***************************************************/
#include <iostream.h>
#include "employee.h"

int main()
{
  employee *ep;
  lineManager m1("Susan", 6, 1350.00, 150.00);
  lineManager m2("Martin", "580925", 5,
    POSTGRAD, 1700.00, 200.00);

  ep = &m1;
```

```
    ep->pay();
    ep->displayStatus();

    ep = &m2;
    ep->pay();
    ep->displayStatus();

    return(0);
}
```

The base class **employee** now contains two virtual functions and a virtual destructor function ~**employee**(). Each of the derived classes overrides **employee::pay()** and **employee::displayStatus()** and includes its own destructor function.

The polymorphic nature of this program is exemplified by the virtual function **pay**. The base class and each derived class contain an instance of **pay**. Using a pointer of any of the class types, the programmer can call the **pay** function. Calls with each of the pointer types results in a different instance of **pay** being called and in a different result being produced.

The base-class function **employee::pay()** is declared as a pure virtual function: in itself, **employee::pay()** has no meaning and is empty. A pure virtual function such as **employee::pay()** must be overridden by definition in derived classes of one or more functions of the same name, return type and argument list. If this is not done, a compilation error results.

Virtual functions declared in a base class must either be defined or made pure by assignment of zero in the declaration. Virtual functions declared in a derived class need not either be defined or made pure.

A pure virtual function must not be directly called.

An abstract class contains at least one pure virtual function. As such, it is an incomplete type and instances of the abstract class cannot be created. To attempt an instantiation of employee:

```
    employee e1;
```

now results in a compilation error.

When making the call to the generic function **pay**, the programmer does not have to be aware which class object is in use. The semantics of virtual functions ensure that payment is performed appropriately for each class type.

Note that the implementation of each virtual function instance is different, while the function header (and hence the interface to the programmer) is the same. The programmer using the **employee** classes does not have to know the internals of the member functions or the differences between the instances to get the appropriate results for a given class type.

When the program files in EMPLOY69 are compiled and run, the output results are these:

```
Supervisor Susan is hired
Manager Susan is hired
Line Manager Susan is hired
Supervisor Martin is hired
Manager Martin is hired
Line Manager Martin is hired
Line Manager 1000 paid 1350
Line Manager 1000 is of grade 6
    and has been paid 1350 so far
    this year
Line Manager 1001 paid 1700
Line Manager 1001 is of grade 5
    and has been paid 1700 so far
    this year
Line Manager Martin is fired!
Manager Martin is fired!
Supervisor Martin is fired!
Line Manager Susan is fired!
Manager Susan is fired!
Supervisor Susan is fired!
```

OTHER RULES FOR VIRTUAL FUNCTIONS

Some rules for uses of virtual functions that are less often encountered than those already shown are summarised here:

- Static member functions cannot be declared **virtual**.

- Overloaded-operator functions can be declared **virtual**.

- If either of the **new** or **delete** operators is overloaded, it becomes a static class member and must not be declared **virtual**.

- Constructors must not be declared virtual.

- Declaring a base class destructor virtual makes the destructors of all derived classes virtual also.

- All destructors for non-virtual base classes are executed before destructors for virtual base classes.

- A virtual function member of the same class may be called directly from a constructor or destructor.

- The virtual nature of a function call may be suppressed by explicitly resolving the scope of the instance of the function being called. In the employee example, the function call:

```
eptr = &m1;
eptr->employee::displayStatus();
```

causes the displayStatus function for the base class employee to be called, and not lineManager::displayStatus().

- Unions must not contain virtual member functions.

- A virtual function can be declared a friend of another class.

- Pointers and references to an abstract class may be defined. The ability to define a pointer to an abstract class is necessary to allow class object pointers to be used to reference instances of virtual functions, including pure virtual function members of an abstract class, in a hierarchy.

- The only way a pure virtual function can be called is with a pointer.

- An abstract class must not be used as an argument type or as a function return type or in a typecast operation.

- Abstract classes may have constructors and destructors. Member functions of the same class may be called from an abstract class constructor.

6.10 Example: A Generic List

This section presents a virtual implementation of the linked list program first shown in Section 4.8.

In that program all the nodes on the list are of a fixed type, node, which in turn defines the components of each node as being objects of the types int, double and node *. The example in this section implements a list of nodes that contain data of many types. Each node on the list is a class object declared in a class hierarchy with base class shape. Each of the class objects represents a geometric figure derived from the base class shape.

To keep the program to a reasonable length, the shapes are restricted to triangles and rectangles. This is sufficient to demonstrate a list of nodes of different class types derived from the class shape, which are accessed using class pointers and virtual functions. It is possible to add other shapes, such as circles and polygons, to the list by extending the program.

The essence of the program is in traversing a list of objects of different types in a way that is transparent to the programmer. Presented with the shape class hierarchy, the programmer must simply call the virtual function print to find the area of the class object currently being pointed to. The programmer does not have to be aware of how the area is calculated for each kind of shape.

LIST610: The Generic List Class

Here are the class declarations, in the file list.h:

```
/*
 *
 *  list.h -  declares list, node and user-prompt
 *     classes as well as 'shape' and derived
 *     classes which are the list items.
 *
 *  The 'list' class is declared with 'node'
 *  as a private member. The nested
 *  instance of 'node' contains pointers to
 *  the data for that node as well as access
 *  functions. The data pointer is assigned
 *  the address of an instance of one of the
```

```
*    classes 'rectangle' or 'triangle' derived
*    from 'shape'. The virtual function 'display'
*    is used to display information about the
*    node depending on which derived-class
*    type is pointed to.
*/

class shape    // base class, defines dimensions
{
protected:
   float dim1, dim2;
public:
   shape(float d1, float d2) // constructor
   {
      dim1 = d1;
      dim2 = d2;
   }
   virtual void display()
            // virtual 'display' function
   {
      cout << "Generic shape " << dim1
            << " " << dim2 << "\n";
   }
};

class rectangle : public shape
{
   // no dimensions added, but could be
public:
   rectangle(float d1, float d2) : shape(d1, d2)
   {
   }
   // Overriding virtual 'display' function,
   // redefines 'shape::display'
   void display();
};

class triangle : public shape
{
   // no dimensions added, but could be
public:
   triangle(float d1, float d2) : shape(d1, d2)
   {
   }
   // Overriding virtual 'display' function,
   // redefines 'shape::display'
   void display();
};
```

```
class node
{
private:
  shape *ob;  // pointer to 'shape' class object
  node *next;    // pointer to next list node
public:
  // constructor, assigns to list node pointer
  // to newly allocated 'shape' class object
  node(shape *ob_in)
  {
     ob = ob_in;
  }
  // access function, returns pointer to next node
  node * &Next() { return (next); }
  // access function, returns pointer to shape
  // object pointed to by node
  shape * &item() { return (ob); }
};

class list    // 'list' class, points to list nodes
{
private:
  node *head, *tail, *curr;
public:
  list() { head = tail = curr = NULL; }
  void get_node_data(float&, float&);
  void add_node(shape *);
  void dump_list();
  ~list() { destroy (); }
  void destroy();
};

class message
{
public:
  void prompt ()
  {
     cout << "Press 'r' to add rectangle: \n";
     cout << "Press 't' to add triangle: \n";
     cout << "Press 'p' to display list: \n";
     cout << "Press 'q' to quit: \n";
  }
};
```

A class hierarchy based on shape is declared. There is one virtual function, display, which is defined inline for shape and defined later for the derived classes rectangle and triangle.

The list class contains pointers to the list of nodes. The crucial class declaration here is that of node. node no longer directly defines its data members; instead, the pointer ob points to an object of the shape class hierarchy. This makes it possible to access the list members using pointers and virtual functions.

The message class defines a series of user prompts. The definitions of all the class member functions not defined inline are contained in the file 'listfunc.cpp':

```cpp
/*
 * 'listfunc.cpp'
 */
#include <iostream.h>
#include "list.h"

void list::get_node_data (float& d1, float& d2)
{
  cout << "Enter first dimension: ";
  cin >> d1;
  cout << "Enter second dimension: ";
  cin >> d2;
}

// add to the list a pointer to a 'shape' class object

void list::add_node(shape *ob)
{
  // Create new list element

  curr = new node(ob);

  //    Add the element to the end of the list

  if (head == NULL)
    head = curr;
  else
    tail->Next() = curr;
  tail = curr;
  tail->Next() = NULL;
}

void list::dump_list()
{
  shape *s;

  //    Display the current state of the list

  if (!head)
    cout << "List is empty\n";
  curr = head;
```

```
   // The virtual function 'display' is called
   // here for every list node, using a pointer
   // of the base class type.

   while (curr)
   {
      s = curr->item();
      s->display();
      curr = curr->Next();
   }
}

void list::destroy()
{
   while (head)
   {
      curr = head;
      head = head->Next();
      delete curr;
   }
}

// Virtual redefinitions of the 'display' function

void rectangle::display()
{
   cout << "Rectangle....\n";
   cout << "Dimensions are " << dim1 << " "
            << dim2 << "\n";
   cout << "Area is " << dim1*dim2 << "\n";
   if (dim1 == dim2)
      cout << "It's also a square \n";
}

void triangle::display()
{
   cout << "Triangle....\n";
   cout << "Dimensions are " << dim1 << " "
            << dim2 << "\n";
   cout << "Area is " << dim1*(dim2/2) << "\n";
}
```

The code to drive these classes and their member functions is contained in the program file 'list.cpp':

```
/*
 *   Program 'list.cpp' - creates a
 *   singly-linked-forward list of nodes
 *   of different types, using a virtual
 *   'display' function to select correctly
```

```
 *    each node type and display
 *    information about it accordingly.
 */

#include <iostream.h>
#include "list.h"

int main()
{
  int c;
  float d1, d2;

  list l;
  message user;

  user.prompt();
  while (c = cin.get(), c != 'q' && c != EOF)
  {
    switch (c)
    {
      case 'r':
      case 'R':  l.get_node_data(d1, d2);
                 rectangle *r =
                 new rectangle(d1, d2);
                 l.add_node(r);
                 break;
      case 't':
      case 'T':  l.get_node_data(d1, d2);
                 triangle *t =
                 new triangle(d1, d2);
                 l.add_node(t);
                 break;
      case 'p':
      case 'P':  l.dump_list();
                 break;
      default:   cout << "Invalid option chosen\n";
                 break;
    }
    c = cin.get();
    user.prompt();
  }
  return(0);
}
```

The user prompt is displayed and, for each possible response, the case statement carries out a set of actions.

If the response is r (rectangle), a new instance of the class object rectangle is allocated and initialised, using the rectangle constructor, to the floating-point values accepted as user input by the function list::get_node_data. The address in memory to the new rectangle class object is assigned to the pointer r, which is then used as the argument to the function list::add_list. This function adds the pointer-to-rectangle to the list.

If the response is t (triangle), the triangle information is added to the list in the same way.

After some nodes have been added to the list, it is reasonable for the user to want to view the contents of the list nodes. The function list::dump_list is called by entering 'p' at the prompt. It defines a pointer s of the base class type shape * and uses this pointer repeatedly to call the virtual display function.

Depending on the type of pointer (either triangle * or rectangle *) the appropriate version of display is called to display the contents of the shape pointed to by each of the list nodes.

If the user makes three entries:

```
rectangle 12 12
triangle   3 4
rectangle  5 6
```

and then enters 'p' to display the list contents, the output is this:

```
Rectangle....
Dimensions are 12 12
Area is 144
It's also a square
Triangle....
Dimensions are 3 4
Area is 6
Rectangle....
Dimensions are 5 6
Area is 30
```

The entry 'q' is used to stop the program.

7 ANSI Standard C++ Facilities

7.1 C++ Standardisation

The First Edition of this book covered C++ as defined by language Release 3.0. This Edition uses as a reference the most recent ANSI C++ Draft Standard Working Paper. The Draft Standard incorporates four major changes from C++ Release 2.0: templates, exception handling, namespaces and runtime type identification. These topics are the subject of this chapter.

The Draft Standard also introduces a host of smaller changes, some of which are referred to at appropriate points throughout this text. The changes include syntactic additions to the language such as keyword operators like **or_eq** (see Appendix A) and tightening of semantic definitions (see Section 5.3).

The ANSI C++ Standardisation Committee, X3J16, is responsible for drafting the American C++ Standard, with corresponding international responsibility being vested in the ISO C++ committee WG21. The meetings of the two committees are joint and, as is the case with ANSI C and ISO C, there will be no technical differences between ANSI C++ and ISO C++ when the respective Standards are approved, probably in 1997.

7.2 Function Templates

C++ provides the syntax of function templates so that a function can be defined as a family of functions capable of operating on arguments of any type. Function templates are declared by prefixing a function declaration with the **template** keyword followed by a pair of angle-brackets containing one or more identifiers that represent parameterised types. This construct is called the *template specification*.

Here is the general form of a function template declaration:

```
template<class T1, class T2,..., class Tn>
function prototype
```

The corresponding template definition is of the form:

```
template<class T1, class T2,..., class Tn>
function definition
```

In both cases, the angle-brackets are part of the syntax.

Using function templates, a function can be declared and defined in terms of arguments and return values of any type. The programmer's interface to the function is thus parameterised. When the function template is invoked by means of a function call with arguments of specific data types, the compiler generates an instance of the function – a *template function*, as opposed to a *function template*! – in the program for those types. Function templates effectively implement an unlimited set of overloadings of a function.

C++ is a strongly typed language. This is mostly a benefit, promoting program reliability, but it causes problems when a simple function needs to be called with arguments of types that may vary from call to call. A good example is a function, called min, that must find the minimum of two values supplied as arguments.

INSTANTIATING TEMPLATE FUNCTIONS

If the function on a first call is to compare two ints and on the second two doubles, then conventionally two definitions of the function must be made to handle the two different calls.

FTMPL721: A SIMPLE FUNCTION TEMPLATE

Templates provide an elegant solution to this problem as the following example program shows.

```
#include <iostream.h>

// template declaration
template<class num>
num min(num n1, num n2);
```

```
int main()
{
  int i1, i2;
  double d1, d2;

  cout << "Enter two integers: ";
  cin >> i1 >> i2;
  cout << "minimum is: " << min(i1, i2) << endl;

  cout << "Enter two doubles: ";
  cin >> d1 >> d2;
  cout << "minimum is: " << min(d1, d2) << endl;

  return(0);
}
//   template definition
template<class num>
num min(num n1, num n2)
{
  if (n1 < n2)
     return (n1);
  return (n2);
}
```

In this program, a function template is defined that
expects one type parameter, represented by the placeholder num specified between angle-brackets following
the template keyword. On the first call to min:

```
min(i1, i2)
```

an instance of the function template is created. This
process is said to *instantiate* a template function. The
resulting template function has the type of the two
arguments, int, substituted for the placeholder num and
compares two integers. On the second call to min:

```
min(d1, d2)
```

a second template function is instantiated. This function
has double substituted for num and compares two double
floating-point numbers. The program's input-output
sequence is this:

```
Enter two integers: 3 4
minimum is: 3
Enter two doubles: 3.5 4.5
minimum is: 3.5
```

It can be seen that two template functions called min are
instantiated in the program. In general, template functions
are instantiated when the function is called or its address
taken. The types of the arguments used in the function
call, not the return type specified in a function template,
determine which template function is instantiated:

```
float result = min(i1, i2);
```

This causes a template function to be instantiated with the
type parameter num becoming int, regardless of the fact
that the return type specified in the call is float.

It must not be impossible for the compiler to instantiate a
template function:

```
template<class num>
num min(num *n1, num *n2)
{
   if (*n1 < *n2)
      return (*n1);
   return (*n2);
}
```

Here, both arguments to the function min are specified as
pointers to objects of the type represented by num.
Therefore, pointer arguments must be supplied in calls to
the function:

```
int i1, i2;
int *ip1 = &i1;
int *ip2 = &i2;
     .
     .
//   min(i1, i2)   // illegal
//   must use pointer args in call to min
cout << "minimum is: " << min(ip1, ip2)
     << endl;
```

Using arguments that are references to num:

```
template<class num>
const num&
   min(const num& n1, const num& n2)
{
   if (n1 < n2)
      return (n1);
   return (n2);
}
```

the min function can be instantiated with integer arguments:

```
cout << "minimum is: " << min(i1, i2)
    << endl;
```

FUNCTION TEMPLATE PARAMETER LIST

In the function template declaration:

```
template<class num>
num min(num n1, num n2);
```

<class num> is the template's formal parameter list. The keyword **class** in this context means *type parameter following*. The type parameter, as we shall see in a following example, may be any basic or user-defined type. The **class** keyword must always be used in a parameter list. If there is more than one type parameter, **class** must be used for each parameter. Each parameter in the list must be unique and must appear at least once in the argument list of the function. These points are illustrated by modifying the min template:

```
//   legal template
template<class num1, class num2>
num min(num1 n1, num2 n2)
{
  //
}

//   illegal, missing class
template<class num1, num2>
num min(num1 n1, num2 n2)

//   illegal, duplication
template
  <class num1, class num1, class num2>
num min(num1 n1, num2 n2)

//   illegal, num3 not used
template<class num1, class num2, class num3>
num min(num1 n1, num2 n2)
```

If a type parameter appears more than once in the function argument list:

```
template<class num>
num min(num n1, num n2)
```

then the types of the arguments used in a call to the function must be identical:

```
char c = a;
int  i = 5;

min(c, i);          // error: char not converted
min(i, i);          // OK
min(c, c);          // OK
```

The template type parameters can be used anywhere in the scope of the function template following their definition. Type parameters are only in existence in that scope and must not be used outside it.

The names of the template type parameters do not have to match in the template declaration and definition:

```
//   declaration
template<class x, class y, class z>
num min(x n1, y n2, z n3);

//   definition
template
  <class num1, class num2, class num3>
num min(num1 n1, num2 n2, num3 n3)
{
  //
}
```

DECLARATION AND DEFINITION

A function template must at least be declared at a point in the code before a template function is instantiated. If this is done, the template may be defined later; the min example above uses this approach. As with any ordinary function, a function template's definition is its declaration if the definition precedes the first function call. The first call to the function following the definition instantiates a template function.

Both the declaration and definition of a function template must be in global scope. A function template cannot be declared as a member of a class.

FTMPL722: USER-DEFINED ARGUMENT TYPES

Class types, as well as other user-defined types, may be used in the parameter list of a function template and in a call to a template function. If this is done, basic operators used within the template function on class arguments must be overloaded in the class. Here is an example:

```cpp
#include <iostream.h>

class coord
{
private:
  int x_coord;
  int y_coord;
public:
  coord(int x, int y)
  {
    x_coord = x;
    y_coord = y;
  }

  int GetX() { return(x_coord); }
  int GetY() { return(y_coord); }
  int operator<(coord& c2);
};

//   function template declaration
template<class obj>
obj& min(obj& o1, obj& o2);

int main()
{
  coord c1(5,10);
  coord c2(6,11);

  //   compare coord objects in min,
  //   using overloaded < operator
  coord c3 = min(c1, c2);
  cout << "minimum coord is: " << c3.GetX()
          << " " << c3.GetY() << endl;

  double d1 = 3.14159;
  double d2 = 2.71828;

  //   compare double objects in min,
  //   using basic < operator
  cout << "minimum double is: " << min(d1, d2)
          << endl;
  return(0);
}
```

```
template<class obj>
obj& min(obj& o1, obj& o2)
{
  //   < operator overloaded if function
  //   instantiated for class type, otherwise
  //   built-in < used
  if (o1 < o2)
     return (o1);
  return (o2);
}
//   define overloaded < operator
int coord::operator<(coord& c2)
{
  if (x_coord < c2.x_coord)
     if (y_coord < c2.y_coord)
           return (1);
  return (0);
}
```

A class coord is declared. The min function, if instantiated
for the coord type, must find the minimum of two objects
of type coord. To do this, the basic < operator must be
overloaded in the coord class. Two coord objects, c1 and
c2, are defined and initialised. The function call:

```
coord c3 = min(c1, c2);
```

instantiates a min template function for the coord type
and assigns the lesser of the two coordinates to the coord
object c3. The comparison of c1 and c2 is done with the
overloaded <. When min is called with arguments of the
basic type double, the basic < operator, rather than the
overloaded version, is used to compare the double floating-
point numbers. The results displayed by the program are
these:

```
minimum coord is: 5 10
minimum double is: 2.71828
```

OVERLOADING FUNCTION TEMPLATES

Function templates may be overloaded with other function
templates. They may also be overloaded with non-template
functions, in which case a type-specific function is created,
which will be called for objects of that type.

In the case of overloaded function templates, instantiated
functions must be distinguishable by the compiler by
having different types of arguments or a different number

of arguments. Return type is not used to resolve overloaded function instances.

FTMPL723:

MULTIPLY-OVERLOADED FUNCTION TEMPLATES

Here is an example program, again based on the min example, that exercises many of the possibilities in overloading function templates.

```
#include <iostream.h>
#include <string.h>

class coord
{
private:
  int x_coord;
  int y_coord;
public:
  coord(int x, int y)
  {
     x_coord = x;
     y_coord = y;
  }

  int GetX() { return(x_coord); }
  int GetY() { return(y_coord); }
  int operator<(coord& c2);
};

//   dummy class to demonstrate multi-type
//   template
class point
{
};

//   general function template declaration
template<class obj> obj& min(obj& o1, obj& o2);

//   function template overloaded to
//   compare against two specified co-ordinates
template<class obj> int min(obj& o1, int x, int y);

//   override template for string arguments
int min(const char *, const char *);
```

```
//   new function template to somehow compare
//   three parameterised types
template<class obj1, class obj2, class obj3>
void comp(obj1& o1, obj2& o2, obj3& o3)
{
  cout << "Comparing objects in comp\n";
}

int main()
{
  //   define coord objects
  coord c1(5,10);
  coord c2(6,11);

  //   general function template called with
  //   coord objects
  coord c3 = min(c1, c2);
  cout << "minimum coord is: " << c3.GetX()
          << " " << c3.GetY() << endl;

  //   compare coord object against two ints
  if (min(c1, 7, 13))
    cout << "coord object smaller" << endl;

  //   define strings for comparison
  char str1[] = "parameterisation - British";
  char str2[] = "parameterization - US";

  //   use min to compare two strings
  if (min(str1, str2))
    cout << "First string less than second"
            << endl;

  //   define point object for call to comp
  int i;
  point p1;

  comp(c1, p1, i);

  return (0);
}

//   define general template for coord objects
template<class obj>
obj& min(obj& o1, obj& o2)
{
  //   overloaded < used here only
```

```
  if (o1 < o2)
     return (o1);
  return (o2);
}

//   define special template to test x and y
//   coordinates
template<class obj>
int min(obj& o1, int x, int y)
{
  if (o1.GetX() < x)
     if (o1.GetY() < y)
             return (1);
  return (0);
}

//   type-specific min overloaded to
//   compare strings
int min(const char* s1, const char *s2)
{
  if ((strcmp(s1, s2)) < 0)
     return (1);
  return (0);
}

//   define overloaded < operator function
int coord::operator<(coord& c2)
{
  if (x_coord < c2.x_coord)
     if (y_coord < c2.y_coord)
             return (1);
  return (0);
}
```

Two classes are declared: coord and point. A function template is declared for min:

```
template<class obj> obj& min(obj& o1, obj& o2);
```

to do a general comparison of two objects of any type. The min template is overloaded by another:

```
template<class obj>
int min(obj& o1, int x, int y);
```

This compares an object with two specific coordinates. The type-specific function min:

```
int min(const char *, const char *);
```

is a further overloading and overrides the general function template when a call is made to min to find the alphabetic minimum of two strings. Additionally, just to show a function template with multiple type parameters, a new template comp is defined to compare any three objects.

When the program is run, min is called three times. For the first two calls, a min function is instantiated after the template overloading is resolved. The third call to min overrides both templates and calls the specialised version of min designed for comparing strings.

When comp is called with three arguments of arbitrary type, a matching instantiation of comp is generated and the function executes simply by displaying a message. The output results of the program are these:

```
minimum coord is: 5 10
coord object smaller
First string less then second
Comparing objects in comp
```

The compiler resolves calls to overloaded functions, including template functions, according to the following steps:

- If an exactly matching (see Section 5.2) non-template function is found, it is called. This happens in FTMPL723 with the version of min that compares strings.

- If an exactly matching function can be generated from a template, it is instantiated and called.

- If a matching function cannot be found or instantiated, or if the function call is ambiguous, a compilation error results.

A function template can specify that its instantiated function will be any of extern, inline or static. In each case, the keyword must be placed between the template specification and the function header. The following example is representative:

```
template<class obj>
inline obj& min(obj& o1, obj& o2);
```

7.3   Class Templates

Class templates are declared by prefixing a class declaration with a template specification. This is the **template** keyword followed by a pair of angle-brackets containing one or more identifiers that represent parameterised types or constant initialising values. Here is the general form of a class template declaration:

```
template<class T1, class T2,..., class Tn>
class classname;
```

The corresponding template definition is of the form:

```
template<class T1, class T2,..., class Tn>
class classname
{
   //   member declarations here
};
```

In both cases, the angle-brackets are part of the syntax. Each of the template parameters **T1, ..., Tn** is either a placeholder or a variable declaration. Type specifiers used when an instance of the class is defined are substituted for the placeholders. Initialising constants used in the class definition are copied to the variables. Both the placeholders and variables may be used within the scope of the class template as would any other type specifiers or variables. They must not be used outside that scope.

INSTANTIATING TEMPLATE CLASSES

Using class templates, a class can be declared and defined in terms of any type. Such a class is said to be parameterised. If classes generalise objects, then class templates can be said to generalise classes. Consider this simple example of a generic **number** class:

```
//   class template declaration
template <class numtype>
class number;

   .
   .
//   definition of a class instance
number<int> ni;
```

```
      .
      .
// class template definition
template <class numtype>
class number
{
private:
  numtype n;
public:
  number()
  {
     n = 0;
  }
  void get_number() { cin >> n; }
  void print_number() { cout << n << endl; }
};
```

Using conventional C++ syntax, defining a class or
structure capable of representing numbers of arbitrary
types is difficult, if not impossible. Class declarations
cannot be overloaded; it is therefore usually necessary to
take the 'brute force' approach and declare a class type for
every type of number that is required. With the class
template shown, it is possible to instantiate that class for
a number of any type. Instantiation occurs when the
template name is used with its list of parameters. An
instance of the class for integer numbers is defined thus:

```
number<int> ni;
```

Now the identifier ni is a class object of type number<int>
that specifies the characteristics of an integer number,
including some operations which are possible on it. The
above definition causes the built-in type specifier int to be
substituted for the class template parameter numtype
and to be used thereafter in the class declaration in place
of numtype. This is exactly as if the class declaration:

```
class number
{
private:
  int n;
public:
  number()
  {
     n = 0;
  }
```

```
    void get_number() { cin >> n; }
    void print_number() { cout << n << endl; }
};
```

were explicitly made and the instance ni defined in the ordinary way:

```
number ni;
```

The class template above is declared, instantiated and defined in that order. In practice, the forward template declaration is often dispensed with and the template is defined at a point in the program source code before the instantiation.

CTMPL731: NUMBER CLASS TEMPLATE

Here is the full number class program:

```
#include <iostream.h>

template <class numtype>
class number
{
private:
  numtype n;
public:
  number()
  {
    n = 0;
  }
  void get_number() { cin >> n; }
  void print_number() { cout << n << endl; }
};

int main()
{
  number<char> nc;
  cout << "Enter a character: ";
  nc.get_number();
  cout << "Character is: ";
  nc.print_number();

  number<int> ni;
  cout << "Enter an integer: ";
  ni.get_number();
  cout << "Integer is: ";
  ni.print_number();
```

```
    number<double> nd;
    cout << "Enter a double: ";
    nd.get_number();
    cout << "Double is: ";
    nd.print_number();

    return(0);
}
```

Three template class instantiations are made, one each for
char, int and double types. For each instance, the private
member n is defined in turn as char, int and double. The
member function get_number extracts a value from the
standard input stream and stores it in n. The first time it
is called, cin uses the extractor that has a standard
overloading for type char and expects a character to be
input. On the second call to get_number, cin expects
input of an int and on the third call a double. If the
numbers are not input in this order, the input operation
fails. When the program is executed, its input-output
sequence is this:

```
Enter a character: r
Character is: r
Enter an integer: 7
Integer is: 7
Enter a double: 2.64575
Double is: 2.64575
```

CLASS TEMPLATE SYNTAX

The syntax of class templates appears daunting. While
certainly not simple, all template syntax has an equivalent
usage for simple classes. The basic equivalence is this:

```
//  instance of template class
number<int>      ni;
//  instance of non-template class number
number    ni;
```

For the template declaration template<class numtype>
class number; the class name number is a parameterised
type and numtype (when replaced by a type specifier) is
its parameter. Therefore:

```
number<double>
```

is a type specifier that can be used to define a double
instance of the template class number in any part of the

program for which the template is in scope. Within the template definition, the type specifier number may optionally be used as a shorthand for number<numtype>, as it is in the constructor function:

```
number()
{
   n = 0;
}
```

Outside the template definition, the type specifier must be used in its full form. If the function get_number is defined outside rather than within the template, the following function declaration and definition is used:

```
//   function declaration in template
void get_number();

//   function definition externally
template <class numtype>
void number<numtype>::get_number()
{
   cin >> n;
}
```

The header syntax is complex but may make sense when we see that the equivalent non-template header is:

```
void number::get_number()
```

The definition of the template function get_number must be prefixed with the template specification template<class numtype> and specified as being in the scope of the type number<numtype>.

From this we can see that a member function of a template class, such as get_number, is implicitly a template function that uses the class template parameters as its own parameters.

CLASS TEMPLATE SCOPE

Class templates obey the normal scope and access rules that apply to all other C++ class and data objects. They must be defined in file scope (never within a function) and must be unique in a program. Class template definitions must not be nested:

```
template <class type1>
class outside
{
private:
  type1 n;
public:
  //   illegal! nested template definition
  template <class type2, class type3>
  class inside { };
  //
};
```

Class templates may be of structures and unions as well
as classes.

CLASS TEMPLATE PARAMETER LIST

In the class template declaration:

```
template<class numtype>
class number;
```

<class numtype> is the template's formal parameter
list. The keyword class in this context means *type
parameter following*. The type parameter may be any
C++ basic or user-defined type. The class keyword must
be used for each type specified in a parameter list. If there
is more than one type parameter, class must be used for
each parameter.

A class template parameter list can also contain*expression
parameters*, usually numeric values. The arguments
supplied to these parameters on instantiation of a template
class must be constant expressions. The class template
parameter list must not be empty and, if there is more than
one parameter, the parameters must be individually
separated by commas:

```
template <class T1, int exp1, class T2>
class someclass
{
  //
};
```

The someclass template specifies an expression as its
second parameter and type placeholders as its first and
third parameters. Instantiation of someclass might look
like this:

```
someclass<double, 500, coord> sc;
```

Built-in types, user-defined types and constant expressions may be used as class template parameters. They may be intermixed in any order. The parameters specified in an instantiation must, however, be in the same order and be of the same types as those specified in the template definition. For example, the following instantiation causes a compilation error:

```
someclass<double, 500U, coord> sc;
```

The error occurs because the expression parameter int exp1 in the template definition does not match the type (unsigned int) of 500U.

The Container Class

Class templates are often used to make very general and flexible definitions of a special kind of class called the *container class*. A container class is one that defines a collection of data objects of a particular type and also defines operations that may be carried out on that collection. Typical examples of container classes are arrays and linked lists.

This section builds a simple container class, defined using class templates, for an array. That definition is later extended with a derived class defining the additional characteristics of a terminated array. This might be a null-terminated character array (a string) but could be an array of any type containing an element of a given value representing an array terminator. The terminated-array example shows, with a minimum amount of code, how class templates can be used in hierarchies.

CTMPL732: The Container Class

First, here is the class template implementation of the array container class:

```
#include <iostream.h>

template <class slottype>
class array
{
private:
  int      size;
  slottype *aptr;
```

```cpp
public:
  array(int slots = 1)
  {
    size = slots;
    aptr = new slottype[slots];
  }
  void fill_array();
  void disp_array();
  ~array() { delete [] aptr; }
};

int main()
{
  array<char> ac(10);
  cout << "Fill a character array" << endl;
  ac.fill_array();
  cout << "Array contents are: ";
  ac.disp_array();

  array<double> ad(5);
  cout << "Fill a double array" << endl;
  ad.fill_array();
  cout << "Array contents are: ";
  ad.disp_array();

  return(0);
}

//  This would be the function header if it
//  were not a template member:
//
//  void array::fill_array()

template <class slottype>
void array<slottype>::fill_array()
{
  for (int i = 0; i < size; i++)
  {
    cout << "Enter data: ";
    cin >> aptr[i];
  }
}

template <class slottype>
void array<slottype>::disp_array()
{
  for (int i = 0; i < size; i++)
    cout << aptr[i] << " ";
  cout << endl;
}
```

A class template is defined for the array class. The private data members of the class are an integer used to represent the size of the array and a pointer to an array of objects of a type specified by the programmer when a template class is instantiated.

The type parameter slottype is also used in the class constructor function to allocate an array of the objects, which is of a size specified in the template class definition:

```
array<char> ac(10);
```

This defines and allocates memory space for an array, called ac, of ten objects of type char. Two class member functions, fill_array and disp_array, are then called. Both functions are declared as part of the class template and defined externally. The header of the fill_array function:

```
template <class slottype>
void array<slottype>::fill_array()
```

specifies that the function is part of a class template with a single type parameter; that it is in the scope of an instance of the class array defined with a type represented by slottype; and that the function returns no value.

When the char type is used to instantiate a template class, slottype is substituted with char and the fill_array member function of that class operates on characters. In the second instantiation shown in the example, a double type is used and fill_array for that instance of the class operates on double floating-point numbers. Arrays of elements of arbitrary types could be instantiated; to do so would require definition of an overloaded extractor function for every non-basic type used. To keep the size of the program small, only basic types are used in this example.

If the template were instead a simple class called array, the header of fill_array would undergo two simplifications: removal of the template specification and of parameter list before the scope-resolution operator:

```
void array::fill_array()
```

The program first accepts input from the user of a sequence of characters which it stores in an array. In the example, if the input data is not of integral or character type, the program fails. After instantiation of the template class for the **double** array, the same operations are done. User-defined types are not handled.

CTMPL733: THE CONTAINER CLASS

Here is the container-class program modified to use both type and expression parameters in the template parameter list:

```cpp
#include <iostream.h>

template <class slottype, int slots>
class array
{
private:
  int  size;
  slottype *aptr;
public:
  array()
  {
    size = slots;
    aptr = new slottype[slots];
  }

  void fill_array();
  void disp_array();
  ~array() { delete [] aptr; }
};

int main()
{
  array<char, 10> ac;
  cout << "Fill a character array" << endl;
  ac.fill_array();
  cout << "Array contents are: ";
  ac.disp_array();

  array<double, 5> ad;
  cout << "Fill a double array" << endl;
  ad.fill_array();
  cout << "Array contents are: ";
  ad.disp_array();

  return(0);
}

template <class slottype>
void array<slottype>::fill_array()
{
```

```
  for (int i = 0; i < size; i++)
  {
    cout << "Enter data: ";
    cin >> aptr[i];
  }
}

template <class slottype>
void array<slottype>::disp_array()
{
  for (int i = 0; i < size; i++)
    cout << aptr[i] << " ";
  cout << endl;
}
```

The main change to the program is in the function
template definition, which now takes two parameters,
one a type and the other an integer quantity, **slots**, to
represent the number of elements in the array. The
syntax of the template class instantiation is changed
accordingly.

```
  array<char, 10> ac;
```

replaces:

```
  array<char> ac(10);
```

The constructor function, consequently, has an empty
argument list. The template expression parameter, in this
case 10, must be a constant expression.

CTMPL734: TYPE-SPECIFIC CLASS DECLARATION

It is possible to override a template class declaration for
a particular type. Adapting the **array** example, two class
declarations are made: one a template definition with a
single type parameter; the other a class declaration of the
same name but with the **char** parameter hard-wired into
the code.

```
  #include <iostream.h>

  template <class slottype>
  class array
  {
  private:
    int size;
    slottype *aptr;
```

```
public:
  array(int slots = 1)
  {
    size = slots;
    aptr = new slottype[slots];
  }
  void fill_array();
  void disp_array();
  ~array() { delete [] aptr; }
};

//   this class declaration, for type char,
//   overrides template
class array<char>
{
private:
  int size;
  char *aptr;
public:
  array<char>(int slots = 1)
  {
    size = slots;
    aptr = new char[slots];
  }
  void fill_array();
  void disp_array();
  ~array() { delete [] aptr; }
};
```

The fill_array and disp_array functions declared as template members are overloaded for the class type array<char>. The overloading functions do processing which is specific to character arrays.

```
//   template fill_array unchanged
template <class slottype>
void array<slottype>::fill_array()
{
  for (int i = 0; i < size; i++)
  {
    cout << "Enter data: ";
    cin >> aptr[i];
  }
}

//   template disp_array unchanged
template <class slottype>
```

```
void array<slottype>::disp_array()
{
   for (int i = 0; i < size; i++)
      cout << aptr[i] << " ";
   cout << endl;
}

//   overloaded definitions of fill_array
//   and disp_array, designed to operate on
//   character strings
void array<char>::fill_array()
{
   cout << "Enter a string: ";
   cin >> aptr;
}

void array<char>::disp_array()
{
   cout << "String is: " << aptr << endl;
}
```

The main function defines two array class instances, ac
and ad. The first is defined with the class declaration
specific to the type char, overriding the class template.
The char-specific overloadings of the member functions
are called to manipulate the character array. The second
class instance is generated from the class template and
creates and manipulates an array of double floating-
point numbers.

```
int main()
{
   array<char> ac(10);
   ac.fill_array();
   ac.disp_array();

   array<double> ad(5);
   cout << "Fill a double array" << endl;
   ad.fill_array();
   cout << "Array contents are: ";
   ad.disp_array();

   return(0);
}
```

STATIC CLASS TEMPLATE MEMBERS

Just as it is possible to declare static members of an ordinary class, it also possible to have static members of a class template.

As is explained in Section 3.2, declaring a class with a static data member does not define that data member by allocating memory space for it. The static data member must be separately defined. The same is true for static data members of class templates. The separate definition must be done in global scope, never within a function or class. The resulting static variable is shared for all template class objects of each instantiation: the variable is global to class objects defined with the same type parameters.

CTMPL735: STATIC TEMPLATE MEMBERS

Here is an example based on the number class template:

```
#include <iostream.h>

template <class numtype>
class number
{
private:
  static numtype n;
public:
  static void inc_number() { n++; }
  void print_number() { cout << n << endl; }
};

//   Define and initialise static member at
//   file scope

template <class numtype> numtype
                number<numtype>::n=5;

//   If this were not a template, the
//   definition would be this:
//
//   int number::n=5;

int main()
{
  //   static member shared for all objects
  //   (i1, i2) of each instantiation (int)
  //   of a class
  number<int> i1;
```

```
    i1.inc_number();
    cout << "Integer is: ";
    i1.print_number();

    number<int> i2;
    i2.inc_number();
    cout << "Integer is: ";
    i2.print_number();

    number<float> f1;
    f1.inc_number();
    cout << "Float is: ";
    f1.print_number();

    return(0);
}
```

The number class contains two static members, a data member n of type specified by the parameter numtype, and the function inc_number, which adds one to n. The static data member n is explicitly defined in file scope with the following rather forbidding syntax:

```
template <class numtype>
numtype  number<numtype>::n=5;
```

It is not as bad as it looks. The first line above is the template specification, which must precede all template definitions. The placeholder numtype preceding number specifies the type of n. Finally, n is in scope of the type number<numtype> and is initialised with the value 5. Cutting away the template syntax, for a static int member of a simple class, the external definition would be:

```
int number::n=5;
```

Two template class objects, i1 and i2, are instantiated for the int type and one for float. The program shows that one static int variable is shared by i1 and i2, while a separate one is defined for f1. For each template class object instantiated with a distinct type, a new static data member n is defined. The output results of the program are these:

```
Integer is:  6
Integer is:  7
Float is:  6
```

CTMPL736: TEMPLATE HIERARCHIES

Template classes can be derived from both template and
non-template classes and can themselves be derived
from either template or non-template classes. Here is a
simple example of a hierarchy of class templates that is
used to generate base and derived template classes.

The example used is the familiar **array** container class
with the addition of a class template that uses the **array**
class template as its base. First, the base and derived class
templates are defined:

```
#include <iostream.h>

template <class slottype>
class array
{
protected:
  int size;
  slottype *aptr;
public:
  array(int slots = 1)
  {
    size = slots;
    aptr = new slottype[slots];
  }
  void fill_array();
  void disp_array();
  ~array() { delete [] aptr; }
};

template <class slottype>
class term_array : public array<slottype>
{
public:
  term_array(int slots) :
    array<slottype>(slots)
  {
  }
  void terminate();
  void disp_term_array();
};
```

The class template **array** is unchanged from its original
definition earlier in the section. The **term_array** class
template derived from it is defined with the same parameter
list and with the class type **array<slottype>** publicly
derived.

Within the term_array class template, the constructor
header is interesting. It takes a single argument, slots,
from the instantiation of term_array, and passes that
argument along to the constructor of the base class
template array. Note that the type of the base class must
explicitly be given outside the scope of that class as
array<slottype>.

Finally, the term_array template declares two member
functions that operate on instances of the derived class
template term_array. The member functions of the
array class template are defined as before:

```
template <class slottype>
void array<slottype>::fill_array()
{
   for (int i = 0; i < size; i++)
   {
      cout << "Enter data: ";
      cin >> aptr[i];
   }
}

template <class slottype>
void array<slottype>::disp_array()
{
   for (int i = 0; i < size; i++)
      cout << aptr[i] << " ";
   cout << endl;
}
```

The term_array member functions are defined similarly,
specifying that they are in the scope term_array<slottype>:

```
template <class slottype>
void term_array<slottype>::disp_term_array()
{
   cout << "Contents of terminated array are: ";
   for (int i = 0; aptr[i] != (slottype)0 ; i++)
      cout << aptr[i] << endl;
}

template <class slottype>
void term_array<slottype>::terminate()
{
   cout << "Null terminating the array"
            << endl;
   aptr[size] = (slottype)0;
}
```

The main function defines an instance of the derived class template term_array. It then calls the fill_array member function of the base class array to accept input values and to store those values in the array. This is an operation common to all arrays.

The characteristics of terminated arrays which are additional to those of general arrays are dealt with by the term_array member functions terminate and disp_term_array. The terminate function null-terminates the array and disp_term_array displays it using the insertion operator for the basic type in use.

```
int main()
{
   term_array<char> ac(10);
   cout << "Fill a character array" << endl;
   ac.fill_array();
   ac.terminate();
   ac.disp_term_array();
   array<double> ad(5);
   cout << "Fill a double array" << endl;
   ad.fill_array();
   cout << "Array contents are: ";
   ad.disp_array();
   return(0);
}
```

FRIEND DECLARATIONS

Class templates can contain declarations prefixed with the keyword friend. Such declarations are not members of the class templates within which they appear.

A non-template function or class can be a friend of a template class:

```
template <class slottype>
class array
{
protected:
   int  size;
   slottype *aptr;
public:
   friend void fill_array();
   friend class Document;
   void disp_array();
   ~array() { delete [] aptr; }
};
```

Here, fill_array is no longer a member of array but is a friend to all instantiations for all types of the template class array. Similarly, the class Document is a friend of all instantiations of array, and Document member functions have access to the private data members of array template classes.

The friend relationship can be restricted to a particular type:

```
template <class slottype>
class array
{
protected:
  int size;
  slottype *aptr;
public:
  friend void fill_array(array<slottype>);
  friend class Document<slottype>;
  void disp_array();
  ~array() { delete [] aptr; }
};
```

The class Document is a friend of instances of the class template array for, and only for, the type specifier represented by the placeholder slottype. Similarly, the function fill_array is a friend of instances of the class template array for the specified type.

Templates can contain friends of templates:

```
template <class slottype>
class array
{
protected:
  int size;
  slottype *aptr;
public:
  template <class othertype>
  friend void fill_array(array<othertype>);

  template <class othertype>
    friend class Document;
  void disp_array();
  ~array() { delete [] aptr; }
};
```

Now, all instantiations of fill_array and Document are friends of all template class instances of array.

7.4   Exception Handling

This section deals with the exception-handling mechanism
provided by the C++ language and environment to aid
recovery from error conditions that may arise during
program execution.

The exception-handling syntax of C++ makes procedures
used for finding and dealing with error conditions more
uniform and reduces unwieldy error-processing code.

At the time the first edition of this book appeared in
1993, there were few commercially-available
implementations of C++ environments that catered for
exception handling. This has changed and exception
handling is now widely implemented. Some of the
syntax is difficult and existing descriptions of the subject
seem to lack clarity. A series of short programs is now
presented that illustrate the essential characteristics and
usage of exception handling.

EXCPT741: EXCEPTION HANDLING BASICS

The program below implements exception handling of
the most straightforward kind.

```
#include <iostream.h>
void throw_test(int);
class ob
{
public:
  int member;
};
int main()
{
  int flag = 2;
  try
  {
    throw_test(flag);
  }
    catch(const char * p)
  {
    cout << "Into character catch-handler"
      << endl;
    cout << p << endl;
  }
```

```
  catch(ob& ob_inst)
  {
    cout << "Into object catch-handler"
      << endl;
    cout << "Member value is "
      << ob_inst.member << endl;
  }
  return(0);
}
void throw_test(int flag)
{
  if (flag == 1)
    throw "Panic!!!";
  else
  if (flag == 2);
  {
    ob ob_inst;
      ob_inst.member = 5;
    throw ob_inst;
  }
}
```

A function, throw_test, is called from within a *try block* in main. The function call is the only code enclosed in the try block. If an error condition of some kind arises within throw_test or code called from it, an exception may be *thrown*, to be *caught* by the *catch handlers* that immediately follow the try block.

In this case, the generation of 'exceptions' is contrived: if the value of the parameter flag received by throw_test is 1, an exception of type **const char *** is thrown; if the value is 2, the exception is of the class type **ob**. The two catch handlers following the try block in main respectively match these types. If the value of flag is 1, throw_test exits by throwing the character-string exception "Panic!!!".

The resulting program output is:

```
Into character catch-handler
Panic!!!
```

If the value of flag is 2, throw_test exits by throwing the ob exception ob_inst. Its only data member has the value 5 and the resulting program output is:

```
Into object catch-handler
Member value is 5
```

EXCPT742: NESTED FUNCTIONS IN THE TRY BLOCK

The catch handlers invoked by the exceptions thrown
from the function throw_test in the last example are also
invoked by exceptions thrown from a function indirectly
called from throw_test.

```cpp
#include <iostream.h>

void nest1(int);
void nest2(int);
void throw_test(int);

class ob
{
public:
  int member;
};
int main()
{
  int flag = 1;
  try
  {
    throw_test(flag);
  }
  catch(const char * p)
  {
    cout << "Into character catch-handler"
      << endl;
    cout << p << endl;
  }
  catch(ob& ob_inst)
  {
    cout << "Into object catch-handler" << endl;
    cout << "Member value is "
      << ob_inst.member << endl;
  }

  return(0);
}

void throw_test(int flag)
{
  nest1(flag);
}

void nest1(int flag)
{
  nest2(flag);
}
```

```
void nest2(int flag)
{
   if (flag == 1)
     throw "Panic!!!";
   else
   if (flag == 2);
   {
     ob ob_inst;
      ob_inst.member = 5;
     throw ob_inst;
   }
}
```

In this case, throw_test calls nest1, which in turn calls nest2. All three functions are subject to the try block and the exceptions thrown from nest2 are caught by the catch handlers following that block. The output results of the program are the same as those for EXCPT741.

EXCPT743: CATCH-HANDLER SELECTION

The matching catch handlers closest to the thrown exceptions are those invoked, as in the following example.

```
#include <iostream.h>

void nest1(int);
void nest2(int);
void throw_test(int);

class ob
{
public:
     int member;
};

int main()
{
   int flag = 1;
   try
    {
        throw_test(flag);
    }
    catch(const char * p)
    {
        cout <<
           "Into 'char' catch-handler" <<endl;
        cout << p << endl;
    }
```

```
    catch(ob& ob_inst)
    {
      cout << "Into object catch-handler" << endl;
      cout << "Member value is "
          << ob_inst.member << endl;
    }

    return(0);
}

void throw_test(int flag)
{
   try
   {
      nest1(flag);
   }
   catch(const char * p)
   {
      cout << "Into 'throw_test' character ";
      cout << "catch-handler" << endl;
      cout << p << endl;
   }
}

void nest1(int flag)
{
   nest2(flag);
}

void nest2(int flag)
{
   if (flag == 1)
          throw "Panic!!!";
   else
   if (flag == 2);
   {
      ob ob_inst;
      ob_inst.member = 5;

      throw ob_inst;
   }
}
```

Here both main and throw_test contain try blocks, while
the nested function nest2 generates the exceptions. If
nest2 throws a character-string exception, the matching
catch handler in throw_test is invoked. If it throws an
exception of type ob, the effect is to call the second catch
handler in main.

EXCPT744: Errors in the Exception Handler (1)

For cases where the exception handling facilities are themselves wrongly used or there is an internal failure, the functions terminate and unexpected are provided by the C++ library to perform final error processing. The example following shows the terminate facility in use, while the succeeding example EXCPT745 illustrates use of unexpected.

In the code following, the type of the exception thrown (5) in throw_test is int. This does not match either of the catch handlers defined following the try block in main. Resulting from the call to the set_terminate library function in main:

```
set_terminate(myTerminate);
```

the value of the terminate function is set to myTerminate, defined later in the program.

```cpp
#include <iostream.h>
#include <except.h>

void throw_test(int);
void myUnexpected();
void myTerminate();

class ob
{
public:
    int member;
};

int main()
{
    int flag = 1;
    set_terminate(myTerminate);
    try
    {
        throw_test(flag);
    }
    catch(const char *p)
    {
        cout << "Into character catch-handler"
            << endl;
        cout << p << endl;
    }
```

```
    catch(ob& ob_inst)
    {
        cout << "Into object catch-handler" << endl;
        cout << "Member value is "
            << ob_inst.member << endl;
    }

    return(0);
}
void throw_test(int flag)
{
    if (flag == 1)
        throw(5);
    else
    if (flag == 2);
    {
        ob ob_inst;
        ob_inst.member = 5;

        throw ob_inst;
    }
}
void myUnexpected()
{
    cout << "(My) Unexpected program end"
            << endl;
}
void myTerminate()
{
    cout << "(My) abnormal program termination"
        << endl;
}
```

The program's displayed output is this:

```
(My) abnormal program termination
```

EXCPT745: ERRORS IN THE EXCEPTION HANDLER (2)

To govern the types of exception that may be thrown by a function, an exception specification may be suffixed to the function's header:

```
void throw_test(int flag) throw(const char *, ob)
```

If an exception thrown by the code within the function does not match one of the types specified in the

parentheses following throw, the unexpected facility is
invoked. Resulting from the call to the set_unexpected
library function in main:

```
set_unexpected(myUnexpected);
```

the value of the terminate function is set to
myUnexpected, defined later in the program.

```cpp
#include <iostream.h>
#include <except.h>

void throw_test(int) throw(const char *);
void myUnexpected();
void myTerminate();

class ob
{
public:
    int member;
};

int main()
{
    int flag = 1;
    set_unexpected(myUnexpected);

    try
    {
        throw_test(flag);
    }
    catch(const char *p)
    {
        cout << "Into character catch-handler"
             << endl;
        cout << p << endl;
    }
    catch(ob& ob_inst)
    {
        cout << "Into object catch-handler" << endl;
        cout << "Member value is "
             << ob_inst.member << endl;
    }

    return(0);
}

void throw_test(int flag) throw(const char *, ob)
{
    if (flag == 1)
        throw(5);
```

```
    else
    if (flag == 2);
    {
        ob ob_inst;
         ob_inst.member = 5;

        throw ob_inst;
    }
}
void myUnexpected()
{
    cout << "(My) Unexpected program end"
            << endl;
}
void myTerminate()
{
    cout << "(My) abnormal program termination"
          << endl;
}
```

The program's displayed output is this:

```
(My) Unexpected program end
```

Finally, throw used without an exception specification:

```
    throw;
```

causes the most recently thrown exception to be re-thrown to the catch handlers following the nearest try block.

7.5 Namespaces

The *namespace* is a new scope specification introduced in ANSI C++. Its purpose is to eliminate the kind of name clashes that are common in large ISO C and pre-ANSI C++ programs.

The ISO C language specifies three levels of scope:

- File (translation unit).
- Function (goto-label).
- Local (enclosing block).

Traditional C++ introduced one more, the class scope.

Variables and functions declared and defined in File scope are what we commonly refer to as global variables. The more formal name for a program file is translation unit. If a variable is defined in one translation unit:

```
int glob = 5;
```

it is accessed in another translation by means of an **extern** declaration:

```
extern int glob;
```

and, if glob has not been assigned to after its initialisation, it will in the second translation unit have the value 5.

The C++ class scope makes necessary use of the scope-resolution operator, ::, as explained in Chapter 3:

```
class ob
{
public:
    void func();
};

void ob::func()
{
    //
}
```

None of the levels of scope referred to deals with the problem of the global name clash exemplified by the case of two header files containing similar declarations that may need to be included in the same translation unit:

```
// header1.h

class ob
{
public:
    int x;
};
int func(int);
int func(double);

// header2.h

class ob
{
public:
    double x;
    void f();
};
int func(int);
```

Using the two header files in the same program file causes clashes between the declarations of the class **ob** and the prototypes of the functions **func**. The solution adopted in ANSI C++ is the namespace scope specification coupled with the using declaration:

```
// header1.h
namespace ns1
{
   class ob
   {
   public:
      int x;
   };
   int func(int);
   int func(double);
}
// header2.h
namespace ns2
{
   class ob
   {
   public:
     double x;
     void f();
   };
   int func(int);
}
```

The function **func** declared in the scope of namespace **ns1** is defined as follows:

```
void ns1::f()
{
    //
}
```

and is thus distinguished from the **func** referenced in namespace **ns2**. Equally, the class objects can be distinguished. To define an instance of **ob** as declared in namespace **ns2**, we use any of the three forms:

```
ns2::ob ob_inst;
```

or

```
using ns2::ob; // now using ob as declared in ns2
ob ob_inst;   // define instance of ns2::ob
```

or

```
using namespace ns2;
                    // all ns2 names now current
ob ob_inst;         // define instance of ns2::ob
ns2::func();        // call func as declared by ns2
```

Namespaces are an elegant solution to a problem that has existed since the inception of the C language. They can be viewed as a generalisation of the class-scope specification. At the time of this writing, namespaces are not widely implemented, especially by commercial C++ compilers, but they are mandated for inclusion in the ANSI C++ standard.

7.6   Run Time Type Identification (RTTI)

The fourth major extension to the C++ language as it was defined by Release 2.0 is *run time type identification*, usually referred to as *RTTI*. (The other three are templates, exception handling and namespaces, all subjects of this chapter).

In essence, the facilities of RTTI are applied to a given object to determine its type. The typical usages are:

* Checking that a given pointer is of a type derived from a specified base type.

* Identifying the actual type of a pointer.

RTTI should be used sparingly and with care. The whole point of the inheritance and virtual function mechanisms described in Chapter 6 is that the programmer *need not* know the type of a derived-class pointer in order to use it to call a virtual member function of that derived class. RTTI runs contrary to polymorphism and it is easy to use it badly, allowing degeneration into an alternative form of multi-way switch construct:

```
if (typeid(d1) == typeid(supervisor))
    cout << "It's a supervisor" << endl;
else
if (typeid(d1) == typeid(manager))
    cout << "It's a manager" << endl;
else
if (typeid(d1) == typeid(lineManager))
    cout << "It's a line manager" << endl;
```

Legitimate use of RTTI is found in the case where, for a particular type of derived class, an exception needs to be made. The problem inherent in this is expressed thus: "Given a base class pointer previously assigned an unknown value, how can we ascertain that it points to an instance of the base class or one of its derived classes and, further, how can we determine its actual type?" The answer in both cases, with traditional C++, is that we cannot. RTTI is introduced to realise both of these objectives.

RTTI761: IDENTIFYING DERIVED CLASS OBJECTS

To illustrate RTTI, a shortened form of the employee class hierarchy introduced in Chapter 6 is used. From the main function, a base class pointer is passed as an argument to a global function. That function must determine whether or not the pointer holds a pointer value of derived-class type. If it does, then in the case of managers, the employee is paid. Striking supervisors, on the other hand, are not paid.

The program is organised in the familiar one-include-file and two program-file format.

```
/****************************************************
 *
 *      employee.h
 *
 ****************************************************/
enum qualification {NONE, CERT, DIPLOMA,
DEGREE, POSTGRAD};

class employee
{
protected:
  char *name;
  char *dateOfBirth;
  int individualEmployeeNo;
  static int employeeNo;
  int grade;
  qualification employeeQual;
  float accumPay;
public:
  // constructor
  employee();
```

```cpp
  // destructor
  ~employee();

  virtual void pay();
  void promote(int);      // scale increment
  void displayStatus();
};

class supervisor : public employee
{
private:
  float monthlyPay;
public:
  // constructor
  supervisor();

  // destructor
  ~supervisor();

  void pay();
  void displayStatus();
};

class manager : public employee
{
private:
  float monthlyPay;
  float bonus;
public:
  // constructor
  manager();

  // destructor
  ~manager();

  void pay();
  void displayStatus();
};

//     Global function to demonstrate RTTI
void pay_managers_only(employee *);
```

The include file **employee.h** is very similar to that found in Section 6.2. It makes the **pay** function **virtual**, eliminates the **technician** class from the hierarchy and declares a new function **pay_managers_only**. The definitions of the member functions, presented for completeness in the program file 'empfunc.cpp', are unchanged.

```
/***************************************************
 *
 *      empfunc.cpp
 *
 ***************************************************/
#include <iostream.h>
#include <string.h>
#include "employee.h"

//    define and initialise static member

int employee::employeeNo = 1000;

//    define 'employee' member functions first

employee::employee()
{
  char nameIn[50];

  cout << "Enter new employee name ";
  cin >> nameIn;

  name = new char[strlen(nameIn) + 1];
  strcpy(name, nameIn);
  dateOfBirth = NULL;
  individualEmployeeNo = employeeNo++;
  grade = 1;
  employeeQual = NONE;
  accumPay = 0.0;
}

employee::~employee()
{
  delete name;
  delete dateOfBirth;
}

void employee::pay()
{
}

void employee::promote(int increment)
{
  grade += increment;
}

void employee::displayStatus()
{
}
```

```
//     define 'supervisor' member functions
supervisor::supervisor()
{
  monthlyPay = 1700.00;
  cout << "Supervisor " << name
    << " is hired" << endl;
}

supervisor::~supervisor()
{
  cout << "Supervisor " << name
    << " is fired!" << endl;
}

void supervisor::pay()
{
  accumPay += monthlyPay;
  cout << "Supervisor " << individualEmployeeNo
      << " paid " << monthlyPay << endl;
}

void supervisor::displayStatus()
{
  cout << "Supervisor " << individualEmployeeNo
    << " is of grade " << grade
    << " and has been paid " << accumPay
    << " so far this year" << endl;
}

//     define 'manager' member functions
manager::manager()
{
  monthlyPay = 2100.00;
  bonus    = 210.0;
  cout << "Manager " << name << " is hired"
    << endl;
}

manager::~manager()
{
  cout << "Manager " << name << " is fired!"
    << endl;
}

void manager::pay()
{
  accumPay += monthlyPay;
  cout << "Manager " << individualEmployeeNo
    << " paid " << monthlyPay << endl;
}
```

```
void manager::displayStatus()
{
   cout << "Manager " << individualEmployeeNo
      << " is of grade " << grade
      << " and has been paid " << accumPay
      << " so far this year" << endl;
}
```

The interesting part of the program is in the client code, the main function and the function it calls. This is in the program file 'emp.cpp':

```
/***************************************************
*
*      emp.cpp
*
***************************************************/
#include <iostream.h>
#include "employee.h"

int main()
{
   supervisor s1;
   manager   m1;
   employee  *ep = &s1;

   pay_managers_only(ep);

   ep = &m1;

   pay_managers_only(ep);
   return(0);
}

void pay_managers_only(employee *base)
{
   manager *mp;
   supervisor *sp;
   if ((mp = dynamic_cast<manager *>(base))
      != 0)
      base->pay();
   else
   if ((sp = dynamic_cast<supervisor *>(base))
            != 0)
      cout << "Don't pay striking supervisors"
            << endl;
   else
      cout << "Unknown employee type" << endl;
}
```

From main, pay_managers_only is twice called with a base class pointer (of type employee) as argument. On entering pay_managers_only, no way exists in traditional C++ of determining the type of base. Using RTTI, this is done using the *dynamic cast* mechanism:

```
if ((sp = dynamic_cast<supervisor *>(base)) != 0)
```

If the contents of the pointer base in fact refer to a base or derived object, that pointer is dynamically typecast and assigned to sp. Otherwise, sp is assigned zero. In the example, on the first call (for supervisors) to pay_managers_only, the virtual pay function is not called, while on the second call it is. The program's displayed output is this:

```
Enter new employee name susan
Supervisor susan is hired
Enter new employee name peter
Manager peter is hired
Don't pay striking supervisors
Manager 1001 paid 2100
Manager peter is fired!
Supervisor susan is fired!
```

Syntax is also provided that allows the programmer to determine the precise type of an object. The typeid() operator yields the actual type, not just the information that a given object is or is not of a type included in a class hierarchy. A simple example of typeid() in use follows in the modified file 'emp.cpp'.

```
/****************************************************
 *
 *      emp.cpp
 *
 ****************************************************/
#include <iostream.h>
#include <typeinfo.h>
#include "employee.h"

int main()
{
  supervisor s1;
  manager   m1;
  employee  *ep = &s1;

  pay_managers_only(ep);
```

```
    ep = &m1;

    pay_managers_only(ep);
    return(0);
}

void pay_managers_only(employee *base)
{
    if (typeid(*base) == typeid(manager))
        base->pay();
}
```

The main function is unchanged. The function
pay_managers_only now does an explicit comparison
of types in deciding whether or not to pay the employee.
typeid() returns a reference to library class type_info.
This class is declared in the standard header file
typeinfo.h, which must be included for the type_info
data to be accessible in client code.

The internal specification of type_info is implementation-
dependent but it minimally provides overloaded
assignment and == operators, as well as a function to
return a character pointer to the name of the type found
in the call to typeid().

8 The C++ Library

8.1 Introduction

ANSI C++ introduces the C++ Library. This is an enormously-expanded set of facilities, strictly not part of the C++ language at all, that provides services in the following areas:

- Language Support.
- Diagnostics.
- General Utilities, including memory-handling.
- String-handling.
- Localisation.
- Container Classes.
- Iterator Classes.
- Algorithms, including sort and search.
- Numeric Operations.
- *Stream I/O*.

No fewer than 32 header files are introduced to declare the facilities provided by the library. (The whole ISO C environment specifies 18). In the current ANSI draft standard document, the sections on the C++ library significantly exceed in size those of the whole language definition, covering around 400 pages. Any treatment or explanation of the non-Stream I/O facilities is therefore outside the scope of this book. For further information on these facilities, the reader is referred to the ANSI Working Paper for the Draft Proposed C++ standard, and to *The Draft Standard C++ Library* [Plauger, 1994].

The Stream I/O library and its associated header files are an alternative to the C Standard I/O functions declared in stdio.h.

The C Standard I/O functions are still available to C++ programmers, but use of the Stream I/O functions is preferred. In ways that are explained later in this chapter, Stream I/O facilities are more easily used with the object-oriented design approach and with C++ language constructs.

Stream I/O facilities mimic those of Standard I/O but present a more uniform interface to the programmer and are, perhaps, easier to use.

C Standard I/O facilities are not part of the C language but are implemented in C. In the same way, Stream I/O is implemented using C++ syntax. Because Stream I/O is not part of the C++ language, it is not covered in some C++ references.

Stream I/O is implemented as a hierarchy of classes. The base class is a stream. A stream may represent a file on disk, a peripheral device such as a terminal or printer, or some other system device. It may be an input stream, an output stream or a stream capable of both input and output.

The base stream class also defines the low-level operations that can be carried out on the stream. These low-level operations are hidden from the programmer, who does not need to know how they operate but only how to use the interface provided by higher-level I/O functions declared in classes derived from the base. These functions include get and read for use on input streams and put and write for use on output streams.

It is a characteristic of the C++ Stream I/O library that all its I/O functions and operators may be applied to any stream, depending on whether it is opened for input, output or both. There is no concept of implementing a function for console I/O and another for file I/O, as is the case with printf and fprintf from the C Standard Library. Instead, a single function, for example put, may be used to send output to any stream if it is opened for output.

In addition, the interface presented to the programmer does not change with data type. If we consider a data object X of one of the types char, int, float and double, but we do not know which, then the statement:

```
cout << X;
```

using the Stream I/O operator <<, correctly sends to the output stream the value of X. On the other hand, the C statement:

```
printf("%d", X);
```

fails if X is, for instance, of type double. There is no easy way in C of implementing functions that operate correctly on arbitrary types. Stream I/O functions and operators do this in a *type safe* manner by taking advantage of the C++ function- and operator- overloading capabilities. Stream I/O in these ways provides a uniform programmer interface and eliminates some of the more piecemeal aspects of the C Standard I/O library.

The Stream I/O class hierarchy is declared in the header files iostream.h, fstream.h and iomanip.h, which collectively replace stdio.h. C++ implements the standard I/O streams with the following instances of classes declared in the Stream I/O class hierarchy:

cin	Standard input
cout	Standard output
cerr	Standard error
clog	Buffered cerr for voluminous error text

Any of the functions or operators that are declared as members of those classes may be called using the standard syntax for accessing class members. For example:

```
char c;
cin.get(c);
```

causes a character to be read from the standard input, and:

```
cout.put(c);
```

writes a character to the standard output.

It is important to note that functions and operators are members of the stream classes and can only affect the status of stream objects with which they are called. In the put example above, only the status of the standard output is altered. The character will not appear as output on any other stream.

Similarly, functions such as setf, which sets input and output data formats, set formats only for the class object with which they are called, never globally for all streams.

In many places in previous chapters, the << and >> operators are used for simple Stream I/O with the output and input stream objects cout and cin. Here is some explanation of why these operators are introduced with Stream I/O.

One of the goals of C++ is to implement type-safety: the ability correctly to perform an operation or call a function regardless of the types of the data used as operands or arguments. This is done in two ways: with overloaded functions and overloaded operators. As we have seen, the function call:

```
printf("%d",X);
```

is only good when X is an integral data type. Using C++ function overloading syntax, it might be possible multiply to define printf so that it could be called appropriately for the data types to be output. This, however, would be clumsy and would result in a large number of overloadings of printf.

Instead, the operators << for output and >> for input are overloaded. The<< operator overloaded for stream output is called the *insertion operator* or *inserter*. When used, it is said to insert bytes on the output stream. The >> operator overloaded for stream input is called the *extraction operator* or *extractor*. When used, it is said to extract bytes from the input stream.

The extractor and inserter operators are basic C++ bit-shift operators overloaded to have multiple definitions as operator functions. The multiple overloadings allow the operators to be used for input and output of objects of many different data types; they take care of type-safety, not the programmer.

The << and >> operators are the ones overloaded because they are easy to relate intuitively to the output and input operations and because their precedence is lower than that of the arithmetic operators. This makes possible the following (unparenthesised) statement:

```
cout << 5 + 5;
```

which sends the value 10 to the standard output stream.

The insertion and extraction operators, together with methods of formatting data sent to output and input streams by them, are examined in the next three sections.

Here is a highly simplified diagram of the Stream I/O class hierarchy with a short summary of the relevant functions and operators that are members of the various classes:

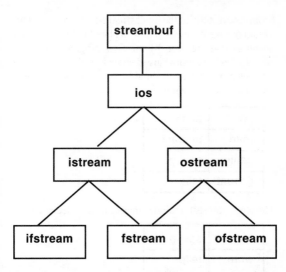

The streambuf class is declared in the header file iostream.h. It describes the stream buffer objext and defines low-level I/O operations such as these:

- The sgetc function looks at the next character on the stream without reading it.

- The sputn function writes a number of characters to a stream.

Usually, C++ programmers do not have to be concerned with the definitions contained in the streambuf class or the details of the low-level I/O performed by it.

The ios (I/O state) class, also declared in iostream.h, inherits streambuf and additionally contains information about the state of the stream. This includes the stream open mode, seek direction and format flags, all of which are dealt with later in this chapter. The following functions are also declared in the ios class:

| flags | setf | unsetf | width | fill | precision | |
| tie | rdstate | eof | fail | bad | good | clear |

The functions in the first row are for data formatting and are explained in the next section. The functions in the second concern the state of the stream and are covered in Section 8.8.

From ios are derived the input stream istream and output stream ostream classes. These declare I/O functions and operators that are used by the C++ programmer. Both istream and ostream are declared in the header file iostream.h. istream contains function declarations including the following:

get	peek
read	putback
getline	seekg
gcount	tellg

The class ostream includes these function declarations:

put	seekp
write	tellp

istream also contains the definitions of the overloaded extractor >>, while ostream contains the definitions for the inserter <<.

The class iostream inherits both istream and ostream. It is declared in iostream.h. It additionally defines *manipulators* (explained in Sections 8.3 and 8.4), which can be used on both input and output streams, and the four standard streams cin, cout, cerr and clog.

The file I/O classes ifstream and ofstream are declared in the header file fstream.h. ifstream inherits all the standard input stream operations defined by istream and adds a few more, such as constructors and functions for opening files. ofstream similarly augments the inherited definitions of ostream.

Finally, fstream, declared in the header file fstream.h, inherits iostream and contains functions and constructors that allow files to be opened in input-output mode.

A more detailed list of Stream I/O functions, the classes of which they are members, their return types and arguments is given in Section 8.9.

8.2   Formatted I/O

All Stream I/O done in earlier chapters is unformatted: the manner in which data is written to the standard output stream and read from the standard input stream is not explicitly specified. The formats of output and input data are default settings used by the insertion and extraction operators. It is possible for the C++ programmer to specify these formats explicitly. This is done in three ways:

- The setf, unsetf and flags functions use format flags to alter input and output data. The ios class enumerates the flag values and also declares the functions.

- The ios class member functions width, precision and fill, are used to set the format of input and output data.

- Using manipulators, special functions that combine the above two techniques and add some more.

This section deals with the first two methods of formatting data. Manipulators are covered in the next three sections.

FORMAT FLAGS

Every C++ input and output stream has defined for it (in the ios base class) a number of format flags that determine the appearance of input and output data. These flags are represented in bit form within a long integer and are defined as an enumerated type within the class ios as follows:

```
class ios
{
public:
  // formatting flags
  enum
  {
    // skip white space on input
    skipws= 0x0001,
    // left-adjust output
    left         = 0x0002,
    // right-adjust output
    right        = 0x0004,
```

```
        // pad after sign or base indicator
        internal      = 0x0008,
        // decimal conversion
        dec           = 0x0010,
        // octal conversion
        oct           = 0x0020,
        // hexadecimal conversion
        hex           = 0x0040,
        // show integer base on output
        showbase      = 0x0080,
        // show decimal point and trailing zeros
        showpoint     = 0x0100,
        // uppercase hex output
        uppercase     = 0x0200,
        // explicit + with positive integers
        showpos       = 0x0400,
        // scientific notation
        scientific    = 0x0800,
        // floating notation (e.g. 123.45)
        fixed         = 0x1000,
        // flush output after each output
        // operation
        unitbuf       = 0x2000,
        // flush output after each character
        // inserted
        stdio         = 0x4000
    };
    //
};
```

The actual numeric values associated with the enumerations are implementation-dependent. While they will often be those shown here, this cannot be guaranteed.

Here is a simple example of how to use format flags. An integer is defined and initialised to a decimal value. It is then written to the standard output in its hexadecimal form, showing the base (0X) in uppercase:

```
int number = 45;

// set uppercase hexadecimal and show the base
cout.setf(ios::hex | ios::showbase |
            ios::uppercase);
cout << number << endl;
```

In this example, the trailing newline output to cout is replaced by endl. This is first introduced in Chapter 1.

endl is a manipulator that has the effect of inserting a newline on the stream and flushing the stream. The output of the code is this:

```
0X2D
```

The bit values of the ios flags hex, showbase and uppercase are combined using the logical OR statement and used as the argument to the setf member function of the cout stream. The format flags set in this way cause all subsequent integers written to the standard output to be displayed in hexadecimal, until the flags are changed or unset. The flags may be switched off using the unsetf function:

```
cout.unsetf(ios::hex | ios::showbase |
            ios::uppercase);
```

After this operation, the output format reverts to what it was before the call to setf. Here are the prototypes of the setf, unsetf and flags functions:

```
long setf(long);
long setf(long, long);
long unsetf(long);
long flags();
long flags(long);
```

The function setf called with a single argument of type long turns on the format flags specified in that argument. setf returns the format flag values as they were before the call to setf. An overloaded definition of setf takes two long arguments. A call to this function turns off the flags specified by the second argument and then turns on the flags specified by the first. The function returns the format flag values as they were before it was called. The function call:

```
flaga = cout.setf(flagb, flagc);
```

is equivalent to the two function calls:

```
flaga = cout.unsetf(flagc);
cout.setf(flagb);
```

The function unsetf turns off the flags specified by its argument and returns the format flag values as they were before unsetf was called.

A call to the flags function without arguments returns the current state of the format flags. The flags function called with one long argument sets the format flags to the values specified by that argument and returns the values of the flags as they were before the call to flags. This function is important in being the only one of the five shown that actually clears all previous format flag settings.

FMT821: MANIPULATING FORMAT FLAGS

Here is an example program that exercises all five flag-setting functions as well as a number of the format flags.

```cpp
#include <iostream.h>

int main()
{
  long old_flags; // old flag values
  long tmp_flags; // temporary flag values
  long new_flags; // new flag values
  int number = 45;

  //   store original format flag values
  old_flags = cout.flags();

  //   show + sign if positive
  cout.setf(ios::showpos);
  cout << number << endl;

  //   set uppercase hexadecimal and show
  //   the base
  new_flags = ios::hex | ios::showbase |
    ios::uppercase;
  tmp_flags = cout.setf(new_flags);
  cout << number << endl;

  //   display twice to show that setf
  //   is persistent
  cout << number << endl;

  //   unset the uppercase flag
  cout.unsetf(ios::uppercase);
  cout << number << endl;

  //   revert to showpos only
  cout.setf(tmp_flags, new_flags);
  cout << number << endl;

  //   return to original format flag values
  new_flags = cout.flags(old_flags);
```

```
   cout << number << endl;
   return(0);
}
```

This is the output when the program is run:

```
+45
0X2D
0X2D
0x2d
+45
45
```

Because the individual flag values are members of the **ios**
class, they must be scope-resolved when they are used:
ios::hex is correct, while **hex** alone is not.

Where a number of flags are to be used as arguments to
setf, **unsetf** or **flags**, it is preferable first to assign them
to a long integer and use that as the argument:

```
new_flags = ios::hex | ios::showbase |
            ios::uppercase;
tmp_flags = cout.setf(new_flags);
```

Format flag settings only affect output of the appropriate
types: the flags used in the program above have no effect
on the output of, for example, the contents of a character
array.

Formatting can be done on data being sent to any stream,
input or output. Here is a simple example of formatting
data from the standard input:

```
#include <iostream.h>

int main()
{
   int number;

   cout << "Enter an octal number: ";

   cin.setf(ios::oct);
   cin >> number;

   cout << "Decimal equivalent is: "
            << number << endl;

   return(0);
}
```

If 45 (octal) is entered, the output is 37 (decimal).

Finally, here is a brief description of the characteristics of the format flags not used in the foregoing examples.

- **dec** is used to control the number base, converting output integers to decimal and causing input integers to be treated as decimal; it is the default base value.

- **skipws**, if set (which is the default), causes white space to be skipped on input using the extraction operator.

- **left** and **right** cause field-justification with padding by a fill character; right is the default.

- **internal** causes the fill character to be inserted between any leading sign or base and the value.

- **showpoint** causes a decimal point and trailing zeros to be output for floating-point numbers, whether they are needed or not.

- **scientific** causes floating-point display to be of the form:

m.ppppppex

where **m** is a digit, followed by a decimal point and a number of digits to a precision specified by the current precision value (see **precision()** below). The default precision is 6. The decimals are followed either by **e** or **E** (the latter if **ios::fixed** is set) and an exponent. The value:

3141.592654

displayed in scientific form is:

3.141593e03

- **fixed** causes floating-point values to be displayed in normal (non-scientific) notation.

- **unitbuf** and **stdio**, when set, cause the output buffers to be flushed after each output operation and output character respectively.

Although effective, formatting using flags is clumsy and prone to programmer error. Use of manipulators for formatting is preferred.

FIELD WIDTH AND PRECISION

The ios class member functions width, precision and fill may be used to do further formatting on input or output data. Here are the prototypes of these functions:

```
int width(int);
int width();

int precision(int);
int precision();

char fill(char);
char fill();
```

Each function is overloaded. In each case, a call without an argument returns the current status: the field width; the precision; or the current fill character.

The width function called with an integer argument sets the minimum output field width to the value of that argument. The function returns the field width as it was before the function call. If the data output to the field is not wide enough to fill it, the field is padded; if it is wider than the field, the data is not truncated. The effect of the width function is not persistent. The minimum field width is reset to zero after the first insertion or extraction operation which follows a call to width. If zero is specified as the value of the argument to width, it is interpreted to mean no minimum width.

The precision function called with one integer argument sets the number of places of decimals that should be shown on output of a floating-point number. The function returns the precision value as it was before the function call. The effect of a call to precision is persistent and must be explicitly reset. The default precision is 6.

The fill function called with one argument of type char specifies that character as the fill character used to pad fields that are incompletely filled. The previous fill character is returned. The effect of the fill function is persistent; the fill character must be explicitly reset. The default fill character is the space.

FMT822: FILL, PRECISION AND WIDTH

Here is an example program which exercises all three functions:

```cpp
#include <iostream.h>

int main()
{
    double pi = 3.141592654;

    //  default display is left-justified with
    //  precision 6
    cout << pi << endl;

    //  set precision 4, field width 12 and
    //  fill character +
    cout.precision(4);
    cout.width(12);
    cout.fill(+);

    cout << pi << endl;

    //  width setting is not persistent
    //  fill setting is

    cout.width(12);
    cout << pi << endl;

    //  precision without argument keeps
    //  previous value
    cout << "Current precision: "
            << cout.precision() <<  endl;
    cout.precision(8);

    //  width does not truncate
    cout.width(2);
    cout.fill(-);
    cout << pi << endl;
    return(0);
}
```

The results output when the program is run are these:

```
3.141593
++++++3.1416
++++++3.1416
Current precision: 4
3.14159265
```

As with the **setf** family of functions, **width**, **precision** and **fill** may be used with any stream, input or output, although they are better suited to use with output streams.

8.3   Stream Output

The overloaded inserter << is used for stream output. It
can be used to direct output to any stream, not just cout.
All insertion operations on the standard output are equally
valid on other programmer-defined streams, such as
files. In this section, the standard output stream cout is
used to illustrate insertion, manipulators and functions
for stream output.

INSERTERS

Stream I/O provides the insertion operator overloaded to
handle a number of data types. These types are referred
to as built-in insertion types. Overloading of the insertion
operator is done according to the rules of operator
overloading, explained in Chapter 5. This short program
illustrates how the insertion operator is overloaded:

```
#include <iostream.h>

int main()
{
   float f = 2.71828;

   cout << f;

   cout.operator<<(f);
   return(0);
}
```

The insertion operations on cout are equivalent and
identical in their effect. In the second, full form, the
operator function operator<< is explicitly called for the
output stream cout. operator<< returns a reference to a
class (stream) object of the type with which it is called,
in this case ostream. This makes it possible to chain
insertion operations in the way we have already seen
many times:

```
cout << "Value of e is: " << f << endl;
```

The built-in Stream I/O inserter types are listed below. It
is possible to define further overloaded operator functions
for insertion. These are of the same form and behaviour
as the built-in inserters. Customised inserters are dealt
with in Section 8.5.

| char (signed and unsigned) |
| short (signed and unsigned) |
| int (signed and unsigned) |
| long (signed and unsigned) |
| const char * (string) |
| float |
| double |
| long double |
| void * (void pointer, hex address) |

MANIPULATORS

When data is directed to an input or output stream, it can be formatted using a notation, known as the manipulator, which is more compact and easier to use than the format flags and setf functions explained in Section 8.2.

Manipulators are formatting functions that may be used between insertion or extraction operators instead of beforehand, as is the case with functions of the setf family. Here are simple equivalent examples:

```
cout.setf(ios::oct);  // set flags octal
cout << number << endl;  // octal output

//    equivalent manipulator operation
cout << oct << number << endl;
```

A manipulator function returns a reference to a stream object of the type with which it is called. Overloaded inserter and extractor operators also return a reference to a stream object. This makes it possible for a manipulator to be part of a bigger I/O operation and to be embedded between insertion and extraction operators.

Stream I/O provides a set of built-in manipulator functions. The operations allowed by these manipulators closely parallel those explained in Section 8.2 for format flags. The list of built-in manipulators for output to any stream is shown below.

Manipulator	Purpose
dec	decimal conversion (default)
endl	insert newline and flush stream
ends	insert null character
flush	flush the output stream
hex	hexadecimal conversion
oct	octal conversion
resetiosflags(f)	reset format bits specified by f
setbase(b)	set number to base b
setfill(c)	set fill character to c
setiosflags(f)	set format bits specified by f
setprecision(p)	set precision to p
setw(w)	set field width to w

MANIP83: MANIPULATORS

The following example program shows all of these manipulators in use.

```
#include <iostream.h>
#include <iomanip.h>

int main()
{
   char string[20] = {a,b,c,d,e,f};
   double pi = 3.141592654;
   int n_dec = 35;
   int n_oct = 035;

   //  Demonstrate simple output manipulators
   cout << "Octal: " << oct << n_dec << endl;
   cout << "Decimal: " << dec << n_oct << endl;
   cout << "Hex: " << hex << n_oct << endl;

   //  Rightmost manipulator overrides others
   cout << "Hex: " << hex << dec << n_oct
           << endl;

   //  Convert octal number to decimal, pad
   //  output field of width 6 with blanks
```

```cpp
    cout << "Padded: " << setw(6) << dec
            << n_oct << endl;

//   Equivalent operation: convert using
//   setbase and pad field with zeros
    cout << "Padded: " << setw(6)
            << setfill(0)
            << setbase(10)
            << n_oct
            << endl;

//   PI output in field-width 8, precision 4
    cout << "Rounded PI: " << setw(8)
            << setprecision(4)
            << pi
            << endl;

//   Precision 8, field width 4: output is
//   expanded
    cout << "Rounded PI: " << setw(4)
            << setprecision(8)
            << pi
            << endl;

//   Output null-terminated character array
    cout << "String: " << string << ends
            << endl;

//   Display PI in scientific notation
    cout << "Exponent PI: "
            << setiosflags(ios::scientific)
            << pi << endl;

//   Display an integer left-justified
//   in hex
    cout << "Hex: " << setw(10)
            << setiosflags(ios::left | ios::hex)
            << n_dec
            << endl;

//   Display an integer right-justified
//   in hex
    cout << "Hex: " << setw(10)
            << resetiosflags(ios::left)
            << n_dec
            << endl;

//   Flush output and stop
    cout << "Finished...." << flush << endl;
    return(0);
}
```

The output displayed by the program is this:

```
Octal: 43
Decimal: 29
Hex: 1d
Hex: 29
Padded:    29
Padded: 000029
Rounded PI: 003.1416
Rounded PI: 3.14159265
String: abcdef
Exponent PI: 3.14159265e+00
Hex: 2300000000
Hex: 0000000023
Finished....
```

The manipulators **setiosflags** and **resetiosflags**, combined in use with the format flags defined in the class **ios**, are equivalent to **setf** and **unsetf**, while promoting shorter and more concise coding. The include file **iomanip.h** must be included if manipulators taking arguments are used.

FUNCTIONS

There are two functions, in addition to the inserters and manipulators already described, for simple output to a stream. The **put** member function of the **ostream** class writes a single character to an output stream. Its lone prototype is:

```
ostream& put(char);
```

The class **ostream** contains a member function **flush**, with this prototype:

```
ostream& flush();
```

This definition is overloaded by a manipulator, also called **flush**, which has the prototype:

```
ostream& flush(ostream&);
```

Using either version of **flush** has the effect of flushing and writing the contents of the buffered stream for which it is called.

```
cout.flush();        // function call
//  equivalent use of manipulator
cout << "Finished...." << flush << endl;
```

Further output functions are dealt with separately in Section 8.7, where they are used for the random access of files opened in binary mode.

8.4   Stream Input

The facilities provided by Stream I/O for input are symmetrical to those for output. The overloaded extraction operator >> is used for stream input. It can be used to accept input from any stream, not just cin. All extraction operations on the standard input are equally valid on other programmer-defined streams, such as files. In this section, the standard input stream cin is used to illustrate insertion, manipulators and functions for stream input.

EXTRACTORS

Extractors share many characteristics with inserters:

- Extractors, like inserters, are overloaded operator functions.

- An extractor operator function returns a reference to a class (stream) object of the type with which it is called.

- Extraction operations may be chained in the same way as insertion operations.

- An extractor can be used for any input stream; there is no concept of separate operations for different streams, along the lines of scanf and fscanf in the C Standard Library.

- Extractors may be customised (see Section 8.5).

The following are the built-in Stream I/O inserter types:

char (signed and unsigned)
short (signed and unsigned)
int (signed and unsigned)
long (signed and unsigned)
const char * (string)
float
double
long double

Extraction operations that accept input from the standard I/O stream cin by default skip leading white spaces and white-space-separated input. This can be changed with the skipws format flag or the ws manipulator (see the example below). Extraction fails if data of a type not matching the receiving variables is received. The stream error-state function good can be used to catch and report on such errors. An example of this is shown in Section 8.8.

The long (L), float (F) and unsigned (U) suffixes cannot correctly be used as part of data extracted from a stream.

MANIPULATORS

Stream I/O provides a set of built-in manipulators for input. Input manipulators are defined and used in a way that is essentially the reverse of output manipulators. All the rules surrounding use of input manipulators are the same:

- Input manipulators are embedded between extractor operators.
- The setiosflags and resetiosflags manipulators combine format flags and manipulators.
- setiosflags is equivalent in effect to setf.
- resetiosflags is equivalent in effect to unsetf.
- iomanip.h must be included if input manipulators are used which take arguments.

Here is the list of built-in manipulators for input from any stream:

Manipulator	Purpose
dec	decimal conversion (default)
hex	hexadecimal conversion
oct	octal conversion
ws	skip white space characters
resetiosflags(f)	reset format bits specified by f
setfil(c)	set fill character to c
setiosflags(f)	set format bits specified by f
setw(w)	set field width to w

MANIP84: MANIPULATORS

The following example program shows a number of these manipulators in use.

```
#include <iostream.h>
#include <iomanip.h>

int main()
{
   //   do a numeric conversion
   int n_dec;

   cout << "Enter a hexadecimal number: ";

   //   dont skip leading white spaces!!
   cin >> resetiosflags(ios::skipws) >> hex
            >> n_dec;
   cout << "Decimal conversion of hex input: "
            << n_dec << endl;

   //   break an input string
   char buf1[20];
   char buf2[20];

   cout << "Enter a string\n";
   cin >> setw(10) >> buf1;
   cin >> buf2;
   cout << "String 1 " << buf1 << endl;
   cout << "String 2 " << buf2 << endl;
   return(0);
}
```

The first interesting aspect of this program is the unsetting of the default flag ios::skipws. Ordinarily, white space before input of the hexadecimal number is ignored. The new flag setting causes leading white spaces to be treated as part of the number, with predictably unpleasant results.

The second part of the program accepts an array of characters of arbitrary length from the input stream. If the input contains more than 10 characters, it is broken into two parts. If the input is abcdefghijklmnopq then the contents of buf1 are displayed at the end of the program as a null-terminated string of nine characters:

  abcdefghi

The remainder of the characters are stored, null-terminated, in buf2.

The setw manipulator is useful for ensuring that the length of data input to an array with an extractor does not exceed the array bounds; the data that cannot be accommodated in the array is discarded or used by the next input operation.

FUNCTIONS

Stream I/O provides a number of functions, in addition to the inserters and manipulators already described, for simple input from a stream.

The get function has a number of overloadings allowing different definitions of the function to perform different tasks on an input stream. These are the get prototypes:

```
int         get();

istream&    get(char&);

istream&    get(char *, int l, char d = '\n');
```

The second and third forms are also overloaded to accept an unsigned first parameter; these prototypes are not shown. Given these definitions:

```
char c;
int  i;
char carr[20];
```

and extracting from the input stream, cin, the following calls to get are valid:

```
i = cin.get();      // read one character, white
                    // space or not

cin.get(c);  // read one character, white
             // space or not

cin.get(carr,20);   // get at most 20 characters
                    // into the array carr
                    // until default newline
                    // seen but not read from
                    // the stream
```

The peek function has only one definition. Its prototype is:

```
int peek();
```

peek looks ahead at, without reading, the next character on the input stream.

This is the prototype of putback:

```
istream& putback(char);
```

putback pushes an already-read character back onto the input stream; it will be read by the next input operation.

The getline function is equivalent to the third definition of get above, except that it also reads the delimiter which is, by default, a newline character. get leaves the delimiter on the input stream. This is the prototype of getline:

```
istream& getline(char* b, int len, char d = '\n');
```

getline reads at most len characters, delimited by the character d or by default a newline, into the array pointed to by b.

The gcount function returns the number of characters read by the last read operation on an input stream. Its prototype is this:

```
int gcount();
```

The ignore function is similar to a flush function for an input stream. (No input-stream flush function is defined in Stream I/O.) This is its prototype:

```
istream& ignore(int len = 1, int d = EOF);
```

When ignore is called, it discards up to len characters (default value 1) or until a delimiter character is encountered on the input stream. The delimiter character is also discarded. Examples of these functions in use are given in file-processing programs in Sections 8.6 and 8.7.

8.5   Customising Stream I/O

Using the function and operator-overloading facilities of C++, it is possible for the programmer to define new extractors and inserters and to define new manipulators for use with input and output streams.

INSERTERS AND EXTRACTORS

The << and >> operators can be overloaded to have meanings additional to those specified by the built-in insertion and extraction types and listed in the last two sections. In this way, objects of types other than the built-in extractor and inserter types (see Sections 8.3 and 8.4) can be inserted on an output stream or extracted from an input stream.

The general form of an overloaded-operator function for insertion is this:

```
ostream& operator<<(ostream& s, <classname> c)
{
    //   operator-function statements
    return (s);
}
```

Elsewhere in the program, the newly-defined operator might be used like this:

```
class classname
{
    // declarations
}c;
    .
    .
cout << c;
```

The overloaded insertion operator can be used with any output stream, not just cout. If an object to the right of the << operator is of the type of class specified as the second argument of the operator function, the overloaded meaning of the operator is used; otherwise the appropriate built-in meaning is used. An overloaded inserter function must return an output stream object of the same type as the stream with which the function is called, in this case cout. This makes it possible for overloaded insertion operations to be chained.

The left operand of the overloaded << is an output stream object, cout. This is supplied as the first argument to operator<<. The right operand of << is a class object, c, and is passed as the second argument to operator<<.

The overloaded inserter must not be a member of the same class as that of the class object to its right. In the example above, it must not be a member of the class classname. When the overloaded inserter is used, a this pointer referring to the stream object used to call it, in this case cout, is quietly passed as the first argument.

If operator<< were a member of classname, the this pointer would refer to a class object of that type, not the required output stream object.

Recall that, for all overloaded operators, at least one operand must be an object of the class of which the operator is a member. Because the left operand of the overloaded inserter must be a stream object, the right operand must be a class object of this type.

Because the overloaded inserter function cannot be a member of the class on which it operates, it is normal to declare it as a **friend** of that class:

```
class classname
{
  // declarations
  friend ostream& operator<<(ostream&,
classname);
}c;
```

The gives the overloaded operator function full access to all members of the **classname** class while preserving its non-member status.

INSERT85: OVERLOADED INSERTER

Here is a full example program that implements an operator function to overload the inserter:

```
#include <iostream.h>

class coord
{
private:
  int x_coord, y_coord;
public:
  coord(int x, int y)
  {
    x_coord = x;
    y_coord = y;
  }
  void print()
  {
    cout << x_coord << " " << y_coord
              << "\n";
  }
  //   declare overloaded inserter
  friend ostream& operator<<(ostream&, coord);
};

int main()
{
  coord point1 = coord(5,10);
```

```
    cout <<
      "Coordinates with built-in inserter: ";
    point1.print();

    cout <<
      "Coordinates with overloaded inserter: ";
    cout << point1;
    // operator<<(cout, point1);  // also legal!
    return(0);
  }

  ostream& operator<<(ostream& s, coord p)
  {
    s << p.x_coord << " " << p.y_coord << endl;

    return(s);
  }
```

The inserter is overloaded so that, when an object of the class type **coord** is encountered as part of an insertion statement, the processing specified by the **operator<<** function is done. While the **operator<<** function may specify any statements, the processing carried out by it should be related to the semantics of the << operator. The function should not, for example, do unrelated graphic output or mathematical calculations. This piece of good practice also applies to overloaded extractors and manipulators, described below. The program's output is:

```
Coordinates with built-in inserter:
5 10
Coordinates with overloaded
inserter: 5 10
```

It is worth noting that the statement **operator<<(cout, point1);** is equivalent to **cout << point1;** and probably helps make clearer the mechanism by which the overloaded inserter is called.

The extractor >> can be overloaded in a parallel manner to that already shown for insertion. The general form of the overloaded extractor function is this:

```
  istream& operator>>
    (istream& s, <classname> c)
  {
    //  operator-function statements
    return (s);
  }
```

The overloaded extractor might be used like this:

```
class classname
{
  // declarations
}c;
    .
    .
cin >> c;
```

The overloaded extraction operator can be used with any input stream, not just cin. If an object to the right of the >> is of the class type specified as the second argument of the operator function, the overloaded meaning of the operator is used; otherwise the appropriate built-in meaning is used. The other rules surrounding overloading of the insertion operator also apply to overloading the extractor.

EXTRACT85: OVERLOADED EXTRACTOR

Here is a program that implements an overloaded extractor:

```cpp
#include <iostream.h>

class coord
{
private:
  int x_coord, y_coord;
public:
  void get_coords()
  {
    cout << "Enter x and y coordinates: ";
    cin >> x_coord >> y_coord;
  }
  void print()
  {
    cout << "Coordinates: " << x_coord << " "
                    << y_coord << endl;
  }
  //   declare overloaded extractor
  friend istream& operator>>(istream&, coord&);
};
int main()
{
  coord point1;

  //   get co-ordinate values with built-in
  //   extractor
```

```
    point1.get_coords();
    point1.print();

    //   get co-ordinate values with overloaded
    //   extractor
    cin >> point1;    // standard notation
    // operator>>(cin, point1);      // legal

    // equivalent
    point1.print();
    return(0);
}

istream& operator>>(istream& s, coord& p)
{
    cout << "Enter x and y co-ordinates: ";
    s >> p.x_coord >> p.y_coord;

    return(s);
}
```

Here, **operator>>** prompts the user for input of a pair of coordinates. These are directly copied using the (non-overloaded) extractor to the data members **p.x_coord** and **p.y_coord**. The changed input stream is then returned to the point at which **operator>>** is called.

MANIPULATORS

Overloading input and output manipulators is similar in technique to overloading extractors and inserters.

The built-in manipulators are used to allow formatting operations to be integrated concisely into I/O statements. Sometimes, the programmer will want to group a number of operations under the heading of a customised manipulator, especially if these operations are often repeated.

MANIP851: OVERLOADED OUTPUT MANIPULATOR

The following example program implements a customised output manipulator called **format**.

```
#include <iostream.h>
#include <iomanip.h>

//   prototype for output manipulator
ostream& format(ostream&);
```

```cpp
int main()
{
   double pi = 3.141592654;

   // default display is left-justified with
   // precision 6
   cout << pi << endl;

   // use custom manipulator to set
   // precision, width and fill character
   cout << format << pi << endl;

   // effects of width and fill are not
   // persistent, use custom manipulator
   // again

   // display left-justified and with
   // trailing fill characters
   cout << format << setiosflags(ios::left)
            << pi << endl;
   return(0);
}

ostream& format(ostream& s)
{
   s.precision(4);
   s.width(12);
   s.fill(+);

   return(s);
}
```

Both the return value and the single argument of the customised manipulator format must be an output stream object of the type with which the function is called. In this case, that type is ostream. The format manipulator sets output precision to 4, field width to 12 and the fill character to + before returning the output stream in its changed state. The output of the program is this:

```
3.141593
++++++3.1416
3.1416++++++
```

MANIP852: Overloaded Input Manipulator

Similarly, a customised input manipulator can be defined. In the example below, the manipulator is called truncate and is used in place of the standard setw manipulator to set the field width to 10.

```
#include <iostream.h>
#include <iomanip.h>

//  prototype for custom input manipulator
istream& truncate(istream&);

int main()
{
  //  break an input string
  char buf1[20];
  char buf2[20];

  cout << "Enter a string\n";

  //  use custom manipulator to set field
  //  width
  cin >> truncate >> buf1; cin >> buf2;
  cout << "String 1 " << buf1 << endl;
  cout << "String 2 " << buf2 << endl;
  return(0);
}

istream& truncate(istream& s)
{
  s >> setw(10);

  return(s);
}
```

8.6   File I/O

Using Stream I/O, a file is opened by linking it with an input, output or input-output stream. This is done either by explicitly calling the stream member function **open** or allowing the stream constructor to open the file implicitly.

All of the I/O functions so far described may be used to access files other than the standard streams. Input functions must be used on files opened for input, and output functions on files opened for output. Both input and output functions may be used to access files opened in input-output mode.

Similarly, the extraction operator and input manipulators may be used to read files opened in input or input-output mode; and the insertion operator and output manipulators may be used to write to files opened in output or input-output mode.

Further Stream I/O functions are introduced in this section and the next; these may similarly be used to access files opened in the appropriate mode.

A file is closed by disassociating it from its stream. This is done either explicitly by the stream member function **close** or implicitly by the stream destructor.

To use files under Stream I/O, the **fstream.h** header file must be included. **fstream.h**, includes the three classes **ifstream**, **ofstream** and **fstream**, for input, output and input-output files respectively. These classes declare all the functions needed to access files in input, output and input-output modes. For example, **ifstream** declares **get**, **ofstream** declares **put** and both declare versions of **open**.

Before a file can be opened, an object of the required stream type must be defined:

```
ifstream ins;
```

Now a file may be opened for input by using the **ifstream** member function **open**:

```
ins.open("infile");
```

The stream **ins** is now linked to the file **infile** and input operations can be carried out on that file using the **ins** stream object name. The file can also be opened automatically using the **ifstream** constructor:

```
ifstream ins("infile");
```

Opening a file with the constructor is more common than explicit use of the **open** function.

If the file **infile** does not exist, it is created. When the file has been opened, the stream object **ins** keeps track of the current state of the file: its size; open mode; access characteristics; current position of the read pointer; and error conditions, if any. The file may explicitly be closed using the stream member function **close**:

```
ins.close();
```

If the file is not closed in this way, it is automatically closed by the **ifstream** destructor when the stream object **ins** goes out of scope.

It is sufficient to open a file using its name only. This is done in the examples above and default values are assumed for the other two arguments that can be supplied. The full prototype of the input stream **open** function, declared in the class **ifstream**, is this:

```
void open(char *n, int m = ios::in,
   int p = filebuf::openprot);
```

The output stream **open** function, declared in **ofstream**, has this prototype:

```
void open(char *n, int m = ios::out,
   int p = filebuf::openprot);
```

The input-output **open** function is declared in **fstream** as follows:

```
void open(char *n, int m,
   int p = filebuf::openprot);
```

The first argument in all cases is a string representing the file name; the second is the open mode; and the third the file access permissions.

The open mode for input files is by default **ios::open**. For output files, it is by default **ios::out**. For input-output files, there is no default and a mode flag must explicitly be specified. The mode flags are defined in stream class **ios** as an enumerated type and are these:

```
class ios
{
public:
  // stream modes
enum open_mode
{
  in  = 0x01,              // open for reading
  out = 0x02,              // open for writing
  ate = 0x04,              // seek to eof upon
                           // original open
  app = 0x08,              // append mode: add
                           // at eof
  trunc = 0x10,            // truncate file if
                           // it exists
  nocreate = 0x20,         // open fails if file
                           // does not exist
  noreplace= 0x40,         // open fails if file
                           // already exists
  binary  = 0x80           // binary file
};
};
```

The actual numeric values associated with the enumerations are implementation-dependent. While they will often be those shown here, this cannot be guaranteed. They are bit-values which can be combined using the logical OR operator:

```
long openmode = ios::in | ios::out | ios::app;
open("iofile", openmode);
```

This opens the file named iofile in input-output mode and appends input to existing file contents, if any, rather than deleting the contents and writing from the start. Whether the flag ios::binary appears or not is system-dependent. Some operating systems, especially UNIX, have no concept of a difference between binary and text files, so this flag is unnecessary. Operating systems such as DOS need a binary open mode to specify that such files must read the same as they were written.

When writing to a file in text mode, DOS replaces '\n' characters with the sequence '\n','\r' (newline-carriage return). When, under DOS, a file is opened in binary mode, no such substitutions are made. For random access applications   under DOS and similar systems, it is necessary to be sure that files read the same as they were written and, hence, that they are opened in binary mode. The default open mode in this case is text.

Apart from ios::in and ios::out, the other modes default to being switched off. The mode ios::app specifies that all data is to be written after the end of the current file contents, and implies ios::out. The mode ios::ate also specifies append mode, but does not imply that the file is opened for output.

The third argument of the **open** functions specifies access permissions. These are implementation-dependent: under DOS, a value of 2 may specify a hidden file; under UNIX, 0777 specifies a file with full read, write and execute permission for all users. The default value is **openprot**, which ensures that files are accessible for ordinary I/O for all systems.

A number of examples of file I/O are now given. They are all based around the same program, which simply copies one text file to another. To do so, a filecopy function is called. The examples concentrate on ways of implementing filecopy using the Stream I/O functions and other facilities so far introduced.

COPY86: BASIC FILE COPY

Here is the basic program, 'filecopy.cpp':

```
#include <iostream.h>
#include <fstream.h>

void filecopy(ifstream &, ofstream &);

int main(int argc, char *argv[])
{
   if (argc != 3)
   {
      cout << "Invalid arguments specified\n";
      return(0);
   }

   ifstream fin(argv[1]);

   if (!fin)
   {
      cout << "Can't open input file\n";
      return(0);
   }

   ofstream fout(argv[2]);

   if (!fout)
   {
      cout << "Can't open output file\n";
      return(0);
   }

   filecopy(fin, fout);
   fin.close();
   fout.close();
   return(0);
}

// Function filecopy copies
//   character-by-character from the input to
//   the output stream.

void filecopy(ifstream &in, ofstream &out)
{
   char c;

   while (in.get(c), !in.eof())
      out.put(c);
}
```

The user may execute the program by entering at the command line:

```
filecopy infile outfile
```

The file infile is linked to the input stream ifstream and
opened. If it cannot be opened, the stream object fin is set
to null, an error is reported and the program stops. If the
file outfile cannot be opened, the program similarly
stops. If both files are successfully opened, their associated
stream objects fin and fout are supplied as reference
arguments to the function filecopy. This function then
reads characters from the input file and writes them to the
output file, stopping when end-of-file is encountered on
the input file. The error-state function, eof, declared in
the class ios, returns TRUE on end-of-file. Error-state
functions are explained in Section 8.8.

In the next example, the files are opened using explicit
open function calls. The output file is opened in input-
output mode and, after the copy, is opened in input mode
and displayed. Only the main function is shown:

```
#include <iostream.h>
#include <fstream.h>

void filecopy(ifstream &, fstream &);

int main(int argc, char *argv[])
{
   if (argc != 3)
   {
      cout << "Invalid arguments specified\n";
      return(0);
   }

   ifstream fin;
   fin.open(argv[1], ios::in);

   if (!fin)
   {
      cout << "Can't open input file\n";
      return(0);
   }

   fstream fout;
   fout.open(argv[2], ios::out);

   if (!fout)
   {
      cout << "Can't open output file\n";
      return(0);
   }

   filecopy(fin, fout);
```

```
    //   now close, open and read the output file
    char c;
    fout.close();
    fout.open(argv[2], ios::in);
    while (fout.get(c), !fout.eof())
       cout << c;

    fin.close();
    fout.close();
    return(0);
}
```

If the output file were opened in append mode:

```
    fin.open(argv[2], ios::app);
```

or:

```
    fstream fin(argv[2], ios::app);
```

the contents of the input file would be added to the end of any existing output file instead of overwriting it. In the case of append mode, if the file does not already exist, it is created.

The filecopy function can be implemented using the multi-character overloading of the get function. The main function is unchanged from the original 'filecopy.cpp' and only the filecopy function is shown:

```
    const int MAX = 100;

    void filecopy(ifstream &in, ofstream &out)
    {
       char instring[MAX];

       while (in.get(instring, MAX, '\n'), !in.eof())
       {
          out << instring;

          // get and copy the newline

          char c;
          c = in.peek();
          if (c == '\n')
          {
                in.get(c);
                out.put(c);
          }
       }
    }
```

A local character array, instring, is defined to act as an input buffer. A line is read from the input file up to, but not including, the trailing newline. If a newline character is not found, a maximum of 100 characters is read. Either way, the characters are stored in instring, the contents of which are then written to the output file using the built-in inserter.

At the end of each line, the newline must be processed. This is done here a little over-elaborately, the peek function being used to check that the next character is indeed a newline before it is copied. The same job could be done in a more crude (and error-prone) way:

```
while (in.get(instring, MAX), !in.eof())
{
  out << instring;
  // get and copy the newline
  in.get();
  out.put('\n');
}
```

In this case, the get call uses the fact that its third argument, the delimiter, has the default value '\n'. The version of the get function that takes no arguments is then used to discard the next character (probably a newline) after the line is read. The put function then writes a hard-coded newline character to the output file.

In the final variant of the filecopy function, the getline function is used to read the input file and the gcount function to count the characters actually read:

```
const int MAX = 100;

void filecopy(ifstream &in, ofstream &out)
{
  long total_chars = 0;
  char instring[MAX];

  while (in.getline(instring, MAX, '\n'),
  !in.eof())
  {
    total_chars += in.gcount();
    out << instring;
  }
  cout << "File copied: " << total_chars
            << " bytes" << endl;
}
```

getline reads from the input file a newline-terminated
line, including the newline character. The line is then
written to the output file using the built-in inserter. On
each iteration, the total number of characters actually
read by getline is incremented. At the end of the function,
the number of characters copied is reported.

8.7 Random Access

This section introduces the facilities provided by Stream
I/O for random access, that is, starting file access at any
point in the file. For portability, random access operations
should be performed on files opened in binary mode. The
six functions provided by Stream I/O to do random
access on binary files are these:

read	Read a string of characters from an input stream
write	Write a specified number of characters to an output stream
seekg	Move the position of the file read pointer to a specified offset
tellg	Return the current position of the file read pointer
seekp	Move the position of the file write pointer to a specified offset
tellp	Return the current position of the file write pointer

The prototypes of the functions are:

```
istream& read(char *b, int c);

ostream& write(const char *b, int c);

istream& seekg(streampos p,
  seek_dir origin = ios::beg);

streampos tellg();

ofstream& seekp(streampos p,
  seek_dir origin = ios::beg);

streampos tellp();
```

The input functions are members of the **istream** class. The output functions are members of the **ostream** class. The **read** and **write** functions are additionally overloaded to take an **unsigned** first argument.

read reads from the input stream exactly **c** characters, regardless of whether or not they are newlines, and stores them at the memory address specified by the buffer **b**. **write** writes to the output stream exactly **c** characters, regardless of whether or not they are null characters, from the buffer **b**.

seekg places the file read pointer at an offset of **p** characters from the **origin**. The offset **p** is of type **streampos**, a **long int** defined with **typedef** in **iostream.h**. The start position **origin** is an enumerated type **seek_set**, defined in the **ios** class, which can have three values:

ios::beg	Start of file
ios::cur	Current position
ios::end	End of file

If the **origin** is not specified, the default value is **ios::beg**.

tellg returns the current read-pointer position in the file to an object of type **streampos**.

seekp places the file write pointer at an offset of **p** characters from the **origin**.

tellp returns the current write-pointer position in the file to an object of type **streampos**.

Use of the random access functions is best illustrated with an example. The example that follows is a class implementation of a program that builds a file of data records input by the user; counts the number of records after input has stopped; and then displays the file contents from a point selected by the user.

The program is called 'randio.cpp' and it uses four of the functions listed above: **read**, **write**, **seekg** and **tellg**.

RANDIO87: Random File Access

Before a file of records can be built, both the file and the format of its records must be defined. This is done in a programmer-written include file, **randio.h**:

```
struct record
{
  char      fname[15];
  char      lname[15];
  char      city[20];
  char      nat_ins_no[8];
  int       age;
  int       height_cm;
  char      sex;

  void      p_cout();
};

class file
{
private:
  record    *rec;
  int       no_recs;
  long      start_off;
public:
  file();
  int       f_count_rec();
  int       f_position();
  int       f_dump();
  ~file();
};
extern const int OK;
extern const int NOT_OK;
extern const int COUNT_ERR;
```

A class type **file** is declared that specifies both the contents of the file and the operations which may be carried out on it. The **private** data members of file are a pointer to an object of type **record**, a count of the number of records in the file, and the start offset for record retrieval.

There are five public functions. The constructor and destructor respectively create the file and free memory. The other functions count the file's records, position the file read pointer and display the file's contents.

The file record type **record** is declared as a structure. The structure members specify the form of a record containing a person's National Insurance details. There is also one member function, for displaying the individual structure members.

The **extern** declarations at the end of the file refer to corresponding definitions in the program file 'randio.cpp' that replace the traditional symbolic constants defined with #define. Here is 'randio.cpp' defining the **main** function:

```cpp
#include <iostream.h>
#include <fstream.h>
#include <stdlib.h>
#include "randio.h"

const int OK    = 0;
const int NOT_OK    = 1;
const int COUNT_ERR  = -1;

int main()
{
  // Create a file of records from user input

  file fio;

  // Find how many records are in the file
  if (fio.f_count_rec() == COUNT_ERR)
  {
    cout << "Error counting records"
                  << endl;
    exit(0);
  }

  //  Request a start-offset position from
  //  the user
  if ((fio.f_position()) == NOT_OK)
  {
    cout <<
    "Start offset requested is out of range"
    << endl;
    exit(0);
  }

  //  Display from the start-offset position
  if ((fio.f_dump()) == NOT_OK)
  {
    cout << "Couldn't print file just created"
                  << endl;
    exit(0);
  }
  return(0);
}
```

First, an object of type file is created. Only one of these is defined; its constructor creates as many instances of record as are required by user input. The main function calls the other file member functions in turn, in each case checking the return status for an error. If there is an error, program execution stops. If all three functions execute successfully, the program terminates normally. The program file 'randfunc.cpp' contains the definitions of the member functions of file and record:

```cpp
#include <iostream.h>
#include <fstream.h>
#include <stdlib.h>
#include "randio.h"

int file::file()
{
  // Create output file

  ofstream outp("file.dat", ios::out | ios::binary);

  if (!outp)
  {
    cout << "Couldnt open output file"
                   << endl;
    exit(0);
  }

  //  Allocate memory space for a record
  rec = new record;
  int c;
  do
  {
    // Enter one record of data

    cout << "Enter first name and last name: ";
    cin  >> rec->fname >> rec->lname;
    cout << "Enter city: ";
    cin  >> rec->city;
    cout <<
          "Enter National Insurance number: ";
    cin  >> rec->nat_ins_no;
    cout <<
    "Enter age, height in cm., sex (M or F): ";
    cin  >> rec->age >> rec->height_cm
                   >> rec->sex;
```

```
      //  discard final newline

      cin.ignore(2,'\n');
      //  c = cin.get(); // OK also
      if (!cin.good())
      {
          cout << "Data of wrong type entered"
                              << endl;
          exit(0);
      }

      // Write the record to the file

      outp.write((char *)(rec), sizeof(record));

      cout <<
          "Press RETURN to enter more data, ";
      cout << "q to quit: ";
   }
   while ((c = cin.get()) != 'q');
   c = cin.get();

   outp.close();
}

int file::f_count_rec()
{
   //  Open file to count its records
   ifstream inp("file.dat", ios::in |
   ios::binary);

   if (!inp)
   {
      cout << "Can't open file just created"
            << endl;
      return(COUNT_ERR);
   }

   //  seek to end of file
   inp.seekg(0, ios::end);

   long no_chars;
   no_chars = inp.tellg();

   cout << "Displacement at EOF is: "
            << no_chars << endl;
   cout << "Size of record is: "
            << (long)sizeof(record) << endl;

   no_recs = no_chars / (long)sizeof(record);
   inp.close();
```

```
    cout << "The file contains " << no_recs
            << " records" << endl;
    return(OK);
}

int file::f_position()
{
    cout << "The file will now be displayed"
            << endl;
    cout << "Print from the start? ";
    cout << " Answer y or n and RETURN: ";

    int c;
    int start_rec;
    start_off = 0;

    if ((c = cin.get()) == 'n')
    {
        c = cin.get();
        cout << "Start with what record no.?"
                    << endl;
        cout << "Enter a number between 1 and "
                << no_recs << " and RETURN: ";
        cin >> start_rec;
        if ((start_rec < 1) > (start_rec > no_recs))
                return(NOT_OK);
        c = cin.get();

        // Subtract one to get offset intended
        start_rec--;
        if (start_rec < 0)
                start_rec = 0;
        start_off =
            long(start_rec) * (long(sizeof(record)));
    }
    return(OK);
}

int file::f_dump()
{
    //  Open file for input
    ifstream inp("file.dat", ios::in | ios::binary);

    if (!inp)
    {
        cout << "Can't open file just created"
                << endl;
        return(COUNT_ERR);
    }
```

```
   if (start_off > 0)
      inp.seekg(start_off, ios::beg);

   rec = new record;

   // Read and display records until end-of-file
   while (!inp.eof())
   {
      inp.read ((char *)(rec), sizeof(record));
      if (inp.bad())
      {
              cout << "Error reading file" << endl;
              return(NOT_OK);

      }
      if (!inp.eof())
              rec->p_cout();
   }
   cout << "End of file reached" << endl;
   delete rec;
   inp.close();
   return(OK);
}
file::~file()
{
   delete rec;
}

void record::p_cout()
{
   cout << "\nName: "
              << fname
              << " "
              << tlname
              << endl;
   cout << "City: " << city << endl;
   cout << "National Insurance number: "
              << nat_ins_no
              << endl;
   cout << "Age, height, sex: "
              << age
              << " "
              << height_cm
              << " " << sex << endl;
}
```

Most of the program is quite simple and only the more
interesting aspects are now highlighted.

The file constructor opens a file called file.dat for output
in binary mode. Memory for a new record is allocated and
rec, the private data member of the file class, is set
pointing to the memory.

Data is then input by the user from standard input. At the
end of the input, the final newline must be discarded. This
can be done equivalently by either of the two statements:

```
//  c = cin.get();
cin.ignore(2,'\n');
```

If any error or type mismatch occurs on input, the error-
state function ios::good returns a FALSE value and an
error status indicator is returned to the main function. The
record is written to the file with the statement:

```
outp.write((char *)(rec), sizeof(record));
```

The write function for the output stream writes a number
of bytes expressed as the size of the record. The write
function expects its first argument to be a character
pointer. The explicit type conversion here from record *
to char * is necessary in C++, which will not carry out
such a conversion automatically. If the typecast is omitted,
a compilation error results.

file::file() keeps creating and writing file records in this
way until the user directs otherwise. The function
f_count_rec is called next. It counts the number of
records in the file by using seekg to seek to the end of the
file, reporting the resulting displacement with tellg and
dividing the displacement by the record size.

The function f_position sets the start-offset for reading
the file to the record number requested by the user. The
byte displacement in the file of this record is found by
multiplying the record size by the requested record
number.

The f_dump function seeks to the offset in the file
requested by the user and allocates memory to hold the
records that will be read. The statement sequence
following reads the records and performs error and end-
of-file checking after the read function call:

```
while (!inp.eof())
{
   inp.read ((char *)(rec), sizeof(record));
   if (inp.bad())
```

```
    {
        cout << "Error reading file" << endl;
        return(NOT_OK);
    }
    if (!inp.eof())
        rec->p_cout();
```

The ios::bad error-state function returns TRUE if the preceding I/O operation has failed. There are six error-state functions, of which we have so far encountered three: eof, good and bad. The error-state functions are explained in full in the next section.

The last statement of the code segment above calls the record member function p_cout to display the contents of the record just read. This process continues until end-of-file is reached. At this point, the program stops.

8.8   Error States

Error states are internally maintained for every open stream. These states are recorded in the stream object as an enumerated type:

```
class ios
{
public:
    // stream status bits
    enum io_state
    {
        goodbit  = 0x00,  // no bit set: status OK
        eofbit   = 0x01,  // end-of-file encountered
        failbit  = 0x02,  // last I/O operation
                          // failed
        badbit   = 0x04,  // invalid operation
                          // attempted
        hardfail = 0x80   // unrecoverable error
    };
};
```

Once again, the actual values assigned to the enumerations are implementation-dependent. Error-state checking can be done for any stream; in RANDIO87 in the last section, the state of the input stream cin is checked as part of the file class constructor. State checking is more usually done on streams that have been linked to files.

There are six functions, all members of the ios class, that check the values of the status bits and return TRUE or FALSE accordingly. The function prototypes are these:

int eof();   TRUE if end-of-file encountered.

int bad();   TRUE if a stream operation has failed.

int fail();   TRUE when stream operation has failed but is recoverable.

int good();   TRUE if eof, bad and fail are all FALSE.

int rdstate();   Returns the current error state.

void clear(int s); Sets to s, or clears if s is zero, the error state of a stream.

The unary negation operator ! is also overloaded for state checking:

```
int operator!();
```

It can be used to check a stream for the bad or fail conditions being set:

```
ifstream inp("file.dat", ios::in | ios::binary);

if (!inp)
{
  // report error
}
```

In RANDIO87, more error-checking could be added, especially after the call to the function write. It is possible to check the status of all the flags individually and perhaps even to overload an operator to do so. A useful check is simply to test for *not good*:

```
outp.write((char *)(rec), sizeof(record));

if (!outp.good())
{
  cout << "Error writing to file" << endl;
  return(NOT_OK);
}
```

8.9   Stream I/O Functions

This section gives the signatures of all commonly-used I/O functions declared in the classes ios, istream, ostream and fstream.

Formatting Functions

Class::return	Function-name
ios::long	setf(long);
ios::long	setf(long,long);
ios::long	unsetf(long);
ios::long	flags();
ios::long	flags(long);
ios::int	width();
ios::int	width(int);
ios::char	fill();
ios::char	fill(char);
ios::int	precision();
ios::int	precision(int);

STREAM ACCESS FUNCTIONS

Class::return	Function-name
fstream::void	open(const char *, int, int=filebuf::openprot);
ifstream::void	open(const char *, int=ios::in, int=filebuf::openprot);
ofstream::void	open(const char *, int=ios::out, int=filebuf::openprot);
fstream::void	close();

INPUT FUNCTIONS

Class::return	Function-name
istream::int	get();
istream::istream&	get(char&);
istream::istream&	get(char *, int, char=\n);
istream::istream&	getline(char *,int, char=\n);
istream::int	gcount();
istream::istream&	read(char *, int);
istream::int	peek();
istream::istream&	putback(char);
istream::istream&	seekg(streampos, seek_dir=ios::beg);
istream::streampos	tellg();

OUTPUT FUNCTIONS

Class::return	Function-name
ostream::ostream&	put(char);
ostream::ostream&	write(const char *, int);
ostream::ostream&	flush();
ostream::ostream&	seekp(streampos, seek_dir=ios::beg);
ostream::streampos	tellp();

ERROR-STATE FUNCTIONS

Class::return	Function-name
ios::int	rdstate();
ios::int	eof();
ios::int	fail();
ios::int	bad();
ios::int	good();
ios::void	clear(int=0);

The offset argument streampos for seekg and seekp is
defined in iostream.h:

```
typedef long streampos;
```

The origin argument for seekg and seekp is defined as
an enumerated type in the class ios:

```
class
{
  // stream seek direction
  enum seek_dir { beg=0, cur=1, end=2 };
};
```

Appendix A Migrating to C++

A.1 Introduction

The C++ language is a significant extension to the syntax of C. The major innovations are the constructs that facilitate the object-oriented approach to software design and development. These include, principally, the class, which is a generalisation of the C structure; templates, which generalise classes; constructor and destructor functions; overloaded functions and operators; and virtual functions.

C++ also includes many changes to the syntax of C which are less fundamental but nonetheless important in improving the language and in removing ambiguities and inconsistencies to be found in C.

This Appendix deals with the language constructs included in C++, other than classes and related features, that represent changes from the ISO C definition. The changes are considered under six headings:

- Declarations
- Types
- Functions
- Keywords and operators
- Preprocessor
- Other changes

The changes are enumerated and, in most cases, examples are given.

Where 'C' is used in this Appendix to refer to the predecessor language of C++, the ISO definition (ISO C) is intended.

A.2 Declarations

1. In C++, all declarations are statements. In C, this is not
   so and declarations must be placed at the start of a
   compound statement, usually that representing the
   function body.

```
void myfunc()
{
    int x;   //  valid C and C++
    x = 0;
    int y;   //  valid C++, invalid C
    {
        int z;   //  valid C and C++
    }
}
```

2. Because declarations are statements, they may appear
   anywhere in C++ (but not C) code:

```
for (int x = 5; x < 10; x++)
    .
    .
```

3. In C++, a **goto** statement is not allowed to 'jump over'
   an initialised definition. There is no such restriction in
   C. Here is an example:

```
class coord
{
    // member declarations here
};
int main()
{
    goto label1;   // valid C, invalid C++
    {
        int x = 5;
        label1: ;
    }
    goto label2;   // invalid C++

    // class constructor C++-specific
    coord inst(5, 10);
    label2: ;
    return(0);
}
```

4. In C++, an external const declaration is by default only visible within the same program file: it has *static linkage*. An external const declaration is treated by C as having *external linkage*: it is visible throughout all program files in the program. Here is an example:

```
const int x;   // treated by C++ as 'static',
               // visible only in this program
               // file. Visible everywhere in C

int main()
       .
       .
```

5. C++ introduces the reference to a declaration. This allows a variable to be given an alternative name and to be accessed indirectly, without using pointers, as is necessary in C. Passing arguments to functions 'by reference' in C is in fact simulated using pointers; the C++ reference declaration also allows true function call-by-reference. The following program initialises a reference declaration (function call by reference is shown in Section A.4):

```
#include <iostream.h>

int main()
{
    int n1  = 7;
    int n2  = 8;
    int &ref_n = n1;  // ref_n is an alias
                      // for n1

    ref_n *= 5;
    cout << ref_n << " " << n1 << "\n";

    ref_n = n2;
    // n1 changed, not just ref_n
    cout << ref_n << " " << n1 << "\n";

    return (0);
}
```

Once the reference ref_n is initialised to n1, it is simply an alias for n1. ref_n cannot subsequently be made to be an alias to something else, as the example shows. After the assignment:

```
ref_n = n2;
```

the value of n1 is assigned that of n2.

The C++ compiler may implement references to variables with standard C pointers and de-referencing, but this is transparent to the programmer.

6. In C++, the address of a register declaration may be taken, at the cost of forcing the register specification to be ignored. In C, the address of a register must not be taken.

```
register  r;
register *rp;  //  invalid C

rp = &r;   //  invalid C
*rp = 5;   //  invalid C
```

A.3   Types

7. In C++, the name (tag) of a class or enumerator is its type. This means that the name of a structure, union or enumeration type is its type. In C, the type of a structure, union or enumeration type is the tag prefixed with the keywords struct, union or enum.

```
struct filerec
{
    // some member declarations here
};

union one_member
{
    // some member declarations here
};

enum seasons {spring, summer, autumn,
winter};

struct filerec record1;   // valid C++ and C
filerec record2;        // valid C++ only

union one_member union1; // valid C++ and C
one_member union2;     // valid C++ only

enum seasons quarter1;   // valid C++ and C
seasons quarter2;       // valid C++ only
```

8. The enumeration type above declares the four enumerators spring, summer, autumn and winter. The type of an enumerator in C++ is the type of its

enumeration, not int as in C. C++ regards it as an error to assign to a variable of enumerated type an expression not of that type. Most compilers issue a warning rather than an error, but the practice should be avoided.

```
int main()
{
    enum seasons
        {spring, summer, autumn, winter};

    // spring, summer, autumn and winter are
    // of type 'seasons', not 'int'.

    seasons ssaw;    // valid C++, invalid C

    ssaw = 2;     // C++ compiler warning:
                  // type mismatch
    ssaw = winter;    // OK
    return(0);
}
```

9. A structure in C++ defines its own scope. Declarations of structures, enumeration types and enumerators are not by default visible to code outside that scope. In C, such declarations are visible outside the enclosing structure.

```
struct filerec
{
    struct table { /* table members here */ };
    enum quarters
        { spring, summer, autumn, winter };

        .
        .
};
```

In C++, the names table, quarters and all four enumerators are not visible outside the scope of the structure type filerec. In C, all these names are visible in the scope enclosing the declaration of filerec. In C++, the definition:

```
table sales_hist;
```

is illegal because table is not in scope; in C it is in scope. C++ syntax requires:

```
filerec::table sales_hist;
```

with the scope of table being resolved as being within that of filerec by the scope-resolution operator '::'.

10. The type of a literal character constant in C is int. This is reflected by a number of the standard library functions that handle character I/O. For example:

```
int fputc(int c, FILE *fp)
```

writes characters to file and returns the values of the characters written but declares both as int. C promotes a character value supplied to fputc to int. In C++, the type of a literal character constant is char. This makes no effective difference in almost all cases; conversion to int in cases such as that above still takes place. However, the value of:

```
sizeof('x')
```

in C++ is 1, while it is 2 or 4 in C, depending on the natural integer size of the host system.

11. C allows a variable of type void * to be assigned without explicit typecasting to a pointer of another type. This means that, for example, when memory space is dynamically allocated using malloc and that function returns a void pointer to the memory allocated:

```
char *memptr;
```

```
memptr = malloc(sizeof(buf));
```

no conversion of the malloc return value is required before assignment to the character pointer memptr. In C++, all assignments which would implicitly convert void pointers are flagged as errors by the compiler. In the malloc example, this code is required:

```
memptr = (char *)malloc(sizeof(buf));
```

12. C++ allows the form:

```
<type-specifier>(variable)
```

as well as:

```
(<type-specifier>)variable
```

for explicit type-casting operations. Here is an example:

```
#include <iostream.h>

int main()
{
    double pi = 3.1415927;
```

```
    cout << pi << "\n";
    cout << (int)pi << "\n";    // cast valid
                                // for C++ and C
    cout << int(pi) << "\n";    // valid C++ only
    return(0);
}
```

ANSI C++ additionally specifies three new casting operators that are applied depending on how 'far apart' are the types on either side of the conversion:

```
static_cast<T>(expr)        // close
reinterpret_cast<T>(expr)   // must be cast back
                            // to be used safely
const_cast<T>(expr)         // eliminate const
```

The first case might be used to convert a base class pointer to a derived class pointer:

```
derived* dp = static_cast<derived *>(bp);
```

The second form is intended for less-safe conversions, for example one from double * to char *:

```
char *cp = reinterpret_cast<double *>(dp);
```

const_cast allows access to data objects previously defined const or volatile:

```
    const char *ccp;
    char * cp;

    cp = const_cast<char *>ccp;
```

13. In C, the type of a bit-field member of a structure must be one of int, signed int and unsigned int. C++ additionally allows the types of these fields to be one of char, short and long in any of their signed or unsigned forms.

14. ANSI C++ specifies the bool type, and the true and false keywords representing the possible values of a variable of that type.

A.4 Functions

15. Function prototypes

The biggest single change between the original language definition of C and ISO C is the function prototype. The prototype was conceived during the development of C++ and was incorporated into the standardised C by the ISO committee. The function prototype allows the C and C++ compilers to do much better type-checking on arguments used in function calls than was possible with the original C.

The rules for function prototypes differ between C and C++ in only one major respect. In C, the function declaration:

```
double atan();
```

means that the function atan may take zero or more parameters and type-checking on arguments supplied to the function in the function call is suspended. The call to atan:

```
deg = atan(1);
```

is not checked for validity of the integer argument 1 and atan returns an unexpected result. This is corrected in C by changing the prototype:

```
double atan(double);
```

This declaration before the function call causes the conversion to be done correctly.

The fact that an empty function-call argument list causes all number-checking, type-checking and conversion of any such arguments to be suspended is a major weakness in the syntax of ISO C. This is corrected in C++, where the compiler takes:

```
double atan();
```

to mean that atan takes no parameters; this is equivalent to the C declaration:

```
double atan(void);
```

In C++, it is still legal, although unnecessary, to use **void** to specify an empty argument list.

16. In C++, every function which is called before its definition in the code must be announced to the compiler by a function prototype at a point in the code before the function call.

    C does not require this but, if this is not done, the compiler assumes that the function called without a prior prototype declaration is of return type **int**. It also suspends type-checking on the parameters of the called function. In either case, errors are likely.

17. In C++, a function declared by its prototype as returning a value must return a value or compilation errors will result.

18. Inline functions

    In C++, but not in C, a function prototype and definition may be prefixed with the keyword **inline**. This does not in any way change the meaning of the program or of the call to the inline function. Instead, the compiler is requested to optimise the function call by substituting the function's code at the point where the function call is made. If the compiler accedes to the request, the overhead associated with a normal function call is eliminated.

```cpp
#include <iostream.h>

//   prototype declaration
inline int leap(int);

int main()
{
    int year;

    cout << "Enter year number\n";
    cin >> year;

    if (leap(year))
        cout << year << " is a leap year\n";
    return(0);
}
```

```
// 'leap' definition
inline int leap(int year)
{
    if (((year % 4) != 0) &&
        ((year % 400) != 0))
        return (0);
    return (1);
}
```

The function **leap** is declared by a prototype and
defined after the **main** function. If the **inline** request
succeeds, the code of **leap** is substituted at the point
of the **leap** function call in **main**.

Either the declaration or the definition of the inline
function must precede the function call to it.

In the example, **leap** is declared before **main** and the
compiler knows what code to substitute for the function
call in **main**. If the definition of **leap** is before **main**,
the function definition is its declaration; the prototype
may be omitted without affecting program correctness.

Functions which are defined (rather than just declared)
as part of a class in C++ are implicitly inline.

Inline functions must not contain definitions of static
variables, loop statements, **switch** statements or **goto**
statements. Inline functions must not define arrays or
be recursive.

19. Function overloading.

In C++, functions may be overloaded: there may be
two or more functions with the same name but with
differences between their parameters. Here is an
example:

```
#include <iostream.h>

// function prototypes
void display();
int display(int, double);

int main()
{
    display();
    if (display(5, 6.78))
        cout << "OK\n";
    return(0);
}
```

```
//  function definitions
void display()
{
    cout << 3 << " " << 4.56 << "\n";
}

int display(int x, double y)
{
    cout << x << " " << y << "\n";
    return (1);
}
```

The compiler chooses whichever function definition is matched by a given call to the function display, checking first for an exact match and then for a match after type conversions. If there is no match, a compilation error results. If two function definitions are identical in name and argument list, a compilation error also results.

20. Default arguments.

C++ syntax includes, unlike C, the default argument as part of the function-calling sequence. A parameter in the called function may be assigned a default value if there is no matching argument in the function call. Here is an example:

```
#include <iostream.h>

void myfunc(int = 3, int = 4);

int main()
{
    int param1 = 5;
    int param2 = 6;

    myfunc();
    myfunc(param1);
    myfunc(param1, param2);
    return(0);
}

void myfunc(int a, int b)
{
    cout << "Parameters are " << a << " "
         << b << "\n";
}
```

The function myfunc may be called with zero, one or two arguments, as it is from the main function in the example. Here are the results of the function calls:

```
Parameters are 3 4
Parameters are 5 4
Parameters are 5 6
```

The default values are specified in the prototype of myfunc. It is legal, but unnecessary, to include argument names in the prototype:

```
void myfunc(int a = 3, int b = 4);
```

The default values must be specified in the prototype and not in the function header, unless the function definition is also a declaration:

```
#include <iostream.h>

void myfunc(int a = 3, int b = 4)
{
    cout << "Parameters are " << a << " "
         << b << "\n";
}

int main()
{
    int param1 = 5;
    int param2 = 6;

    myfunc();
    myfunc(param1);
    myfunc(param1, param2);
    return(0);
}
```

This produces the same results as the first form of the program.

The specification of all default arguments must be to the right in the list of any arguments that do not have defaults. There must be no arguments without defaults to the right of default arguments.

Here are examples:

```
void myfunc(int, int = 4);    // OK
void myfunc(int = 3, int);    // invalid
```

21. Function call-by-reference.

Reference declarations may be used to accomplish true function call-by-reference. In C, it is only possible to simulate call-by-reference using pointers and de-referencing. Call-by-reference is implemented in C++ like this:

```
#include <iostream.h>
void myfunc(int&);  // prototype
int main()
{
    int x = 5;
    myfunc(x);
    cout << "Changed value: " << x << "\n";
    return(0);
}
void myfunc(int& x)
{
    x = 10;
}
```

The change caused in myfunc to x is reflected in main. Here is the equivalent C code:

```
#include <stdio.h>
void myfunc(int *); /* prototype */
int main()
{
    int x = 5;
    myfunc(x);
    printf("Changed value: %d\n", x);
    return(0);
}
void myfunc(int *x)
{
    *x = 10;
}
```

22. const arguments.

Passing arguments to a function using either references or pointers causes any change made by the called function to that argument also to have effect in the calling function.

If an argument is passed to a function as a reference or a pointer and if the called function is not intended to change that argument, it is good practice to qualify the argument as const in the called function's argument list. Any attempt by the function to change the parameter is then flagged as an error at compilation time.

```
void myfunc(const int& x)
{
    x = 10;//   error, cannot change a 'const'
}
```

In this case, since the purpose of myfunc is to change the value of x, the const qualification is not sensible. One of the major reasons for passing a reference to a variable as an argument is for efficiency: it is more efficient to pass between functions a reference to a large data object such as a class than to copy it.

Often, a reference to a class object is passed between functions without the intention of having the calling function change its contents. In this case, the variable should be qualified const in the function argument list:

```
#include <iostream.h>

class myclass
{
public:
    int x;
};

//   prototype specifying invariant argument
void myfunc(const myclass&);

int main()
{
    myclass myc;

    myc.x = 5;

    cout << "Initial value: " << myc.x << "\n";
    myfunc(myc);
    cout << "Changed value: " << myc.x << "\n";

    return (0);
}

void myfunc(const myclass& myc_ref)
```

```
{
    myc_ref.x = 7; //   error
}
```

There is no error in not passing the class argument as a reference qualified const. Doing this, however, leaves open the possibility of class object data being corrupted. This may or may not be detected at run time. It is better clearly to define the function interface so that such errors are caught at compilation time.

23. mutable Type Qualifier.

   ANSI C++ introduces the *can't ever be* const qualifier, mutable:

```
class ob
{
    int x;
    mutable int y; // cannot be cast to const
    .
    .
}
```

A.5 Keywords and Operators

24. The following keywords are reserved for use by ANSI C++ and not by C. Any C program that uses one of these as an identifier is not a valid C++ program.

bool	catch	class
const_cast	delete	dynamic_cast
false	friend	inline
namespace	new	operator
private	protected	public
reinterpret_cast	static_cast	template
this	throw	true
try	typeid	using
virtual		

The purpose and use of the other keywords are described elsewhere in the text. All the C keywords are also C++ keywords.

25. C++ includes the following new operators, in addition to all the existing C operators:

Operator	Meaning
new	Allocate memory space
delete	De-allocate memory space
::	Scope resolution
->*	Member pointer operator
.*	Member pointer operator

ANSI C++ also introduces the following keyword operators as equivalents to operators containing national-language-specific characters:

Keyword operator	Traditional operator
and	&&
and_eq	&=
bitand	&
bitor	|
compl	~
not	!
or	||
or_eq	|=
xor	^
xor_eq	^=
not_eq	!=

26. new and delete are the C++ replacements for the C library functions malloc and free. malloc and free may still be called, but new and delete are easier and safer to use. In addition, new and delete are extensible: they can be used to implement class-specific memory management.

The new operator is almost always used in one of the following general forms:

```
<ptr> = new <type>(<initial value>);

<ptr> = new <type>[<size>];
```

The angle-brackets indicate that the value within is replaced by an actual literal value. new returns to the pointer on the left-hand side of the assignment a pointer to the memory allocated. The pointer is of the type specified on the right-hand side of the assignment. If for any reason the memory cannot be allocated, new returns a NULL pointer, which may be used in application code to check for a memory allocation error.

The general forms of the delete operator are these:

delete <ptr>;

delete [] <ptr>;

These deallocate the space pointed to by the pointer <ptr> which was previously allocated by new.

Here is a program that summarises these uses of new and delete:

```cpp
#include <iostream.h>

int main()
{
    int *iptr1, *iptr2, *iptr3;

    iptr1 = new int (5);
    iptr2 = new (int) (6);
    if ((iptr3 = new int[20]) == NULL)
        cout << "Couldn't allocate array\n";

    //   Display first two integer values
    cout << "Integer 1: " << *iptr1 << "\n";
    cout << "Integer 2: " << *iptr2 << "\n";

    delete (iptr1);
    delete iptr2;
    delete [] iptr3;
    return(0);
}
```

The displayed results are:

5
6

These are the values of the dynamically-allocated integer variables pointed to by iptr1 and iptr2.

27. C++ introduces the scope resolution operator ::, which is used to render unambiguous the scope of an

identifier. It is used mainly in defining and referring to functions that are class members and to access variables that are hidden by an enclosed scope.

Use of this operator in the context of classes is dealt with in some detail in Chapter 2. Here is an example in which a hidden variable is accessed.

```
int rec;

void myfunc()
{
    struct rec
    {
        int      sales;
        double   revenue;
        double   forecast;
    };

    // In C++, integer rec hidden
    // In C, integer rec in scope
    cout << rec << "\n";

    // This allows C++ access integer rec
    cout << ::rec << "\n";
}
```

This example also highlights the differences between the structure-scoping rules of C++ and C.

28. C++ introduces the member pointer operators ->* and .*. These operators are used only with pointers to class members. They are explained in Section 3.6.

29. In addition to the new, delete, :: and member-pointer operators, C++ also gives new meanings to several existing operators. It is said that these operators are overloaded. They are:

Operator	C Meaning	Overloaded Meaning
~	1's complement	destructor
&	address, bitwise AND	reference
<<	left bit-shift	stream output
>>	right bit-shift	stream input

C++ provides facilities for overloading the meaning of almost all its operators. Operator overloading is not provided in C syntax. Operator overloading is explained fully in Chapter 5.

30. The table of precedence and associativity for all the C++ operators, including the C operators, in decreasing order of precedence, follows:

Level	Operators	Associativity
17	:: (unary)	right to left
17	:: (binary)	left to right
16	() [] -> .	left to right
15	! ~ ++ -- (typecast) sizeof	right to left
15	+ (unary) — (unary)	right to left
15	* (indirection) & (address)	right to left
15	new delete	right to left
14	->* .* (member pointers)	left to right
13	* / %	left to right
12	+ -	left to right
11	<< >>	left to right
10	< > <= >=	left to right
9	== !=	left to right
8	&	left to right
7	^	left to right
6	|	left to right
5	&&	left to right
4	>	left to right
3	?:	right to left
2	= += -= *= /= %= &= ^=	right to left
2	|= <<= >>=	right to left
1	,	left to right

A.6 Preprocessor

31. Symbolic constants.

    The #define preprocessor directive traditionally used
    in C in this way:

    #define PI 3.1415927

    may be used in the same way in a C++ program. This
    usage of #define has been largely supplanted in C++,
    however, by definition of a variable with the const
    qualifier:

    const double PI = 3.1415927;

    Replacing preprocessor definitions with const
    variables helps avoid problems which can arise in such
    definitions when a #define pattern is expanded more
    than once:

    ```
    #include <iostream.h>

    #define ONE 1
    #define TWO ONE+ONE
    #define FOUR TWO*TWO

    const int UN = 1;
    const int DEUX = UN + UN;
    const int QUATRE = DEUX * DEUX;

    int main()
    {
        cout << "Preprocessor result "
                << FOUR << "\n";
        cout << "C++ code result "
                << QUATRE << "\n";

        return(0);

    }
    ```

    The program output is:

    ```
    Preprocessor result 3
    C++ code result 4
    ```

32. Macros.

    Preprocessor macros are often used in C for efficiency:
    they avoid the overhead of a function call. In C++, their
    use is often replaced by inline functions. Here is an
    example involving a well-known preprocessor pitfall:

```cpp
#include <iostream.h>
// preprocessor macro
#define min(a,b) ((a) < (b) ? (a) : (b))
// Equivalent C++ inline function
inline int MIN(int A, int B)
{
    return (A < B ? A : B);
}
int main()
{
    int x = 5;
    int y = 5;

    cout << "Preprocessor minimum "
         << min(x++, 7) << "\n";
    cout << "C++ code minimum "
         << MIN(y++, 7) << "\n";
    return(0);
}
```

The output of this program is:

```
Preprocessor minimum 6
C++ code minimum 5
```

which shows that an inline function can be used to avoid preprocessor problems while equalling the gain in efficiency offered by preprocessor macros.

33. Duplication of class declarations.

Declaring hierarchies of derived classes can require a special use of the #ifndef and #endif preprocessor directives to ensure that base classes are not multiply defined. Here is an example, involving the base class **clock** and the derived class **digital**. There are two header files, clock.h and digital.h:

```cpp
// clock.h - defines 'clock' class
#ifndef CLOCK
#define CLOCK

class clock

{
    //
};
#endif
```

```
// digital.h - defines 'digital' class
#ifndef DIGITAL
#define DIGITAL

#include clock.h

class digital : public clock
{
    //
};
#endif

// clock.cpp - source file
#include "clock.h"
#include "digital.h"
//
```

In this example, care is taken to ensure that the contents of the header file clock.h are not redeclared in digital.h after clock.h has already been included in the source code file.

At the start, CLOCK is not defined. When clock.h is included in the source file, it defines CLOCK. This acts as a semaphore to prevent clock.h being included again.

The header file digital.h in turn includes clock.h. When digital.h is included in the source code file, CLOCK is defined. The class clock is not redeclared, while the derived class digital is declared for the first time.

The technique is often found useful when developing large class hierarchies. In the case above, if it is not used, the multiple class declarations will cause compilation errors.

A.7   Other Changes

34. The ISO C standard does not guarantee that an identifier may have more than 31 significant characters. The number of significant characters in the identifier of an externally-defined variable is not guaranteed by the ISO standard to be more than six.

The compiler may also ignore the distinction between upper- and lower-case characters for such externally-defined names.

C++ removes all these restrictions and allows an identifier to comprise an arbitrary number of significant characters.

35. The underscore character is treated as a letter if embedded in a C++ or C identifier:

```
int run_total;
```

The underscore should not be used as the first character of either a C++ or C identifier because identifiers beginning with underscore are used by the C run-time environment and as the names of C library functions.

The double-underscore sequence __ is reserved for use by the C++ environment and libraries. Users should not define identifiers containing this sequence. In C, the double-underscore embedded in an identifier is harmless.

36. C++ allows one-line comments starting with a double-slash sequence:

```
// This is a comment
```

This is the equivalent of the C form:

```
/* This is a comment */
```

The C comment form remains part of C++ and is useful for multi-line comments.

37. In C++, when a character array is being initialised with a string literal, the bounds of the array must be empty or one greater than the length of the initialising string. This is to provide space for the string terminating character, \0.

ISO C, on the other hand, allows the initialising string literal to equal in length the array it is assigned to, with the terminating null character being quietly included in memory after the end of the character array. Here is an example:

```
// Valid C, invalid C++
char ch_arr[15] = "Now is the time";
```

```
// Valid C and C++
char ch_arr[16] = "Now is the time";

// Valid C and C++
char ch_arr[] = "Now is the time";
```

38. C++ allows general (non-constant) expressions as initialisers for static objects:

```
void myfunc()
{
    int a = 5;
    int b = 6;

    // valid C++, invalid C
    static int c = a + b;

    // valid C++ and C
    static int c = 5 + 6;
}
```

39. In C, the main function may be explicitly called and may also have its address taken. This is rarely a good idea. In C++, main must not be called, have its address taken, be overloaded or declared inline or static.

Index

Symbols

#define directive 398
#include directive 10
% 6
& 18
* 6
+ 6
- 6
->* 89
.* 89
/ 6
:: 32
::* 109
<< 24, 329, 341
== 42
>> 33, 329

A

Abstract class 258
   Pointer and reference to 268
Access function 69
Access level conversion 216
Access permissions
   DOS and Unix 360
Access restriction
   Overriding 217
Access-control keywords 57
Access-specifier keywords 214
Address operator 18
Aggregate data object 15
Aggregates 59
Ambiguity and name overloading 143
ANSI C++
   Keyword operators 394
   Keywords 393
ANSI C++ class library 133
ANSI C++ Draft Standard 277, 327
ANSI C++ Standard 51
ANSI C++ Standardisation Committee 277
ANSI Working Paper for the Draft C++ standard 327

P

Diskette Offer

The reader is offered a diskette containing all the source code of all complete non-trivial programs presented in *The C++ Pocket Book*, Second Edition. The offer is of one diskette in the 1.44MB, 3.5-inch Windows/DOS format. In many cases, the diskette will also be readable in OS/2 and UNIX environments.

The price for a copy of this diskette is £10.00. Non-residents of the European Union are charged £2.50 extra to cover shipping costs. (Prices in U.K. Pounds Sterling.) You may pay by Banker's Draft or Money Order in Sterling or by personal cheque made out in your local currency which, when converted, will approximate closely (allowing for conversion charges) to the Sterling price.

Please allow 28 days for delivery.

Please send me _____ copies, at UK£10.00 each (plus UK£2.50 p&p for non-EU residents) or the equivalent in local currency, of the programs in *The C++ Pocket Book*, Second Edition on an IBM-compatible diskette.

Name _ _ _ _ _ _ _ _ _ _ _ _ _ _

Address _ _ _ _ _ _ _ _ _ _ _ _ _

_ _ _ _ _ _ _ _ _ _ _ _ _

City/Country _ _ _ _ _ _ _ _ _ _ _ _

Telephone _ _ _ _ _ _ _ _ _ _ _ _

Signature _ _ _ _ _ _ _ _ _ _ _ _

Send to:
Conor Sexton,
14, Castleside Drive,
Rathfarnham,
Dublin 14, Ireland
Phone: +353-1-4906727   Fax: +353-1-6682166

This offer is solely of the author, Conor Sexton. Butterworth-Heinemann takes no responsibility for this offer or its fulfilment. This offer is subject to change or cancellation at any time. Conor Sexton accepts no liability for consequential or other damage arising from use of the programs that are part of this offer.